THE HISTORY OF CRICKET.

FROM THE WEALD TO THE WORLD.

PETER WYNNE-THOMAS.

THE HISTORY OF CRICKET

From The Weald to The World

THE HISTORY OF CRICKET

From The Weald to The World

Peter Wynne-Thomas

The Stationery Office

© Crown copyright 1997

Applications for reproduction should be made to
The Copyright Unit, Her Majesty's Stationery Office
St Clements House, 2–16 Colegate, Norwich NR3 1BQ

ISBN 0 11 702048 6

Peter Wynne-Thomas has asserted his right under the Copyright,
Designs and Patents Act 1988 to be identified as the author of the work

British Library Cataloguing in Publications Data

A CIP catalogue record for this book is available from the British Library

Designed and produced by the Stationery Office: Design by Jennifer Hannaford

Printed in the United Kingdom for the Stationery Office
0 11 702048 6/1 C50 6/97

Published by The Stationery Office and available from:

The Publications Centre
(mail, telephone and fax orders only)
PO Box 276, London SW8 5DT
General enquiries 0171 873 0011
Telephone orders 0171 873 9090
Fax orders 0171 873 8200

The Stationery Office Bookshops
49 High Holborn, London WC1V 6HB
(counter service only and fax orders only)
Fax 0171 831 1326
68–69 Bull Street, Birmingham B4 6AD
0121 236 9696   Fax 0121 236 9699
33 Wine Street, Bristol BS1 2BQ
01179 264 306 Fax 01179 294 515
9–21 Princess Street, Manchester M60 8AS
0161 834 7201 Fax 0161 833 0634
16 Arthur Street, Belfast BT1 4GD
01232 238 451 Fax 01232 235 401
The Stationery Office Oriel Bookshop
The Friary, Cardiff CF1 4AA
01222 395 548 Fax 01222 384 347
71 Lothian Road, Edinburgh EH3 9AZ
(counter service only)

Customers in Scotland may
mail, telephone or fax their orders to:
Scottish Publications Sales
South Gyle Crescent, Edinburgh EH12 9EB
0131 479 3141 Fax 0131 479 3142

Accredited Agents
(see Yellow Pages)

and through good booksellers

CONTENTS

Maps and charts

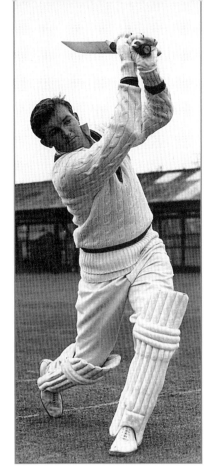

*Richie Benaud
in England in 1956.*

My first cricket book was the *NSW Cricket Association Yearbook* of 1937, which had in it all the scorecards and details of the 1936–7 Ashes series, where the teams were captained by Don Bradman and Gubby Allen. I played all my Test Matches before the age of ten using those teams, and alongside these written words I had the booklet concerning batting and bowling where the instructors were Bradman and Clarrie Grimmett. My first real and proper cricket book was Jack Fingleton's *Cricket Crisis*, in which he talked of the Maynard Arms at Main Road Grindleford, in Derbyshire, where the Australian team stayed in 1938. I desperately wanted to be a good cricketer but, almost as much, I wanted to be an Australian cricketer staying at the Maynard Arms and be on the bus when it crested the hill. Then the industrial smoke could be seen above Sheffield where we would be playing that day against Yorkshire and where Yorkshire Annie would be calling our abilities into question. It was the written word that did that for me. In the modern day, computers and CD–ROMS and talking books are wonderful and, no doubt, this *History of Cricket* will encompass all of those and do it very well, but I regard myself as being fortunate that my love of the game began with print on paper.

I've always been of the opinion that luck plays a great part in cricket, something which I found of great benefit in my playing days. It has worked out the same way in life away from the playing side of the game, in matters involving the written word, the opportunity to spend 40 years as a journalist and commentator and to be part of a short but very effective change in the game 20 years ago. Nothing I have read in Peter Wynne-Thomas's excellent *History* dissuades me from the view that cricket remains the most controversial game of all. It's not so much that the people playing it are necessarily controversial; they are sometimes ordinary, occasionally brilliant, they will do unusual things, sometimes their feats will be flashy or heroic. It is the politics in the game which makes it so controversial, and the wheeling and dealing of cricketing matters throughout the world comes to light in these pages. It is a wonderful game and has made a great contribution to world sport and the culture of various countries; its controversial and often confrontational aspect provides added spice.

So too the manner in which the game has fluctuated with spectator interest, financial ups and downs and the way in which its future has changed from decade to decade and where administrators have been able, or failed, to take advantage of a great number of important challenges.

A strong reminder is in these pages of one of the reasons why Australian cricket is strong: because of the club system which has operated from the time contests began in Sydney in the 1830s. The establishing of cricket in Australia had to be different from that of England because of short twilight time and the fact that only Saturdays and Public Holidays could be used for matches. Sunday play came much later. The club system has meant fierce but friendly competition, where everyone has the opportunity to play for Australia, and the difference between club standard and Sheffield Shield means that only those of skill and temperament will survive later to play for their country.

There is a wealth of information in these pages, much of it new to me, and a framework has been created so that it is by no means a dry chronicling of events but a narrative which gives a clear picture of the manner in which the game has evolved in different countries. The Empire, and what used to be the colonies, played a great part in this, but there were other aspects as well which had a bearing on events. Could the Americans have become cricket lovers and players but for the Civil War? That may be doubtful but what is less in doubt is that soon a World Cup may be staged in America even if audiences there would be small. Television audiences though would be massive, with number-crunchers talking of more than one billion.

The catalyst for this was the series played in 1996 in Toronto, Canada, between Pakistan and India, the politicians of neither country really permitting cricket to be played against one another. This Sahara Cup was the brainchild of the International Management Group and while paying audiences struggled to breach the 1,000 mark, television audiences ran to hundreds of millions.

Although every day's cricket I watch produces something new and exciting, it paradoxically remains the same. This book tells of the coloured clothing worn before whites became the standard dress and it talks of the one-day game and its offshoots. It discourses on the betting which was part of the game for both spectators and, it seems, occasionally, the players. Nothing could be closer to 'spread betting' than the note about newspapers reporting details of the changes in the odds as matches progressed in the 18th and early 19th centuries.

I like the sound of William Clarke, an entrepreneur who was much admired, other than perhaps by James Dark and, in the light of present-day events, my attention certainly has

THE HISTORY OF CRICKET

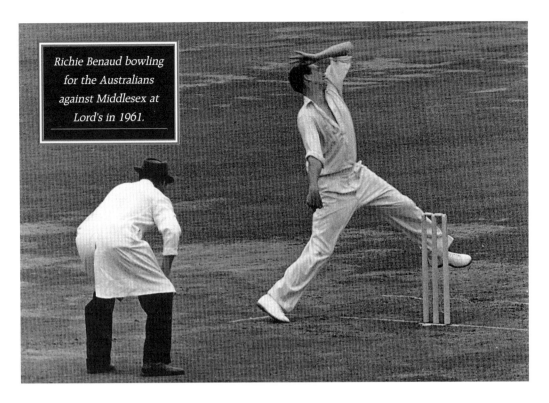

Richie Benaud bowling
for the Australians
against Middlesex at
Lord's in 1961.

been caught by the chapter concerning the proliferation many years ago of cricket's professional coaches who were attached to universities and clubs.

And, having played in front of audiences in England where spectators were allowed to sit behind the rope but on the playing area, I had forgotten the true reason why that is now banned.

It is my belief that cricket, in spite of intense competition, will continue to flourish and may even become far more popular on a worldwide basis than is the case today, providing administrators embrace the challenge. If there is any threat to cricket it lies in the way in which the first-class game is administered and played. Players will always be just as good, or better, than those who have gone before, but the game will only advance if people in control remember that the future belongs to those who plan for it.

pHOTOGRAPHIC ACKNOWLEDGEMENTS

Photographs kindly supplied by the following organisations:

Nottinghamshire County Cricket Club/Trent Bridge: Pages 4, 11, 14, 21, 31, 36 (x 3), 43, 48, 49, 51 (x 2), 52, 55, 56, 58, 59, 72, 75 (x 2), 77, 84, 91, 94, 95, 96, 98, 101, 103 (x 2), 109, 113 (x 2), 119, 120, 127 (x 2), 129, 132, 133, 134, 135 (x 2), 138, 143, 144, 146, 149 (x 2), 154 (left), 157, 159 (right), 163, 164, 170, 171, 176, 185, 189, 224, plate section (Alfred Mynn), front cover (Alfred Mynn, K.S. Ranjitsinhji).

S&G Press Agency Ltd: Pages vii, ix, 201, 203, 216, 217, 220 (top), 221, 227, 229, 234 (x 2), 235, 237 (x 3), 238 (x 2), 239, 247, 249.

ALLSPORT: Pages 220 (bottom), 241, plate section (Lord's Ground, Shane Warne, Ian Botham, Brian Lara, C.L.R. James, Eden Gardens, England Women's XI, Arjuna Ranatunga), front cover (Brian Lara), back cover (bottom) (ALLSPORT/Hulton Getty).

Central Office of Information: Pages 1 (x 2), 87, 90, 122, 136, 154 (right), 159 (left), 170, 199.

Lord's/Bridgeman Art Gallery: Page 32 (Portrait of Thomas Lord, anonymous), plate section (Thomas Hope of Amsterdam by Sablet, 'Cricket in Marylebone Fields' by Hayman), front cover (detail from 'Cricket in Marylebone Fields', Thomas Hope).

Goodwood House: Pages 8 (West Sussex Record Office Goodwood MS 1884), 12, plate section (4th Duke of Richmond). By courtesy of the Trustees of the Goodwood Collections and with acknowledgements to the West Sussex Record Office and County Archivist.

Imperial War Museum: Pages 197, 198 (x 2) (E16922, E4505, by kind permission of The Trustees of the Imperial War Museum, London).

Army Careers: Page 60 (bottom), plate section (advertisement), front cover (detail from advertisement).

Institution of Royal Engineers: Page 86, back cover (top).

Roedean School: Pages 195 (top), 254, with thanks to Andrew England.

Peter Wynne-Thomas: Page vi.

Charterhouse School: Page 38 (by kind permission of The Headmaster of Charterhouse).

Victoria & Albert Museum: Page 60 (top).

British Library (Oriental and India Office): Page 181. By permission of The British Library.

Cheltenham Ladies' College: Page 195 (bottom), with thanks to Janet Johnstone.

Lombard North Central PLC: Plate section (Lombard Under 15 World Challenge).

All 14 maps, and chart on page 44, designed by ML Design.

Captions to back cover photographs:
Top: The Royal Engineers' team and coach about to depart for a cricket match in 1864.

Bottom: The MCC, captained by Colin Cowdrey (bottom right), board the plane for their tour of Ceylon and Pakistan in January 1969.

Front cover photographs are all found within the book.

Two events more than any others have shaped my approach to cricket's history. When I was eight, in 1942, my family moved to Nottinghamshire, and in about 1960 I made the acquaintance of Rowland Bowen.

These observations require an explanation. In 1946 I gravitated to Trent Bridge, began watching and supporting Nottinghamshire, scored the matches I watched and worked out seasonal averages for the county's cricketers. My interest in history in general then took over and I started on my long and indeed continuing search to obtain biographical details of all the Nottinghamshire cricketers. Because Nottinghamshire cricketers were at the centre of the expansion of cricket as an international sport through the second half of the 19th century, the biographies I built up involved research not only throughout the British Isles, but in all the major overseas cricketing countries. My general knowledge of cricket history became extensive, but it was a knowledge which largely accepted the available published facts and my research concentrated on finding missing details rather than testing the given facts.

At this point I met Rowland Bowen, whose critical eye was testing the wisdom of cricket's historians. From him I learnt which writers to study and which to ignore. His *Cricket Quarterly* magazine encouraged the questioning of historical data and fresh research. My years of indiscriminately gathering facts ceased and I unloaded the dross.

The formation of the Association of Cricket Statisticians and Historians in 1973 provided a new forum for cricket historians and continued the work which had been led by Rowland Bowen. Over the past twenty or so years I owe a debt to my colleagues in the Association: David Baggett, Philip Bailey, Kit Bartlett, Robert Brooke, Chris Clynes, Brian Croudy, John Featherstone, Peter Griffiths, Les Hatton, David Harvey, Andrew Hignell, Dennis Lambert, Jim Ledbetter (who also kindly read the typescript of this book and made several useful comments on it), Derek Lodge, Malcolm Lorimer, Roger Page, S.S. 'Chandra' Perera, Frank Peach, Mick Pope, William Powell, Steven Sheen, Richard Streeton, Philip Thorn, Ken Trushell, Ken Williams and Tony Woodhouse. I must also mention my co-author of half a dozen books relating to cricket history, Peter Arnold.

In 1989, Michael Blumberg invited me to write a series of articles on cricket history for *Cricket World.* The series ran for some three years and in part forms the opening chapters of this present work. I must therefore thank Michael for his encouragement over the years.

Keith Warsop wrote a number of articles for Rowland Bowen in his *Cricket Quarterly.* Keith and I have worked for many years on historical research, often together, and he was kind enough to read through the first draft of this book and make a number of constructive comments. Throughout the writing of this history, Nigel Pearce of the Central Office of Information has been a tremendous help as the in-house editor, and the way the facts are presented owes more than a little to him. Nigel's colleagues at COI, Paul Webb and John Collis, carried out some very useful picture and other research.

Edith North kindly drove me around Sussex and Shropshire during my research in those two countries, and the index was most efficiently typed by Hazel Crozier.

I must also thank the Corps of the Royal Engineers, Stonyhurst College, Roedean School, Cheltenham Ladies' College, Harrogate Ladies' College, the Women's Cricket Association and Timothy McCann for willingly supplying material which greatly aided my research.

And, last but not least, I am very grateful to Richie Benaud for contributing such a thoughtful and pertinent Foreword.

Finally, the books listed in the Bibliography are recommended for those readers who wish to pursue the subject of cricket's history beyond the scope of this work.

Peter Wynne-Thomas
Trent Bridge
September 1996

'Don't throw stones!'
'Who's chopped the heads off the flowers?'
'You've ruined those shoes!'

Familiar parental cries which have echoed and re-echoed down the corridors of time. They may be clichés, but each child hears them afresh. To pick up a small object from the ground and hurl it as far as strength will permit; to take a stick and flick the heads off dandelions on a country walk; to amble to school kicking a pebble as one goes – these innate childish acts form the rudiments of our games. The child simply requires a companion in order to compete, to see who throws the stone the farthest, who can hit a target, who is most accurate at beheading dandelions, or kicking a pebble.

In 1801 *The Sports and Pastimes of the People of England* by Joseph Strutt was first published. For a century this, with revisions, was the standard textbook on the history of sports and pastimes. Strutt divided ball games into three categories:

1.   Club-Ball (games played by hitting a ball with a stick, bat, racket, club, etc.).
2.   Hand-Ball (games played using the hand to propel the ball).
3.   Foot-Ball (games played by kicking the ball).

1

THE

ORIGINS

An engraving by James Pollard (1797-1859) entitled 'A Cricket Match' and published in 1824. Pollard was noted for the accuracy of his work.

Returning to our child, having mastered throwing, swinging a stick at a stationary object, or kicking a pebble at a target, he and his friends at some time in the very distant past must have invented crude games of bowls or skittles, to see which competitor was best at hitting or reaching a target. The children with sticks tried the same exercise and invented golf, hurling and hockey. Later in the process of evolution a group must have decided that it would be more exciting if the child with the stick tried to prevent the child throwing the pebble from hitting the target. Further down the evolutionary chain it was found that even this combined 'game' was rather dull, and the child with the stick was invited to score 'points' not only by preventing the target from being hit, but also by hitting the pebble with his stick as far as he could. More children were brought into the action in order to stop the pebble being hit too far.

All this sounds exceedingly simple, but it would not have occurred overnight and games such as foot-ball, hand-ball and the simple golf 'club-ball' must have been established many years before cricket came along. The older games of bowls, golf and football require one particular skill, but cricket requires several. These skills do not have to be acquired by every player and this fact alone ensures that cricket is more deeply fascinating than games involving, in broad terms, one skill. Because cricket needs a complexity of skills, because these skills have to be carefully coordinated by the captain of the team, because the spectator requires much more knowledge in order to follow the progress of a match, cricket is bound to take longer to be transferred from one parish to another, from one county to another, from one country to another, and to become assimilated into the social framework.

Once basic rules had been established for soccer, golf, tennis and so on, those games spread throughout the world within a generation or two. The rules of cricket, on a national level in England, were established before those of most other ball games, but only in the last 50 years has cricket begun to obtain a firm foothold outside the former British Empire.

EXPLODING SOME OLD MYTHS

The Revd James Pycroft, who published the first history of cricket in 1851, under the title *The Cricket Field*, had studied Joseph Strutt's volume and concluded that cricket began in the 13th century under the name 'club-ball'. Pycroft quotes sundry stray references to 'cricket' and to other games which he assumes to be cricket under another guise, but the whole of his detection is muddled until he arrives at Hambledon in the middle of the 18th century. His broad conclusion is that cricket came to fruition at Hambledon, his evidence being John Nyren's *The Young Cricketer's Tutor*, edited by Charles Cowden Clarke and published in 1833. This book includes Nyren's reminiscences of Hambledon and its cricketers; Nyren's father, Richard, was the captain of the side in the 1770s. Pycroft was also able to interview William Beldham, one of the old Hambledon cricketers.

Both books, Pycroft's and Nyren's, were to be reprinted frequently through the rest of the 19th century and became source books for anyone interested in cricket. Generations of

Englishmen were thus weaned on the theory that organised cricket began at Hambledon, and this notion remains firmly entrenched even at the present time. As this narrative will demonstrate, organised cricket pre-dates Hambledon.

Some historians of the recent past, having grasped the fact that Hambledon was not the birthplace of modern cricket, have made every attempt to give cricket much greater antiquity than the known facts merit. Strutt's club-ball is fastened upon as 'evidence' when, in fact, no known document that lists games pre-1700 mentions club-ball, which, as noted earlier, is simply a general term for any game in the golf, hockey, cricket family. In itself it does not exist.

'Creag' is another word which some historians have decided refers to cricket. There is only a single known mention of 'creag'. This occurs in a Latin text of 10 March 1300 relating to the accounts of Prince Edward, the son of Edward I. The idea that creag means cricket is based on evidence so flimsy as to be transparent: namely, that no Latin dictionary can provide a meaning for the word; that creag bears a vague similarity to the word 'cricket'; and that the geographical reference is Newenton, which could be Newenden near Rye on the south coast (it is far more likely to be Newington near Chatham in Kent, since Prince Edward lived at Eltham Palace around that time). Creag is thus mentioned in the area of England where most of cricket's 17th-century references are located, and this geographical link is the only supporting evidence for the theory.

'Criquet' is the next word which Rowland Bowen in particular (in his *Cricket: A History of its Growth and Development*, 1970) believes to be cricket. 'Criquet' occurs in a French document written in the Pas-de-Calais in 1478. Scholars of medieval French are divided as to the word's meaning. Bowen supports his idea with two other facts: first, that northern France used at that time a numbering system based on eleven; and, second, that Stonyhurst College was based in northern France until the French Revolution, at which time the college moved to England bringing with it a fossilised form of cricket. A history of Stonyhurst College however reveals that, though based in France, it taught English Catholic boys (Catholic schools being banned in England in the 17th century). Little is known of the origins of Stonyhurst cricket, but it is likely that the English boys, mainly from south-east England, brought the game to the school from their homes, and not that the boys learnt it in France. Had the latter occurred there would surely be evidence of local French boys playing cricket. Such evidence does not exist. Bowen's claim is no more than an interesting hypothesis.

'Handyn and Handoute' is given by Pycroft as an early form of cricket and this assertion has been repeated numerous times. It comes from a statute of Edward IV, dated 1477, which forbids Handyn and Handoute being played indoors or in a house yard. The fact that it is played indoors ought to have killed its cricket connotation dead, but some researchers failed to read the full quote. It is in fact a crude gambling game, in which a player puts his hand in a bag and withdraws it with fist clenched; and the opponent then has to guess either what is in the fist, or whether it is empty.

This twin illustration shows how the illuminated manuscript of c.1340 of the Romance of Alexander *was adjusted in Joseph Strutt's book to give a better impression of 'early cricket'.*

The next evidence to which some experts cling in order to prove cricket's antiquity is pictorial. There are four 14th-century illustrations which have been published in cricket histories or magazines relatively often with the claim that they 'prove' that cricket existed during that period. The most common comes from the borders of the *Romance of Alexander*, an illuminated manuscript of 1340, which was redrawn and carefully adjusted when employed as an illustration in Joseph Strutt's book of 1801. Strutt's adaptation and the original can be seen in the picture reproduced above. It needs a fertile imagination to describe the picture as 'cricket'. The other three examples – the Schilling manuscript of c.1300, shepherds in a mural at Cocking church in West Sussex and a stained-glass window in Gloucester cathedral (the last two dating from about 1350) – come into the same category.

In all these examples one vital piece of cricket evidence is missing – any sign of stumps. Whatever game is depicted, cricket it is not, unless a target for the bowler exists.

Although it may appear to the contrary, it is not the intention of this present work to debunk the writing of Pycroft, Nyren or indeed Strutt. All three based their ideas on the evidence available to them at the time and their deductions come from the few scraps that researchers had found. What is of concern is that 20th-century writers have gone back to those three sources and ignored much of the vast quantity of evidence which has emerged since from the careful combing of 18th-century documents, newspapers, diaries and other source material.

THE WEALD

In the 1890s, H.T. Waghorn and F.S. Ashley-Cooper began to discover and publish numerous cricketing references from 18th-century newspapers. In the 1920s the most erudite of cricketing scholars, P.F. Thomas, analysed these new findings and produced a series of booklets laying out his historical concepts based on this analysis. Thomas's efforts should be the foundation for anyone delving into 17th- and 18th-century cricket.

In the 1930s, G.B. Buckley continued the newspaper combing of Waghorn and Ashley-Cooper and two additional books of newspaper references resulted. After the Second World War, H.F. Squire concentrated on researching references to early Sussex cricket, and was later followed by Timothy McCann, checking 17th-century documents. John Goulstone specialised in early Kent cricket references and filled in many gaps, as well as confirming some early general references. In 1963, Rowland Bowen founded the *Cricket Quarterly*, one object of which was to publish new evidence on early cricket. This magazine printed many of Goulstone's findings as well as more by G.B. Buckley and pieces by other researchers.

P.F. Thomas, using the information available to him up to 1920, concluded that cricket was first established in The Weald, between the North and South Downs, mainly in Sussex, with an overflow into southern parts of Surrey and western parts of Kent. Since Thomas put forward his theories, the number of known cricket references before 1675 with a geographical location has doubled, and every one reinforces Thomas's theory. A map of the area giving all these pre-1675 references to cricket produces the shape of a crescent, with its most westerly point at Selsey in Sussex, its northern point in Eltham, Kent, and its eastern point in Ruckinge, also in Kent (see below).

PLACES WHERE CRICKET WAS PLAYED BEFORE 1675

Places where cricket is known to have been played before 1675. The pattern suggests that the game took its present form in The Weald near the point where the three counties of Kent, Surrey and Sussex meet, and spread outwards from there.

The centre of this crescent is about Horsted Keynes in Sussex – by coincidence the place where the first person was killed playing cricket, in 1624. The earliest surviving reference to cricket involves the game being played by schoolboys about 1550 in Surrey, which would suggest that cricket began as a boys' game. This idea is reinforced by the first dictionary mention of cricket, in 1611, when 'a cricket staffe' is described as 'a staffe wherein boyes play at cricket'.

By the 1620s youths are mentioned as playing the game in West Sussex, and in 1629 the curate of Ruckinge in Kent, Henry Cuffin, is taken to task for engaging in cricket 'in a very unseemly manner with boys, and other very mean and base persons'. Cuffin replied that he simply played with some of his parishioners and they were persons 'of repute and fashion'. Certainly, by 1646 men of some substance are concerned with the game, since a case goes to court at Coxheath, near Maidstone in Kent, to settle some bet involving cricketers.

Further evidence that cricket began in The Weald comes in diary form. Thomas Marchant of Hurstpierpoint and Thomas Turner of East Hoathly (both in Sussex) each kept a diary in the 18th century, the former from 1717 to 1727, and the latter from 1754 to 1765. Both contain references that clearly demonstrate how inter-village cricket was a commonplace in The Weald, and not just a game played on village Feast Days or organised as a special event by the landed gentry. Although we have only scattered references to cricket in the 17th century, I am convinced that what Marchant and Turner describe in the 18th also applied in the previous century, though in a more restricted way.

IRON WORKERS AND SHEPHERDS

The theory that cricket began as a game for shepherds has been often mentioned. A study of the Sussex Weald in the 16th and 17th centuries, however, reveals that the area, then densely wooded and with ample supplies of iron ore, was the 'Black Country' of England of its day, dotted with nearly 200 iron foundries and glass manufacturers (see opposite page). Until 1700, when the 'cottage' iron industry collapsed as the coke furnaces of the Midlands began operation, much of the population of The Weald was therefore employed in iron or its related industries. An inspection of the sites of the ironworks shows that the majority of villages had, or were adjacent to, a foundry. The iron workers and those in allied trades clustered in or near the villages now known to have been associated with cricket, are much more likely to have played in the first organised matches than the more isolated shepherds. When the iron industry ceased, the population turned more to agriculture and, especially, sheep-rearing.

The shepherd theory is based on three main premises: first, that the shepherd's crook was the first 'bat', and crook is somewhat close to the word 'cricket'; second, that the wicket derived from a wicket gate used by shepherds (although by the 14th century 'wicket' already had several meanings, for example, 'a garden gate' in Chaucer's *Merchant's Tale*); and, third,

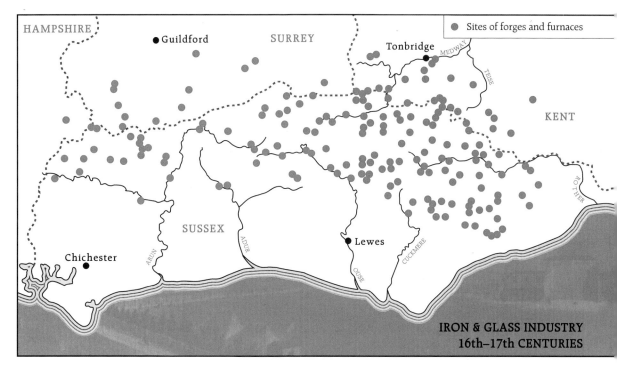

The sites of the iron and glass works of the 16th and 17th centuries in Sussex and neighbouring counties, in the same localities where cricket was played.

that the sheep cropped the grass to provide a suitable pitch. The whole is possible but a little fanciful.

It is worth noting here, though the point will be expanded later, that Nottinghamshire developed into the centre of cricket a century and a half later through its own 'cottage' industry of framework knitting.

OTHER EARLY REFERENCES

There are no 17th-century illustrations of cricket, and no detailed descriptions of games (1706 was the date of the first), but there are references to cricket bats, balls and wickets during the century. The dictionary definition of a bat (or staffe) in 1611 has been noted. A cricket bat is mentioned during the inquest on Jasper Vinall, who died at Horsted Keynes in 1624, and in 1648 another cricketer died as a result of being hit by a cricket bat at Selsey in Sussex. Edward Phillips, a nephew of Milton, specifically mentions a 'cricket-ball' in a piece published in 1658 and the pitching of wickets is noted in a poem of about 1680 (found in Kent). As for a written code of rules, the first extant set is dated 1744, though P.F. Thomas in his *Old English Cricket* (1924) analyses the 1744 version and convincingly argues that it

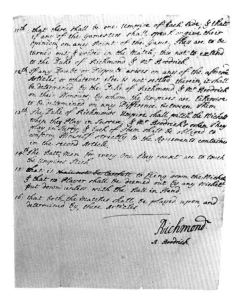

*The 'Articles of Agreement' between the 2nd Duke
of Richmond and Mr Alan Brodrick, drawn up for a match
in 1727. These are additional to the basic laws of the
game. The latter must have been in existence before 1727,
but no copies are known to have survived.*

is the revised version of an earlier code. Since 1924 the discovery at Goodwood House in
West Sussex of the 1727 'Articles of Agreement' confirms Thomas's theory. I shall return to
the Laws later.

SCHOOLS AND UNIVERSITIES

Many of the sons of the nobility and landed gentry living in The Weald, and indeed in
the counties of Surrey, Sussex and Kent as a whole – for cricket had spread throughout
these shires by the end of the 17th century – were educated at one of the four great schools:
Eton, Harrow, Winchester and Westminster. These sons almost certainly established cricket
at their schools before 1700, though the earliest school references are dubious. John Timbs
in his book *School Days of Eminent Men* (published in 1862) states that Thomas Ken 'used
to yield a cricket bat' while at Winchester (*c.*1655), and John Churchill (later Duke of
Marlborough) is referred to as playing cricket at St Paul's School (*c.*1665). There is no
suggestion that inter-schools matches took place this early.

By the end of the 17th century, cricket had moved a stage further, from the four great
schools to Oxford and Cambridge. In 1710, Thomas Blomer, a Fellow of Trinity College,

THE HISTORY OF CRICKET

Cambridge, complains of undergraduates hurrying their meals so they can go to play football or cricket. Samuel Johnson, at Oxford in 1729, later points out to a friend that a certain field was used for cricket in his day. Indeed, a case could be made for cricket of some sort at both universities a century earlier, since several of the people mentioned in the 17th-century notices were educated either at one of the four schools or at Oxford or Cambridge. Thomas Harlackenden, for example, who is mentioned as playing cricket at Coxheath, Kent in 1646, was educated at Oxford, while Henry Cuffin, the curate who played cricket at Ruckinge in 1629, attended King's College, Cambridge.

LONDON AND THEREABOUTS

With this base in the three south-eastern counties, and the playing of cricket by the upper-class boys and undergraduates, it is not surprising that the sport came to London at the turn of the century.

> These are to inform Gentlemen, or others, who delight in cricket-playing, that a match at Cricket of 10 Gentlemen on each side, will be played on Clapham-Common, near Fox-Hall [now Vauxhall] on Easter Monday (April 1st) next; for £10 a Head each game, (five being design'd) and £20 the Odd one.

This notice appeared in *The Post Boy* of 28–30 March 1700. In 1707 two matches, the first at Croydon and the second in Lamb's Conduit Fields, were advertised to be played between London and Croydon. Two years later the first 'inter-county' match is advertised, for £50 a side between Surrey and Kent at Dartford. The names of the players are not mentioned, and the match probably has a title it scarcely deserves.

By this time there existed, not a pictorial record of cricket; rather, a detailed description of a match – an excellent piece in many ways, but unfortunately for cricket historians written in Latin hexameters. The author was William Goldwin, educated at Eton and going up to King's College, Cambridge, in 1700. (Goldwin provides a further example of a cricket enthusiast attending major seats of learning.) From 1710 to his death in 1747 he resided in Gloucestershire. His book, which contains the verse entitled 'In Certamen Pilae' ('On a game of ball', i.e., a cricket match), was published in March 1706. The full verse runs to 95 lines and there are two well-known translations: one appears in H. S. Altham's *A History of Cricket* (1926), another in P.F. Thomas's *Early Cricket* (1923). There are minor differences, but most important, the game described by Goldwin is readily identifiable as the game we know today, as the following extract shows:

> Deinde locum signant, qua se diffundit in aequor
> Plana superficies; Hinc illinc partibus aeque
> Oppositis bifido Surgentes vertice furcae
> Erectas modicum quas distinet intervallum

Infiguntur humo; Tum virgula ponitur alba,
Virgula, qua dubii certaminis alea pendet,
Et bene defendi poscit: Coriaceus Orbis
Vi ruit infesta, quem si fortuna Maligna
Dirigit in rectum, subversaque Machina fulcris
Abripitur, cedas positis inglorius armis.

    The pitch [locum] then's chosen, where the meadows start
More flat. Each end, the proper length apart
And opposite, twin uprights [Surgentes furcae], cleft atop,
With little interval between, upcrop,
Thrust in the ground; a clean bail [virgula] caps their ends,
A bar on which the contest's fate depends,
And well it needs defending: Leather Sphere [Coriaceus Orbis]
May force its downfall; if by chance severe
She's straightly aimed, and strikes the wicket's [Machina] stay,
It falls, and its shamed guardian slinks away.

(TR. P.F. THOMAS)

The poem demolishes yet another of cricket's myths. Nyren's book (1833) notes that about 150 years earlier the two stumps were set two feet apart and were one foot high. In between the two stumps was a hole. To complete a run, the batsman had to put the end of his bat in the hole; to run a man out the fielder had to place the ball in the hole. Nyren goes on, 'Many severe injuries of the hands were the consequence of this regulation.'

This notion has been copied from Nyren's book into many subsequent volumes, but aside from Nyren's piece no other confirmation of such wicket-and-hole exists. How the bowler ever managed to bowl a batsman out with the wicket that shape is not explained. It is not mentioned by Goldwin. It would seem most probable that what Nyren describes is 'cat and dog', in which one player tries to throw a 'cat' into a hole, while another prevents this happening by using a 'dog' (the 'cat' is a small piece of wood, and the 'dog' is a club).

In 1712 cricket is well enough known to the reading public of London to be used as part of a lampoon in a political broadsheet featuring John Churchill, Duke of Marlborough (1650–1722), who had recently lost political power, and Charles Townshend (1674–1738), godson of James II and Viscount Townshend's son.

By the early years of the 18th century, Kent had overtaken Sussex as the principal cricketing county. The Earl of Oxford, travelling through Kent in 1723, noted:

At Dartford upon the Heath as we came out of the town, the men of Tonbridge and the Dartford men were warmly engaged at the sport of cricket, which of all the people of England the Kentish folk are the most renowned for, and of all the Kentish men, the men of Dartford lay claim to the greatest excellence.

THE HISTORY OF CRICKET

The Devil and the Peers : Or,
The Princely Way of Sabbath-breaking.

Being a True Account of a famous **Cricket-Match** between the Duke of M----, another Lord, and two Boys, on *Sunday* the 25th of *May* laft, 1712. near *Fern-Hill* in *Windfor Forreft* ; for Twenty Guineas.

◆ ◆ ◆ ◆ ◆

As the Devil never is wanting in his own Caufe, fo he had taken all imaginable care to fecond the L'uke's Inclinations ; for, *as the Devil won'd have it,* the Duke and Lord found feveral Boys ready to their Hands playing at Cricket. Quoth the Lord, *When I went to Eaton School I underftood this Game better than my Book ;— And I* (fays the Duke) *lov'd it better than Moral Philofophy.* — I'll *play with you* for Twenty Guineas (fays the Lord :) — A Match, cries the Duke ; and fo the Game begun.

The two Nobles agreed to chufe the two beft Boys at Cricket for each a Partner, and promis'd 'em Crowns a piece for their pains when the Match was won or loft, and Twelve-pence to a third Boy to knotch the Game down exact.

The Boy that was Partner againft the Duke whifpers my Lord and tells him, *Sir, I can play ten times better than t'other Boy, and if you'll make my Crown ten Shillings, I'll catch them both out in three or four ftroaks.*' The Lord readily agreed to 't, and the Boy perform'd his promife, and won him the 20 Guineas, but not fo eafily as imagin'd, for the Duke gave 'em feveral Mafter ftroaks before he was outed.

I had this Information from the Mouth of JUSTICE, *and it's queftion'd whether or no thefe Sabbath-Breakers will long efcape the Hands of Juftice ; for the Reformers of Manners, and many Confcientious Diffenters, are ftrangely alarm'd at this Princely Way of Sabbath breaking.*

The Truth hereof you may have Vouch'd and Confirm'd at *Windfor, Oakinghams, Maidenhead, Harford Bridge, Staynes, Slough, Colebrook,* at all the adjacent Villages, and at the *Tower of London* ; where you may find the abovefaid Duke and Lord after the arrival of a Foreign Mail, or any fine Afternoon, playing at Skittles with Mr. *Walpole.*

Hence who can doubt the Wars will ceafe, | For here Fernhillian *Swain fhall fay,*
When Generals take to Games of Peace, | Europe's Chief General loft the Day,
And pafs a Sunday, or an Hour, | Then point you out the very Place,
In Windfor Forreft, or the Tower ; | Here ftood my Lord — and here his Grace ;
There as Cricket, here at Skittles, | And that's the Boy, with Courage ftout,
For Stomachs to their Caufe and VPPeals ? | Who caught the mighty General out ;
Fern-Hill fhall hence as famous be | And on this mournful Spot be paid,
As any Place in Germany ; | With Tears, the Sum for which he plaj'd.

Printed for *J. Barker* in *Pater-nofter-Row,* 1712.

Notices and results in the extant newspapers are so sparse that it would seem impossible to verify the Earl's remark,[1] but John Goulstone discovered the following obituary notice in *Lloyd's Evening Post* from June 1768:

> Died on June 3, Mr William Beddel, a wealthy farmer and grazier aged near 90, at his house near Dartford. He was formerly accounted the most expert cricket player in England.

---

1 Robert Harley, Earl of Oxford (1661-1724), was Speaker of the House of Commons in 1700.

The first cricket clubs, as opposed to *ad hoc* village or town teams, were now being established. For example, in 1718–19 a well-reported match and trial occurred involving the 'Rochester Punch Club Society' and a London Club. In 1722, a letter to *The Weekly Journal* comments, 'A Match at Cricket was made between the little Parish of Dartford in Kent, and the Gentlemen known by the name of the London Club.'

THE FIRST GREAT PATRONS

However, in addition to these clubs, cricket acquired some wealthy patrons who financed their own teams: one in Surrey, one in East Sussex, one in West Sussex, and one in Kent. Of these patrons the most important was the 2nd Duke of Richmond, grandson of Charles II. He was born at Goodwood House in 1701 (Goodwood being in a part of West Sussex long versed in cricket), and the first extant mention of his involvement in the game comes in a letter dated 16 July 1725, which runs as follows:

The 2nd Duke of Richmond, from a portrait by Vanloo. His country seat, Goodwood House in West Sussex, was a centre of cricket in the 1720s. In the 1740s, Slindon, the village on the edge of the Goodwood Estate, possessed one of the best teams in England.

My Lord Duke,

I received this moment your Grace's letter and am extremely happy your Grace intends us ye honour of making one a Tuesday, and will without fail bring a gentleman with me to play against you, one that has played very seldom for these several years.

I am in great afflication from being shamefully beaten Yesterday, the first match I played this year. However I will muster up all my courage against Tuesday's engagement. I will trouble your Grace with nothing more than that I wish you Success in everything but ye Cricket Match and that I am etc. etc.

FIRLE   W. GAGE

THE HISTORY OF CRICKET

This letter to the Duke also brings a first cricketing mention of Sir William Gage (born Firle, East Sussex, in 1695), MP for Seaford. It would seem clear that both the Duke and Sir William had been organising cricket matches and playing for a number of years prior to 1725.

The following summer comes the first appearance of Edwin Stead (1701–35) of Maidstone, when Stead and his team are involved in a lawsuit regarding the outcome of a match against Chingford, played on Dartford Heath. In 1728, Stead's Kent side played matches against both the Duke of Richmond's team and Sir William Gage's side. In 1729, when they opposed the combined forces of Sussex, Surrey and Hampshire, the report closed thus:

> A groom of the Duke of Richmond signalized himself by such extraordinary agility and dexterity, to the surprise of all the spectators, which were some thousands, and 'tis reckoned he turned the scale of victory, which for some years past had been generally on the Kentish side.

As with the Gage letter of 1725, this report demonstrates that these 'inter-county' matches had been a cricketing feature for some years, and the adoption by the organisers of county titles at this time set the style for county teams which is *de rigueur* even now. The notice also suggests that the organisers employed men on their estates for their cricketing ability, a practice which becomes more apparent as the century proceeds. The groom in question is Thomas Waymark – in 1730 a press notice states that the match between the Duke and Sir William Gage is postponed 'on account of Waymark, the Duke's man, being ill'.

As yet no detailed scores exist: indeed, it is not until the next decade that team totals and the margins of victory are published. The individual batsman's scores have to wait until the gambling fraternity move from betting on the results to betting also on the scores of batsmen in the 1740s.

Stead was Kent's patron, Gage and Richmond supported Sussex, but the third major county, Surrey, were not so fortunate. Alan Brodrick of Peper Harow near Guildford raised a team for two games against the Duke of Richmond in 1727; the details only exist through the extant Articles of Agreement for the matches. Brodrick (born 1701) succeeded to the title of Viscount Midleton in 1729. Another early Surrey patron was Mr Andrews, whose team opposed the Duke of Richmond on Merrow Down near Guildford in 1730.

LONDON AND GAMBLING

More important than the Guildford match in 1730 was the first mention of cricket on the Artillery Ground in London. This venue became established as the ground for major matches. At its height in the 1740s some 70 noteworthy games were staged there during the decade, and no doubt numerous lesser ones which went unrecorded in the press. George Smith, the lessee of the ground and of the Pied Horse public house in adjacent

Chiswell Street, was the Thomas Lord of his day. He was also responsible for the first known admission charges, spectators paying 2d to watch matches on the Artillery Ground in 1744. Smith featured as a player in some matches, but later suffered financial problems and in 1752 moved to Marlborough, Wiltshire. On his ground the London Club was established, the organisation of which remains a mystery. Perhaps some Minute Books will one day surface to fill this irritating void. In 1732, the newspapers note, 'This is the thirteenth match the London gamesters have played this year and not lost one match.'

In December 1728, Frederick Louis, eldest son of George II, arrived in England. The following month he was created Prince of Wales. If his mother's opinion is a guide, he was an unpleasant character. His chief passions were women and gambling, and it was not long before he discovered that cricket was an ideal vehicle for the latter. The Prince was first reported attending a match, between London and Surrey, in 1731, 'there being great wagers depending'. The money was also beginning to attract the ruffians at the other end of the social scale. In the same year there are two reports of fighting between the spectators and the players. On 23 August, 'the Duke of Richmond and his Cricket Players were greatly insulted by the mob, some of the men having their shirts tore off their backs'.

The respectability of cricket slid rapidly downwards. In the 1740s an outstanding cricketer of the day was Robert Colchin, known as Long Robin. John Goulstone's biographical piece on Long Robin notes: 'Colchin's abilities as an organiser were never restricted to the cricket field; he was also a leader of the London Underworld – an

18th-century forerunner of the O'Bannions and Capones of more recent times – whose remarkable exploits stamp him as being one of the most original and extraordinary characters in the entire history of crime.'

His cricketing reign lasted from 1743 to the end of the decade. He lived in Bromley, Kent, at the start of his career and is chiefly associated with that county.

THE FAMOUS MATCH OF 1744

Despite these sordid connections cricket came of age in 1744. The *London Magazine* for June of that year does not employ hyperbole when it prints:

> Monday 18, was played in the Artillery Ground the greatest Cricket Match ever known, the County of Kent playing against all England, which was won by the former. There were present their Royal Highnesses the Prince of Wales, the Duke of Cumberland, the Duke of Richmond, Admiral Vernon, and many other persons of Distinction.

Not only is the detailed score of this game preserved – the famous Waymark dropped a vital catch for England, which lost the game by one wicket, and Long Robin was among the most successful of Kent's batsmen – but a certain James Love was commissioned to write a description of the game in the guise of an heroic poem. Also, it cannot be a coincidence that the earliest extant set of Laws are dated 1744. The poem is dedicated to John, 4th Earl of Sandwich (1718–92), who was an active cricketer, having most probably learnt the game at Eton. He later played for the Old Etonians. The poet's real name was James Dance (1722–1774), son of the architect of the Mansion House. The following extract gives a flavour of his poem:

> then poised, and rising as he threw,
> Swift from his Arm the fatal Missive flew.
> Nor with more Force the Death-conveying Ball,
> Springs from the Cannon to the batter'd Wall;
> Nor swifter yet the pointed Arrows go,
> Launched from the Vigour of the Parthian bow.
> It whizz'd along, with unimagined Force,
> And bore down all, resistless in its Course.
> To such impetuous Might compell'd to yield
> The Ball, the mangled Stumps bestrew the Field …
> But while the drooping Play'r invoked the Gods,
> The busy better calculates his Odds.
> Swift round the Plain, in buzzing Murmurs run,
> I'll hold you Ten to Four, Kent. – Done Sir. – Done.

THE ORIGINS

15

Apart from Waymark, the England team contained four players directly connected to the Duke of Richmond and hailing from the village of Slindon, adjacent to the Duke's residence at Goodwood. In the three years prior to the famous 1744 game, Slindon had built up a formidable side. A newspaper report stated in 1742 that Slindon had played 43 matches and lost only one. In 1744 the team challenged any parish in England and the challenge was repeated in 1747. Slindon's most famous matches were two against London in 1742; the Sussex side lost both. The interesting point in the report of the first match is the comment, 'it's to be hoped – nay desired – that gentlemen will not crowd in, by reason of the very large sum of money laid that one of the Sussex gentlemen gets 40 notches himself'.

Most probably the batsman concerned is Richard Newland, one of the three Slindon brothers, all of whom represented England against Kent in 1744. Richard Newland failed to reach 40. However, he succeeded in the 1745 England vs. Kent game, scoring 88. Extant letters show how much the Duke of Richmond was involved in this Slindon side and Richard Newland, its leader, has another important historical role, since he taught his nephew, Richard Nyren, later captain of Hambledon, to play.

The four great patrons were all gone by the mid-1750s. Edward Stead, a prey to his gambling habit, died in reduced circumstances in 1735; Sir William Gage died in 1744; the 2nd Duke of Richmond in 1750; and Alan Brodrick in 1752. The Prince of Wales died in 1751, in some reports as the result of a blow from a cricket ball, his demise being mourned only by those who would have preferred to see his brother the Duke of Cumberland dead. Cumberland was also interested in cricket and an amusing story about him is related in a letter dated 1751 from Robert Ord (Chief Baron of the Exchequer of Scotland) to the 4th Earl of Carlisle (1694–1758). The Duke ordered the 22 best cricketers in England to practise in front of him, so he could select the best eleven. He made his choice, then the rejected eleven played against the Duke's preferred side and easily beat them.

THE LANDED GENTRY

Proof of the growing interest in cricket at public schools through the first half of the 18th century was provided in 1751, when Eton Past & Present challenged the Gentlemen of England to a series of three matches for £1,500. England won two matches to one. A fourth match was played (result unknown) at the Duke of Bedford's estate, Woburn. The games were taken very seriously and such participants as the Duke of Kingston (at Thoresby Hall) and the Earl of Sandwich (at Huntingdon) practised cricket on their estates. The novelist Charlotte Smith, who grew up at Bignor Park in West Sussex in the 1750s (not far from Goodwood), was doubtless drawing on childhood memories in her book *The Old Manor House* in this description of the house and extensive grounds at 'Rayland Hall':

> She was as little capable of disguising as of denying the truth; and the menaces
> of her aunt frightened her into an immediate confession, that it was Mr. Orlando,

who, passing through the court to go to cricket in the park, had seen her sitting at the window, and, 'not thinking any harm', had thrown up his ball 'only in play', to make her jump; but that it had unluckily gone through the window, and hit against the picture.

This enthusiasm, which meant that cricket was being played by a number of the landed gentry throughout the British Isles, has led to a rather confused picture regarding the overall popularity of cricket. Outside the south-east of England, the game was being played in isolated pockets, rather than by all and sundry. An extreme example, somewhat later, is the first mention of a cricket match in Scotland in 1785, which involved house guests at the Earl of Cathcart's. It was not until some 50 years later that the people of Scotland took an interest in the game. It is perhaps appropriate to note here that the so-called first mention of cricket in Wales (in Pembroke in 1763) is incorrect, the reference being to Pembroke College, Oxford.

SPREADING SLOWLY

A survey of the known references to cricket by the middle of the 18th century shows that while the game was attracting great crowds in London and its immediate surroundings, as well as being played extensively in Sussex, Kent and Surrey, the complex nature of the sport meant that it was making slow progress as a pastime for the general population, as opposed to the nobility. It was not until 1749 that the first game was reported in Hampshire: Portsmouth Common against Fareham & Titchfield. The match in 1735 between Brentwood and Romford on Shenville Common would appear to be Essex's first recorded game, although Chingford played matches before this outside the county. The famous Thomas Waymark came originally from Bray in Berkshire and the southern parts of both that county and Buckinghamshire, the latter including Eton, were popular venues for cricket. Nearby Moulsey Hurst on the Thames, but in Surrey, was the venue for a number of major matches from the 1730s.

There is a stray reference to a game in Gloucester in 1729, maybe connected with William Goldwin, who was living in the county at the time. The next cricket notice in that city is a hundred years later! Neighbouring Wiltshire does not come on the scene until the late 1760s. Through the two universities cricket was played at both Oxford and Cambridge in the 18th century, but the first area, away from the vicinity of London and the south-east, where the game achieved widespread acceptance was Suffolk and Norfolk. J.S. Penny's comprehensive search of the Norwich newspapers from 1701 to 1800 was published in 1979, and the fact that the editors felt it worthwhile printing the notices of cricket matches played in the south-east from 1729 indicates that their readers were interested in the game. From the 1740s local matches are relatively common.

In the north of England, the Duke of Cleveland's side opposed the Duke of

Northumberland's side at Raby Castle, County Durham in 1751, but this match is similar to the Scottish example previously noted.

One reference which needs explanation features Ireland in 1656. The notice suggests that Cromwell's Commissioners announced the banning of the game throughout Ireland. This notice came to light in *The Cricketer* magazine of 1956 (p.398). One has to ask oneself, if cricket was so popular in Ireland then that it required banning, would the Irish population have bowed totally to the Cromwellian edict and not played the game for the next 200 years? This seems so unlikely that one can only assume that the document mistook hurling for cricket, because of the use of a similar stick or bat.

THE MID-18TH-CENTURY GAME

Would a cricket match of 1750 be immediately recognised as such by a present-day spectator? The answer is depicted in Francis Hayman's picture, 'Cricket in Marylebone Fields' (see plate section). The exact date of the painting is not known, but it is certainly before 1748, when an engraving of it was published and advertised for sale. Today's viewer can see at a glance all the basic elements of 20th-century cricket. There are eleven fieldsmen of whom one is bowling and another keeping wicket. Two umpires and two batsmen are shown, and even two scorers. The wickets, two stumps and a bail, conform in size to the dimensions laid down in the 1744 Laws. The bowler is delivering the ball under-arm. The players are dressed predominantly in white with most of them wearing a standard jockey-type cap – the use of pads and gloves is still in the distant future. A study of the early extant scores also reveals how close the game was to present-day cricket. The four common ways of being dismissed – bowled, caught, stumped and run out – all appear: only lbw is missing, introduced into the laws in 1774. Byes are recorded separately. One omission is the bowling analyses, but in those days the bowler was not credited with wickets, except the ones he bowled down, and detailed bowling figures were not kept until the 1830s.

The bats are of a single piece of timber and shaped to suit the all-along-the-ground bowling. The regulations concerning the size of the bat did not come in until 1771 as a result of switching the bowling from along the ground to first bounce to the batsman some time in the 1760s. The original 'hockey stick' shape then evolved into a parallel-sided 'pod'.

In the 1740s and 1750s, matches were arranged and teams gathered together in two main ways. The first and principal factor was the patron, whose presence has been noted previously. Lord John Sackville's XI, Lord Montford's XI, Squire Hartley's XI, and J. Tatum's XI are further examples. The second method was teams run by 'clubs'. Their existence, too, has already been noted, but by the middle of the century they were far more common. The following notice is typical:

> Subscribers to the Cricket Club for the ensuing season are desired to meet at Bridge Hill House, on Wed., 22nd inst., at 3 p.m.

This refers to Bridge in Kent in 1751. As with the London Club, the Minute Books or Accounts of all these local clubs appear to have been lost.

Two important clubs in this period, apart from the London Club, were Addington, in Surrey, and a little later Dartford. Addington, which opposed London in 1743 and the two following years, faded away after 1752; Dartford, which was mentioned by the Earl of Oxford in 1723, revived in the 1750s and in 1759 beat the Rest of England twice. Neither of these games was staged on the Artillery Ground, one being at Dartford and the other at Laleham Burway, on the Thames near Staines. The seamier reputation of the Artillery Ground was telling against it as a venue for major matches.

THE HAMBLEDON CLUB

In August 1756 the Dartford Club had played three matches against a side which is described in one source as Hampton in Middlesex and in another as Hambledon in Hampshire (see next page). It would seem to be more likely the latter, this being the same year in which an advert appears about a dog lost at a cricket match on Broadhalfpenny Down (the Hambledon ground). The next reference to Hambledon occurs in 1764, when 'The Gentlemen of Hambledon, called Squire Lamb's Club' played Chertsey. A variety of dates have been given for the foundation of the Hambledon Club, usually in the 1750s and frequently as early as 1750, but these are based purely on a remark of William Beldham to James Pycroft. Beldham states that Mr Powlett had, by 1780, spent 30 years raising the Club. I suggest that this is a mishearing of 13 years, putting the date that Powlett succeeded Lamb (actually Thomas Land) at about 1767.

The Revd Charles Powlett did not come, or move closer, to the Hambledon area until 1763, when he was appointed curate of Itchen Abbas. He was born in 1728, a son of the 3rd Duke of Bolton, and was educated at Westminster and Trinity College, Cambridge, getting his MA in 1755. About the same time as he arrived Richard Nyren, the nephew of the old England and Slindon captain, Richard Newland, moved to Hambledon from Sussex. A third party in the establishment of the Hambledon Club was Philip Dehany (1733–1809), also educated at Westminster; he resided at Kempshott Park in Hampshire. After some initial success, Powlett's Club went into temporary decline, but in 1771 it really blossomed and effectively organised the Hampshire county side for the next two decades.

NEW PATRONS

At the same time as Powlett and Nyren were building up the Hampshire side through the Hambledon Club, fresh patrons were giving support to the three older established cricketing counties. The 4th Earl of Tankerville (1743–1822), educated at Eton, had his country seat at Mount Felix, Walton on Thames, and employed such famous players as 'Lumpy' Stevens (1735–1819) and William Bedster (d.1805). He played his matches at

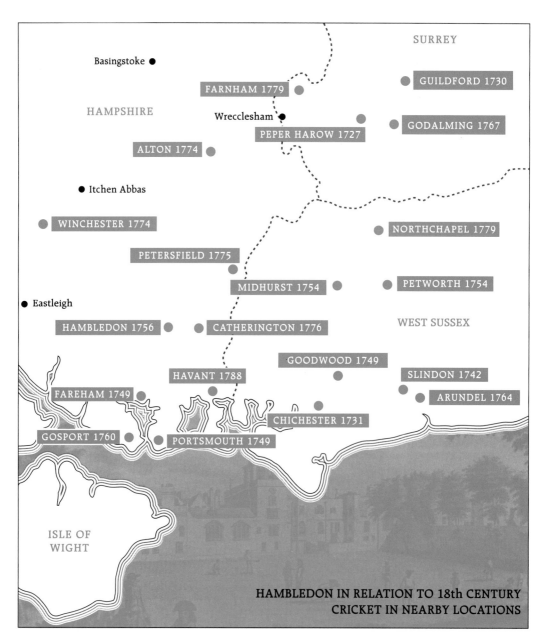

SURREY

Basingstoke ●

FARNHAM 1779 ●

GUILDFORD 1730 ●

HAMPSHIRE

Wrecclesham ●

GODALMING 1767 ●

PEPER HAROW 1727

ALTON 1774 ●

● Itchen Abbas

WINCHESTER 1774 ●

NORTHCHAPEL 1779 ●

PETERSFIELD 1775 ●

● Eastleigh

MIDHURST 1754 ●

PETWORTH 1754 ●

WEST SUSSEX

HAMBLEDON 1756 ● ● CATHERINGTON 1776

GOODWOOD 1749 ●

HAVANT 1788 ●

SLINDON 1742 ●

FAREHAM 1749 ●

ARUNDEL 1764 ●

CHICHESTER 1731 ●

GOSPORT 1760 ● ● PORTSMOUTH 1749

ISLE OF
WIGHT

**HAMBLEDON IN RELATION TO 18th CENTURY
CRICKET IN NEARBY LOCATIONS**

*Relative distances from Hambledon to that earlier seat of cricket, Goodwood, and Winchester.
The Revd Charles Powlett, who combined with Richard Nyren to run the famous Hambledon Club,
was curate of Itchen Abbas from 1763 to 1792.*

THE HISTORY OF CRICKET

Laleham Burway and was the principal supporter of Surrey cricket. The 3rd Duke of Dorset (1745–1799), educated at Harrow, owned the Sevenoaks ground in Kent and was a considerable cricketer in his own right. He also employed several noted players, including William Bowra (1752–1820), Joseph Miller (d.1799) and John Minshull (1741–1793). The last named, while playing for the Duke of Dorset's side in 1769, hit the first recorded century.

The Duke of Dorset was not the sole Kent patron; the county had a second promoter in Sir Horatio Mann (1744–1814). Educated at Charterhouse, he had cricket grounds at Bishopsbourne, near Canterbury; Linton, near Maidstone; and Sissinghurst; then later at Dandelion Paddock, Margate. His expenditure on cricket, among other extravagances, caused his bankruptcy. Dorset and Tankerville were described as 'the two idlest lords in His Majesty's three kingdoms'. Mann employed John and George Ring and James Aylward, but despite his generous hospitality to cricketers and his popularity, he was frequently the object of 'buffooneries of his less decorous associates'. Aylward had made a new record score of 167 for Hampshire in 1777, and this feat, together with other excellent scores, persuaded Mann

The 3rd Duke of Dorset, who played for Kent from 1773 to 1783, was one of the game's greatest patrons. The Duke gave the Sevenoaks Vine Club's ground to the public.

to give him a job as bailiff. Thus Aylward moved from the Hambledon Club to Kent.

Sussex, the oldest cricketing county, were without effective patronage at this time. The 3rd Duke of Richmond raised occasional county sides, but was not the supporter his father had been. The contest for the crown of 'Champion County' was therefore between Kent, Hampshire and Surrey. Outside these select three, the Oldfield Club of Maidenhead raised some Berkshire teams and flourished from 1774 to 1785 (it was later revived); the Hornchurch Club was the principal Essex side in the 1780s and continued through the next decade, sometimes raising county sides.

While the organisation of these clubs remains unknown and their players are little more than names, Hambledon and Hampshire are well known, thanks to John Nyren's book of 1833 and, by good fortune, the survival of their Minute Books and Accounts. However, the majority of the best Hambledon Club cricketers were not natives of that village. James Aylward (born Warnford, 1741), David Harris (born Elvetham, 1755), John Small sen. (Empshott, 1737), Harry and Thomas Walker (Churt, Surrey, 1760 and 1762), Thomas Brett (Catherington, 1747), Noah Mann (Northchapel, Sussex, 1756), as well as Richard Nyren, were all incomers. Edward Aburrow (b.1747), George Leer (b.1749) and Thomas Sueter (b.1750) were the three notable cricketers born in the village. The account book of 1791 shows 52 'Gentlemen Subscribers' paying three guineas each.

MOVING NORTH

While Hampshire, Kent and Surrey arranged the great matches among themselves, or one of the three challenged All England, a lesser, but important, competition was burgeoning in the Midlands. The most likely innovators were the occupants of the Dukeries in north Nottinghamshire (see opposite). The Pelham family, who lived at Halland near Lewes in the 1690s, moved to Clumber early in the next century and inherited the Dukedom of Newcastle. Sir John Pelham (1623–1702) was known to be involved in cricket in Sussex. By the 1740s the estate accounts for the Duke of Portland at Welbeck contain items for the making of cricket bats, and at Thoresby resided the Duke of Kingston, who played for Eton Past & Present in 1751.

The game spread rapidly from the estate workers of the Dukeries northward to Sheffield and Yorkshire, westward to Derbyshire and south to Nottingham and Leicester. The framework knitters of the region, particularly Nottinghamshire, could arrange their own leisure time and therefore soon acquired more cricketing skill than agricultural labourers and others whose working hours were less flexible.

The earliest recorded Nottingham vs. Sheffield game took place in 1771. In the 1780s Leicester formed a club and played against their northern neighbours. These clubs of Sheffield, Nottingham and Leicester were markedly different from the principal sides in the south-east. They were clubs of artisans, largely self-supporting and run by the landlord of one of the town's inns. The peerage residing in the Dukeries had little or nothing to do with the offspring of the game they had introduced to the area, and the players made what money they could from betting on individual performances or the outcome of matches. Their matches were not staged in the park of a private estate, but on common land; later, as a speculation, publicans and others laid out grounds, often adjacent to a public house, to which they could make admission charges. Through this accident of geography and time, the contrast between the way cricket was run in the 'north' and the 'south' led to the legendary north/south divide which lingers still persists.

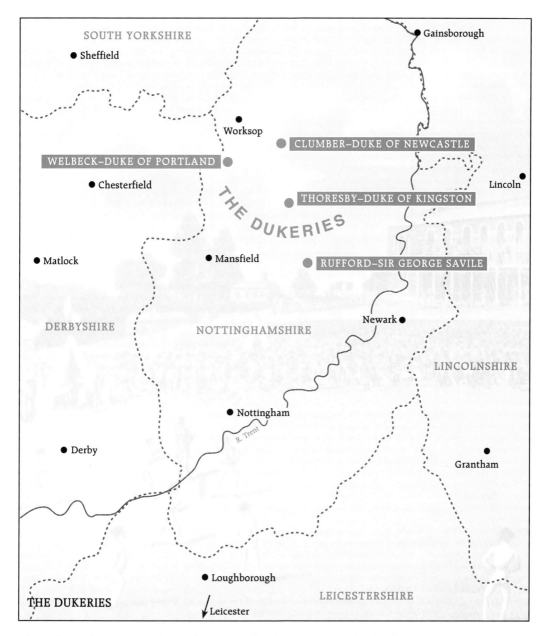

SOUTH YORKSHIRE

● Sheffield

● Gainsborough

● Worksop

● CLUMBER–DUKE OF NEWCASTLE

WELBECK–DUKE OF PORTLAND ●

● Chesterfield

Lincoln ●

THE DUKERIES

● THORESBY–DUKE OF KINGSTON

● Matlock

● Mansfield

● RUFFORD–SIR GEORGE SAVILE

DERBYSHIRE

NOTTINGHAMSHIRE

Newark ●

LINCOLNSHIRE

● Nottingham

R. Trent

● Derby

● Grantham

● Loughborough

LEICESTERSHIRE

THE DUKERIES

↓ Leicester

The earliest references to cricket in this East Midlands area occur on the ducal estates, from where the game spread to Nottingham, Sheffield, Leicester, Chesterfield and Derby.

THE LAWS

The Laws of the game were revised once in the period 1767–86, that is, during the 20 years when the Hambledon Club was raising the Hampshire side to its pinnacle. The actual heading of the document relating to this Law change is as informative as the details of the Laws themselves:

> THE LAWS OF CRICKET
> Revised at the Star and Garter, Pall-Mall, February 25, 1774
> By a Committee of Noblemen and Gentlemen of Kent, Hampshire,
> Surrey, Sussex, Middlesex and London.
> Committee:
> In the Chair – Sir William Draper. Present – His Grace the Duke of Dorset,
> Right Honourable Earl Tankerville, Sir Horace Mann,
> Philip Dehany, John Brewer Davis, Harry Peckham, Francis Vincent,
> John Cooke, Charles Coles, Richard James, Esquires,
> Rev Charles Powlett.

First, the meeting was in London rather than anywhere in the three major cricketing counties of that date. Second, the Committee was representative of the counties, which further emphasises the importance of county teams. Third, of the individuals who attended, General Sir William Draper, the chairman, had played for Eton against England in 1751; while Dorset, Tankerville, Mann, Dehany and Powlett are all known and have been mentioned as promoters of the game. F.S. Ashley-Cooper identifies some of the others as John Brewer Davis, who played for Kent in 1773; and John Cooke and Richard James, who were possibly the former Westminster School pupils of the same name.

In contrast to the 1744 Laws, a definite lbw law appears. According to William Beldham, 'The Law for leg before wicket was not made, nor much wanted, till Ring, one of our best hitters, was shabby enough to get his leg in the way and take advantage of the bowlers, and when Tom Taylor, another of the best hitters, did the same, the bowlers found themselves beaten and the law was passed.' Despite this claim, G.B. Buckley's search through the extant scorecards failed to find lbw recorded until 1795.

The width of the bat is laid down for the first time, but in fact in September 1771, the Hambledon players Richard Nyren, Thomas Brett and John Small had minuted that, because of the action of White of Reigate, the bat should be 4¼ inches wide forthwith. White had used a bat as wide as the wicket. What size of bat White used when scoring 197 runs in his two innings for Surrey and Kent vs. Middlesex and Hampshire in July of the same year is not recorded! Thomas White died in his native town of Reigate in 1831, aged 91.

One point that is not mentioned in the 1774 Laws and indeed does not appear in the official Laws until 1838 is the introduction of a middle stump. Nyren in his book is very precise:

On the 22nd of May 1775, a match was played in the Artillery Ground, between five of the Hambledon Club and five of All England; when Small went in the last man for fourteen runs, and fetched them. Lumpy was bowler upon the occasion; and it having been remarked that his balls had three several times passed between Small's stumps, it was considered to be a hard thing upon the bowler that his straightest balls should be thus sacrificed; the number of the stumps was in consequence increased from two to three.

There is some doubt about the accuracy of this comment since John Nyren was only ten years old at the time. The following year Richard Hayes (1725–1790) of Cobham, Kent, watched Hampshire play England at Sevenoaks and noted afterwards in his diary: 'They talk of having three stumps.' The earliest picture with a definite date which shows three stumps appeared in 1782.

According to F.S. Ashley-Cooper's *Match List*, the Hambledon Club raised teams for 81 matches between 1772 and 1783. In the next ten years only 24 matches were played, a number of which were of a minor nature. John Nyren claims, 'When Richard Nyren left Hambledon (1791) the club broke up, and never resumed from that day. The head and right arm were gone.'

The Revd Charles Powlett, who had founded the Club, was appointed Rector of St Martin's-by-Looe in Cornwall in 1785, which might be expected to restrict his time in Hampshire, but an inspection of the contemporary church registers at St Martin's reveals that Powlett rarely officiated at his parish. Richard Nyren was over 50 in 1785; his active cricketing days, at least at the top level, were at an end.

Meanwhile a rival club was being fostered in the Farnham area by Lord Stowell and Lord George Kerr, son of the Marquis of Lothian. A ground was laid out at nearby Wrecclesham and such notable cricketers as William Beldham and the brothers James and John Wells were recruited. However, above and beyond this, two new cricket patrons had arrived who wanted to set up a private ground in London. The time had come to take the major matches back to the capital.

EARLY CRICKET FACT FILE

The following references to cricket have been used in previous histories, but it is debatable whether many, if any, of them refer to cricket.

c.1180 Joseph of Exeter, writing in Latin, is quoted in translation as saying: 'The youths at cricks did play/Throughout the merry day.'

1300 'Creag' – an unknown pastime referred to in Latin, in the Wardrobe Accounts of Edward I.

c.1300 A bat and ball game illustrating the border of the Schilling manuscript.

c.1340 Pictorial reference on the border of an illuminated manuscript of the *Romance of Alexander.*

c.1350 Shepherds in a mural at Cocking Church, Sussex.

c.1350 A bat and ball game on a stained-glass window in Gloucester Cathedral.

1477 'Handyn and Handoute' among pastimes listed in a statute of Edward IV.

1478 'Criquet' mentioned in a French manuscript, referring to a place in the district of St Omer, north-east France.

1562 'Clyckett' mentioned as an unlawful game played in Malden, Essex.

1598 Sgrillare defined as 'to make a noise as a cricket, to play cricket-a-wicket and be merry' in Florio's *Italian-English Dictionary.*

1656 Cricket banned in Ireland – Cromwell's Commissioners clearly mistook hurling for cricket.

1666 St Alban's Cricket Club formed. No evidence; probably a misread date – 1666 should be 1806.

1668 Landlord of the Ram Inn, Smithfield, rated for a Cricket Field – this is a misreading of the Clerkenwell Rate Book.

The following are authentic English cricket references, some of which are referred to in the main text, and some mentioned only here. The list is meant to be representative rather than exhaustive, particularly as it moves into the 18th century, and, with one exception, it stops short of 1800.

1598   'Creckett' referred to in a court case in Guildford during an argument over a piece of land. A witness, John Derrick, stated that when a schoolboy he and his friends played 'creckett' on the land about 50 years previously.

1611   Two young men fined for playing cricket on Sunday in Sidlesham, West Sussex.

1611   'Crosse' is defined in Randle Cotgrave's *French-English Dictionary* as 'a cricket staffe, or the crooked staff wherein boyes play at cricket'. Cotgrave went to St John's College, Cambridge, in 1587, and was in the Inner Temple in 1591.

1613   An assault with a 'cricket staffe' in a court case, the assault taking place at Wanborough, near Guildford.

1622   A number of youths 'playing at cricket in the churchyard' at Boxgrove, West Sussex.

1624   Inquest on Jasper Vinall, accidentally hit with a 'Cricket batt' while trying to catch the ball – a group were playing cricket on Horsted Green, Sussex.

1629   Henry Cuffin brought before the Archdeacon's Court for 'playing at Cricketts' immediately after divine service. Cuffin was curate of Ruckinge, Kent.

1636   Henry Mabbinck stated he played cricket 'in the Parke', West Horsley, Surrey – a court case on a tithe dispute.

1640   A court case involving land at Chevening, Kent, mentions cricket being played there 'about 30 years since'.

1640   The Revd Thomas Wilson charged some cricketers with playing on a Sunday, smashing a window, endangering the life of a child, Maidstone, Kent.

1646   A court case at Coxheath, near Maidstone, involving a match and betting on cricket.

1648   Court case about the death of Thomas Hatter, wounded when struck by a cricket bat at Selsey, West Sussex.

1652   Court case involving the playing of cricket in Cranbrook, Kent.

1654   Money received for misdemeanours by 'Cricket players' on the Lord's Day, Eltham, Kent.

1658   'Cricket-ball' referred to as such for the first time, in a book by Edward Phillips (1630–1696), nephew of Milton. The book was published this year in London. Phillips was tutor to the son of the diarist John Evelyn, when the latter was living in Deptford.

1666	'He saw your son very well engaged in a game at cricquett on Richmond Green.' Letter from Sir Robert Paston. Richmond in Surrey.
1668	Reference to the sale of drink at cricket matches, in Maidstone.
1668	Court case concerning the 'playinge at crickett and strokebase', at Shoreham, Kent.
1671	Edward Bound charged with playing cricket on Sunday – exonerated. Shere, Surrey.
1677	'Pd to my Lord when his Lordship went to the crekitt match at ye Dicker.' Dicker in East Sussex. From the Earl of Sussex's Accounts.
1678	The first edition of Dr Adam Littleton's *Linguae Latinae Liber Dictionarus. Quadripartitus: A Latine Dictionary in Four Parts* defines cricket as 'a play. Ludus baculi & pilae [Game of stick & ball]'. He also defines the Latin word 'vibia' as: 'A pole or stick laid across on Forks, like the Cricket-bar at bat-play.' Littleton was educated at Westminster (and Christ Church, Oxford) and later taught at the school.
1694	'2/6 paid for a wagger about a cricket match at Lewis.' Steward's Accounts of Sir John Pelham, who lived at Halland, West Sussex.
1697	'The middle of last week a great match at Cricket was played in Sussex; there were eleven of a side, and they played for fifty guineas apiece.' (*Foreign Post*, 7 July.)
1700	A cricket match announced on Clapham Common (*Post Boy*, 28–30 March).
1705	Eleven-a-side match, West of Kent vs. Chatham, arranged for Malling (*Post Man*, 24 July).
1706	Publication of William Goldwin's Latin poem describing a cricket match.
1707	Two matches between Croydon and London, one at Croydon and one at Lamb's Conduit Fields, Holborn, advertised (*Post Man*, 21–24 June).
1708	'We beat Ash Street at Crickets', Diary of Thomas Minter of Canterbury (manuscript in British Museum).
1709	First inter-county match: Kent vs. Surrey at Dartford for £50 (*Post Man*, 25 June).
1710	First mention of cricket at Cambridge University. Noted by Thomas Blomer, Fellow of Trinity College, in a dispute about undergraduates.
1712	Political tract featuring cricket published in London.
1717	Eighteen references to inter-village cricket between 1717 and 1727 by Thomas Marchant of Hurstpierpoint, Sussex, in his diary.
1718	Law suit between two cricket teams, Rochester Punch Club Society and the London Gamesters.

1722	Long letter regarding a match between London and Dartford (*The Weekly Journal*, 21 July).
1724	Probable first reference to cricket in Essex, Chingford vs. Dartford. Venue probably Chingford.
1725	References to matches between the Duke of Richmond's team and Sir William Gage's team.
1726	Single wicket match advertised between Perry of London and Piper of Hampton, Middlesex, to be played at Moulsey Hurst (*London Evening Post*, 27 August).
1727	Articles of Agreement between the Duke of Richmond and Alan Brodrick of Peper Harow, Surrey.
1729	Probable first reference to cricket at Oxford University (Dr Samuel Johnson stated he played at the University. He was only there one year.)
1729	First reference to cricket in Gloucestershire, in Gloucester.
1729	Earliest surviving bat. John Chitty of Knaphill, Surrey, was the original owner. It is now kept in The Oval pavilion.
1730	First mention of a match on the Artillery Ground, London vs. Surrey (*Grub Street Journal*, 3 September).
1730	First mention of cricket in Buckinghamshire – at Datchet.
1731	Prince of Wales attends a match.
	Team totals published in newspaper.
1735	London vs. Kent: teams chosen respectively by the Prince of Wales and the Earl of Middlesex. Advertised to be played for £1,000.
1737	First mention in Hertfordshire – Hertford vs. Stansted.
1739	First pictorial representation of cricket.
1741	Bedfordshire vs. Northamptonshire, home and away, at Woburn and Northampton; first mention in both those counties.
1743	Stradbroke vs. Finningham; first mention in Suffolk.
1744	First full score preserved.
	First extant Laws.
	First recorded charge for admission.
1745	First recorded women's cricket match: at Gosden Common, Surrey, between Bramley and Hambleton, Friday 26 September.
1745	Setting up of a club in Norwich; first mention in Norfolk.
1748	Cricket bats being made at Welbeck; first mention of cricket in Nottinghamshire.
1749	Portsmouth vs. Fareham & Titchfield; first match in Hampshire.

1751	First mentions in Somerset (Saltford, Bath), Warwickshire (Aston, Birmingham), Yorkshire (Standwick) and Berkshire (near Windsor).
1754–65	Several references to cricket in the diary of Thomas Turner of East Hoathly, Sussex.
1755	First edition of Dr Samuel Johnson's *Dictionary* defines cricket as: 'A sport, at which the contenders drive a ball with sticks in opposition to each other.' Johnson then quotes the poet Alexander Pope's use of the word 'cricket' in *The Dunciad*, Book IV, which Pope published 13 years earlier.
1757	Wirksworth vs. Sheffield at Brampton Moor; first mention in Derbyshire.
1766	Cricket on ice in Hexham; first mention in Northumberland.
1767	The Revd Charles Powlett establishes his Hambledon Club.
1767	Hambledon play the Caterham Club at Croydon. Under the patronage of Henry Rowed, Caterham became a powerful club in the 1760s.
1768	Frederick Howard, Fifth Earl of Carlisle, plays cricket with friends in Spa (in what is now Belgium) while on the Grand Tour of Europe.
1769	First individual century – 107 by John Minshull.
1769	First mention of cricket in Wiltshire, at Upford.
1771	Dimension of bat set at 4¼ inches.
1773	First mention of cricket in Devon, at Teignmouth.
1774	Laws revised at the Star and Garter Club, Pall Mall.
1775	Cricket at Huntingdon – first mention in that county.
1776	First known scorecards – in Sevenoaks, Kent.
1776	First mentions of cricket in Dorset (Poole) and Leicestershire (Mount Sorrel vs. Barrow on Soar – although the Laws had been advertised in the local press two years earlier).
1777	John Aylward makes a record score of 167.
1779	Painting of the Countess of Derby's women's match at The Oaks, Surrey.
1781	Cricket on Brinnington Moor; first mention in Cheshire.
1790	First mention of cricket in Rutland, at Burley on the Hill.
1794	First mention of cricket in Shropshire, at Shrewsbury.
1811	First women's 'county' cricket match, between Hampshire and Surrey, on 3 October at Ball's Pond, Newington, Middlesex.

THE HISTORY OF CRICKET

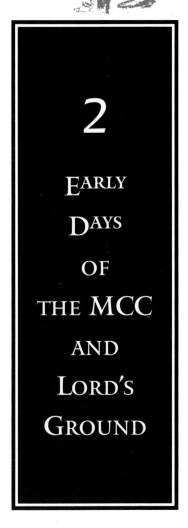

Marylebone Cricket Club, invariably referred to as the MCC, is considered to be the world's premier cricket club and is based at Lord's Cricket Ground in St John's Wood, London. The Club remains the arbiter on the Laws of Cricket and for many years effectively ran English cricket at Test and county level. It is and always has been a private members' club. The details surrounding the establishment of the MCC are obscure, and most reference books give its foundation year as 1787. This is most certainly the year in which Thomas Lord established a new cricket ground in London, but it most certainly is not the year the MCC was founded.

THOMAS LORD

Thomas Lord was born in Thirsk, Yorkshire, on 23 November 1755. His well-to-do family had lost its wealth espousing the cause of Bonnie Prince Charlie and, by the 1760s, the family had moved to Diss in Norfolk. Diss was a major centre of cricket at that time; in 1764, for example, the Diss Club issued a challenge to play any other town in Norfolk or Suffolk. Having learnt his cricket in Diss, young Thomas Lord came to London in or about 1778. At that time the principal London cricket ground was adjacent to White Conduit House, a tavern in Islington to which certain sections of society came for recreation and the air (see page 33).

The Cricket Club, which used the Star and Garter in Pall Mall for its formal dinners, rented the cricket ground on White Conduit Fields three days a week during May, June and July. Thomas Lord, as a capable cricketer, acted as the general factotum for the Cricket Club at White Conduit.

Some time in 1786, the Earl of Winchilsea, who was Treasurer of the Cricket Club, told Thomas Lord that some members of the Club, but principally himself and Colonel Lennox (later Duke of Richmond), would support Lord if he could lay out a private cricket ground and that the Cricket Club would move its activities from White Conduit Fields to this new ground.

Lord, who apart from his cricket activities was making his way in the wine trade, took a lease on a tavern and adjacent field off the New Road in Marylebone. He enclosed the field with a close-boarded fence and prepared the ground for cricket.

2

EARLY

DAYS

OF

THE MCC

AND

LORD'S

GROUND

Thomas Lord. As a result of his connection with the Earl of Winchilsea and the Hon. Charles Lennox, he founded in 1787 the cricket ground which is appropriately named after him and which has been the headquarters of the Marylebone Cricket Club since the ground was laid out.

The Morning Herald of 19 May 1787 contains the following notice:

A grand match will be played on Mon. May 21, in the New Cricket Ground, the New Road, Mary-le-bone, between eleven Noblemen of the White Conduit Club and eleven Gentlemen of the County of Middlesex with two men given, for 500 guineas a side.[2]

2   Men were 'given' to even up the sides for betting purposes.

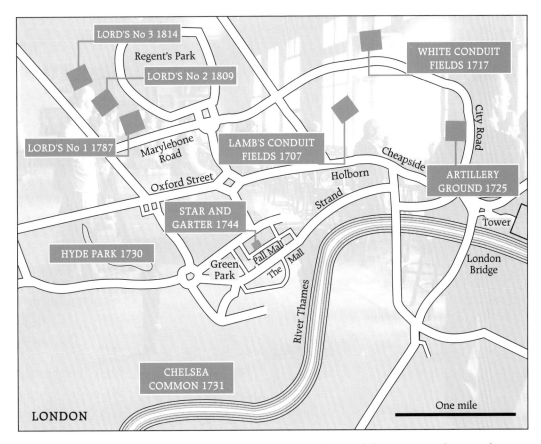

London, showing the principal cricket locations up to the foundation of the present Lord's Ground.

The following month another report notes: 'Mr Lord, the proprietor of the ground and adjoining tavern, deserved much praise for the management and order he displayed.' This was in relation to a match between the White Conduit Club and England.

Lord continued to run the ground, which was situated adjacent to the present Dorset Square, until 1810, but in 1808 he was aware that his ground would shortly be required for building. In 1809 he accordingly laid out a fresh cricket ground about half a mile to the north-west and for two seasons, 1809 and 1810, both cricket grounds were in use. The second ground, however, was not destined to survive long, since it was decided in 1813 to construct the Regents Canal through the land. So in 1814 Lord established a third ground another quarter of a mile north-west on the north side of St John's Wood Road. This remains the Lord's Cricket Ground that we know today. Thomas Lord's wine business, which he established in Upper Gloucester Street, flourished as a result of the contacts he made through the Cricket Club, and at one point he could boast of supplying the Royal Household. Through his enterprise he managed to regain at least part of the fortune his father had lost 40 years earlier.

THE MCC

Turning from the early history of Lord's Ground to the history of the Marylebone Cricket Club, it is obvious that writers have been led astray by the importance placed on the geographical description 'Marylebone'. In seeking the origins of this Cricket Club, the geographical attachment to the present name should be ignored. The key to the riddle is contained in a broadsheet, the only known copy of which is housed in the Leicester Record Office (this broadsheet was unknown to cricket historians until the 1940s).

The date of the document is 1784 and it contains three elements: the Laws of Cricket, the Rules of the Cricket Club, and a list of the Cricket Club members.

It is called simply 'The Cricket Club'; there is no geographical tie. The only location given in the Rules is the Star and Garter, Pall Mall, which the Club was to use for its dinners. Concerning the playing of cricket, the Rules state: 'That all expenses for the hire of ground, umpires, bats, balls, etc., be paid out of the stock purse.'

It is apparent from the Rules that most of the Club's matches were purely pick-up games between members of the Club, rather than a Cricket Club team opposing another club. In general, it is unlikely that the newspapers would have reported pick-up matches of this kind. (Sundry members of the Cricket Club would assemble at the cricket ground and from those present two sides would be formed.)

There are in fact one or two 1784 mentions of matches concerning the 'Star and Garter Club', but no details of the players involved have survived. In 1785 and 1786, however, some scores of 'White Conduit Club' matches were published, and the team comprised members of the Cricket Club, as listed on the broadsheet of 1784. When the White Conduit Club team plays a match at Lord's in 1787, the team again comprises members of the Cricket Club. Going on to 1788, the home team on Lord's Ground is given as 'Marylebone' Cricket Club, and once more is basically the members of the Cricket Club which dines at the Star and Garter.

It can therefore be stated unequivocally that the Cricket Club of the Star and Garter in 1784, the White Conduit Club of 1785–7 and the Marylebone Cricket Club of 1788 onwards are one and the same club. There is a parallel; during the 1780s the Jockey Club also dined at the Star and Garter – simply the Jockey Club, no geographical attachment.

Having thus established that the 'Marylebone' Cricket Club goes back to 1784's broadsheet, is it possible to go back further? *The Morning Post* of 5 October 1778 announced: 'We hear the noblemen and gentlemen of the Grand Cricket Club have established a fund for the purpose of rewarding such players as particularly distinguish themselves in the great cricket match.' The match in question was an all-professional affair between elevens representing Surrey and Hampshire.

Four years earlier, in 1774, the Star and Garter is given as the meeting-place of the Committee which revised the Laws. In 1755, the then published Laws are headed: 'The Game of Cricket as settled by the Several Cricket Clubs, particularly that of the Star and

Garter, Pall Mall.' When the *Reading Mercury* advertised for sale copies of the Laws, it stated: 'The Articles of the Game of Cricket as settled in the year 1744 by the Society of Noblemen and Gentlemen at the Star and Garter in Pall Mall.'

These four notices thus provide continuity from 1744 to 1778 and so on to 1788 and the present Cricket Club based at Lord's. The conclusion to be drawn is that the present MCC was founded in or before 1744. The Jockey Club's date of foundation is given as 1750 – is this pure coincidence or did the Cricket Club spawn the Jockey Club?

Another piece of speculation: the oldest extant Laws of Cricket are those of 1744, presumably issued so that the famous England vs. Kent match of that year could be played without disputes arising. Perhaps a Committee at the Star and Garter was set up to draft these Laws. If so, then it is sensible to settle on 1744 as the date the (Marylebone) Cricket Club was founded.

On a minor point, there is some dispute regarding the exact location of the Star and Garter in Pall Mall. Rowland Bowen discovered that during the 18th century at various times there were three distinct taverns in that street, all called 'Star and Garter'. However, the most likely home of the Cricket Club and the Jockey Club was at numbers 94–95 (now renumbered 100). This was the grandest and longest lasting of the three.

Two loose ends which need a note: first, there was a Marylebone Club in the 1750s, which met at the Rising Sun near Marylebone Church, but it had no connection with the one that became the MCC. Second, there was another White Conduit Club in the 1790s, which was merely a club playing on White Conduit Fields after *the* Cricket Club moved to Lord's.

The three principal men involved in the Cricket Club at the time of its move to Lord's Ground were the 9th Earl of Winchilsea, the Hon. Charles Lennox and Sir Peter Burrell. Winchilsea (1752–1826) was educated at Eton and had his country seat at Burley on the Hill in Rutland, where he also laid out a cricket field and played major matches. As has been noted, he was Treasurer of the Cricket Club in 1784 and he joined the Hambledon Club in 1786. He served as a volunteer in the American War of Independence and, at a cost of £20,000, raised a regiment of infantry. He was a very useful cricketer and a generous patron of the game. In an age when the frequenters of London clubs were given to madcap ideas and practical jokes, Winchilsea stood aside and acted with decorum and rectitude.

Lennox (1764–1819) succeeded as the 4th Duke of Richmond in 1806. He belonged to the more rumbustious school and in 1789 fought a famous duel with the Duke of York on Wimbledon Common. Neither party suffered injury and they made up their quarrel. In 1819, when he was the Governor-General of Canada, he was bitten by a pet fox and died of hydrophobia. He was a talented batsman and played in major matches for over 20 years.

Burrell (1754–1820) was educated at Eton and Cambridge. He was considered one of the best amateur batsmen in the 1780s. He presided over the corruption trial of Warren Hastings (the former Governor-General of Bengal) and in 1796 was created Baron Gwydyr.

On 30 May 1788 the Laws of the game were revised by 'the Cricket Club at St Marylebone'. It is worth noting the precise wording, which reinforces the supposition

The 9th Earl of Winchilsea. As Treasurer of the Cricket Club in the 1780s, he, with others, persuaded Thomas Lord to lay out the first 'Lord's Ground', to which he then moved the Cricket Club. His country seat in Rutland was also the venue for major matches.

Colonel The Hon. Charles Lennox, who succeeded as the 4th Duke of Richmond in 1806. A leading patron and participant in all athletic sports, he was a notable cricketer and encouraged the establishment of Lord's Ground (see also plate section).

Sir Peter Burrell, created Baron Gwydyr in 1796. A leading batsman when the Cricket Club played on White Conduit Fields and during its early days at Lord's. In 1777, it was reported that his sister, Elizabeth Anne Burrell, scored more notches than any other lady cricketer in a match.

already put forward that it was indeed the Cricket Club of the Star and Garter which had transferred to Lord's Ground in Marylebone. The changes were not major and in fact the earliest extant copy of the 1788 Laws was printed in 1796; so one or two of the minor alterations as given in 1796 might have been slipped in any time between then and 1788. One omission from the Laws is any mention of the number of players in a team. It was not until 1884 that the law was introduced: 'A match is played between two sides of eleven players each, unless otherwise agreed to.'

The first report of a match with eleven players appeared in the *Foreign Post* of 7 July 1697: 'The middle of last week a great match at Cricket was played in Sussex; they were eleven of a side, and they played for fifty guineas apiece.' However, the next reference to a specific number of players comes in 1700, when ten per side is noted. In 1727, the Articles of Agreement

THE HISTORY OF CRICKET

between Richmond and Brodrick specify twelve a side, and another game the same year also mentions twelve. P.F. Thomas in *Old English Cricket* devotes a chapter to theories regarding the adoption of eleven as the accepted number in a cricket team, but his answers remain no more than a hypothesis.

THE PUBLIC SCHOOLS AND UNIVERSITIES

Cricket at the principal public schools, and at Oxford and Cambridge, continued to grow and flourish throughout the 18th century. Horace Walpole (Eton 1727–34) makes reference to cricket being played at school in his day, though he himself was not keen on the sport.

In 1742, the Earl of Chesterfield writes to his son at Westminster: '. . . for if you have a right ambition you will desire to excel all boys of your age at cricket, or trap-ball, as well as in learning', and repeats himself in 1745: 'I have often told you that I even wished you played at pitch and cricket, better than any boy at Westminster.'

The poet William Cowper, also at Westminster at that time, later wrote: 'When I was a boy, I excelled at cricket and football, but the fame I acquired by achievements that way is long since forgotten.'

In 1751, the series of three matches between the Old Etonians and the Gentlemen of England (i.e., The Rest) was played at Newmarket, illustrating the keenness of Etonians for cricket in the middle of the century. In 1754 Eton College played Cambridge University. In 1760 James Woodforde, then at New College, Oxford, noted in his diary: 'Plaid at Crikett in Port Meadow, the Winchester against Eaton and we Winton: beat them.'

Cricket was by no means confined to a few major public schools. Of four known illustrations of cricket at school in the second half of the 18th century, two are of Charterhouse (1775) and Harrow (1771), but the other two are of the Free School, Maidstone (1760) and Carmalt School, Putney (1780).

Although games had been arranged between old boys of schools – the most celebrated being Old Etonians vs. Old Westminsters at Moulsey Hurst in 1768 – not one reference has been found to matches between two schools involving *current* pupils before 1794. All cricket activity at schools was of the boys' own making and was not encouraged by the school authorities.

The match of 1794, between Charterhouse and Westminster, was not discovered until the 1960s, when R.L. Arrowsmith researched the biographies of the 22 players in a given match and discovered that one side comprised current Charterhouse pupils and the other current pupils from Westminster. The title of the match in the newspaper report was: 'City of London against City of Westminster' and the game was advertised as being played for 500 guineas. Why was it played under an alias? Possibly the explanation is revealed by an incident two years later. Westminster arranged to play Eton on Hounslow Heath. Edward Harbord of Eton wrote home: 'The masters know nothing about it, nor are they intended to

Boys playing cricket at Charterhouse School about 1780. This is one of several illustrations showing cricket being played at schools in the south-east of England during the second half of the 18th century.

do so, I believe, until it is over.' The boys were wise to keep the game to themselves, for when the Eton headmaster discovered it had been played, he flogged the whole team.

What is more, the next projected Eton match, against Harrow, was seemingly abandoned. The future Lord Palmerston had written home asking for 'two pair of stumps and a good bat ... we have accepted a challenge sent us by the Eton boys, who have challenged us to fight not with cannons (sic) and balls, but with bats and balls, in the Holydays, 18 of our best players against 18 of theirs.' No report of this match appeared, if indeed it ever took place.

THE HISTORY OF CRICKET

Whether the headmaster's flogging was simply because the boys were playing cricket or whether it was more directed against the horseplay and drunkenness which seems to have followed the matches is not known. The latter appears likely if Lord Byron's letter relating to the 1805 match between Eton and Harrow is accurate. Byron tells how both teams got 'rather drunk, and went together to the Haymarket Theatre, where we kicked up a row, as you may suppose . . . and we nearly came to a battle royal'.

From the historian's viewpoint cricket's most disastrous fire occurred at Lord's in 1825 when the pavilion was burnt down. The cause was never discovered, but the fire took place between the ending of the Harrow vs. Winchester match and the start of the Eton vs. Harrow match, when the 'gentlemen' had some sort of wild party overnight in the pavilion.

The 1805 Eton vs. Harrow game is the first of which the score details survive, but from other comments it would seem that games between the two schools had been played for, perhaps, three or four years prior to 1805. Eton won the 1805 game by an innings and two runs, Byron scoring 7 and 2 for Harrow.

With so many Etonians going up to King's College, Cambridge, the university had a clear advantage over Oxford in the development of cricket, and the matches between Eton and Cambridge in 1754 and the following years received notice in the newspapers.

Considering all this activity in the middle of the 18th century, it seems strange that cricket does not really become organised at either university until towards the end of it. At Oxford the Bullingdon Club, which was more or less representative of the university, played home and away games with the MCC in 1795. The first Oxford vs. Cambridge contest did not take place until 1827, though the Cambridge University Cricket Club was formed about 1820.

However, in wondering why cricket at the two universities seemed to lag behind that of the south-eastern schools, one must remember the general principle that cricket travels slowly. Outside the university itself the earliest known match played in Cambridgeshire was March vs. Wisbech in 1744, and apart from a note about cricket being common in Nettlebed in 1720, the first match in Oxfordshire, away from the university, involved Henley-on-Thames in 1766. So even if the undergraduates loved the game from the end of the 17th century, the natives of the two university shires were not steeped in cricket in the same way as those in Surrey, Sussex and Kent were.

EARLY CRICKET OUTSIDE BRITAIN

In broad terms the game of cricket took two hundred years to spread from its south-eastern birthplace to the rest of mainland Britain. It is therefore hardly surprising that in the same two centuries (1600–1800) authenticated references to cricket outside mainland Britain concern, almost without exception, English cricketers who decided to organise some matches among themselves while they were abroad.

Even Ireland is apparently devoid of any references to the game until the 19th century. The dubious Cromwellian reference (see page 18) can be dismissed – hurling remained the game of the Irish people.

The first undisputed mention of the game in France comes in a letter from Quiberon Bay in 1760, from an English ship moored there: 'We live here very happily, have extreme fine weather, go ashore very often and play at cricket.' In 1769 a cricket match was organised in Calais, but the newspaper reference closes with 'the players are to be all English men'.

In 1766 Horace Walpole watched cricket at Neuilly-sur-Seine, near Paris, and in the years immediately prior to the French Revolution the English in Paris and some French aristocrats were playing cricket in and around the capital. This provoked the ambassador in Paris, the Duke of Dorset, previously noted as a patron of cricket in Kent, to organise the visit of an English side to Paris in 1789, led by William Yalden of Chertsey. The team reached Dover, but abandoned the trip because of the Revolution. An excellent pamphlet on the background to the tour was written and published by John Goulstone in 1972.

Apart from France and Ireland, the rest of Europe has no cricketing connections until the last years of the 18th century, except for a stray reference to British naval cricket in Portugal in 1736. By this time a large portion of the English upper class was either involved in or at worst familiar with cricket, from school, university or country seat. Consequently, the principal cities in Europe have occasional mentions of the English expatriates playing cricket, as well as a few Anglophiles. The well-known painting of Mr Hope while he was staying in Rome (see plate section), is a prime example of the latter. In Berlin a German book of sports, published in 1796, includes the rules of cricket and the same book continues to do so when it appears in a Danish version in 1801. This publicity for cricket does not necessarily go hand in hand with Germans or Danes actually organising matches; the French game of boules is included in some English books on sport without any explosion in the playing of it in England.

English soldiers on the continent in the 1790s played cricket in Portugal and the cricket match prior to the battle of Waterloo is often mentioned; but the game remained stubbornly English, and the continentals in general did not copy the matches which they saw being played.

The non-European shores of the Mediterranean provide the first reference, about which there seems to be no dispute, to cricket outside mainland Britain. The reference comes in the diary of Henry Teonge and the year is 1676. Teonge was the chaplain aboard the *Assistance*, one of three English naval vessels which had moored in the Eastern Mediterranean off Antioch. A party from the three ships decided to ride to Aleppo, situated in what is now Syria (then part of the Ottoman Empire). Aleppo was a centre for the Levant Company, founded in 1592, and a clearing house for trade between Europe and the Middle East. Teonge records on 6 May 1676:

> This morning early (as it is the custom all summer longe) at the least 40 of the
> English, with his worship the Consull, rod out of the cytty (Aleppo) about 4 miles

to the Green Platt, a fine vally by a river syde, to recreate themselves. Where a princely tent was pitched; and wee had severall pastimes and sports, as duck-hunting, fishing, shooting, handball, krickett, scrofilo; and then a noble dinner brought thither, with greate plenty of all sorts of wines, punch and lemonads; and at 6 wee returne all home in good order, but soundly tyred and weary.

As Henry Teonge came from Warwickshire it might be said he was only guessing that 'krickett' was being played, but he did go to Christ's College, Cambridge and, what is more important, the ships sailed originally from Dartford and sailed back to Rochester, so the crew were presumably mainly from Kent.

The one country in which the residents did play cricket through much of the 18th century was America, where there are frequent references both before and after the War of Independence. However, the earliest is a matter of heated debate.

William Byrd of Westover, Virginia, kept a diary written in a secret code. This was translated and published in English by Jane Carson in 1965 and apparently contains a number of references to cricket. A typical example reads:

April 25th, 1709
I rose at 6 o'clock and said my prayers shortly. Mr W-l-s and I fenced and I beat him. Then we played cricket, Mr W-L-s and Mr Custis against me and Mr Hawkins, but we were beaten.

If viewed in isolation this can be taken as the English game of cricket, but a careful reading of all the references in context reveals that the game played was a version of 'old-two-cat', which involved four players and was still occasionally being played in the United States in the 19th century. I am indebted to David Creeth of Glendale, California, for his investigation into Byrd's diary and the interpretation of it.

Any doubts about the true nature of the game Byrd played can be dispelled by the fact that he kept a detailed diary on his visits to England and specifically to Kent. Yet, travelling around the early authentic homes of cricket, he makes no mention in his diary of the game he seemed to play so enthusiastically in Virginia.

The second earliest North American reference is also open to question. Judge Samuel Sewell of Boston noted in his diary of 15 March 1725: 'Sam Hirst got up betimes in the morning and took Ben Swett with him and went into the (Boston) Common to play at wicket.' It seems probable that 'wicket' was cricket. Another diarist, William Stephen, educated at Winchester and King's College, Cambridge, gives a number of references to cricket from 1741 onwards, the first being Easter Monday, 30 March 1741: 'Many of our Townsmen, Freeholders, Inmates and servants were assembled in the principal Square, at Cricket, and divers other athletick sports.' Stephen had emigrated to North America because of serious financial losses in England. In 1741 he was President of Savannah County in Georgia.

In New York cricket was noted as being played in 1747 and, much more important, the first North American newspaper notice of the game was printed in the New York *Gazette and Weekly Post Boy* in 1751:

> Last Monday afternoon (May 1st) a match at cricket was played on our common for a considerable wager eleven Londoners against eleven New Yorkers. The game was played according to the London method and those who got the most notches in two hands were to be the winners.

The paper goes on to give the scores; New York won by 87 notches. We are now on firm ground and from this time on cricket developed in New York and other parts of the east of America along the same lines as in England. The War of Independence and the withdrawal of English troops causes a break in the reporting of cricket, but in the 1790s details again become frequent.

Across the border, in Canada, the diary of Robert Hunter notes that cricket was being played while he was visiting Montreal in 1785. Rowland Bowen states that the people playing must have been French Canadians. The reference is so brief that it should be treated with caution. It is some years before a second reference to cricket in Canada appears.

The earliest known reference to cricket in the West Indies mentions a meeting of the St Anne's Cricket Club in Barbados in 1806. Certainly, in both the Caribbean and South America, cricket seems to be virtually unknown until the 19th century. The same timescale applies to Africa and Australasia.

The first note of cricket on the Indian subcontinent is of a similar nature to the Aleppo reference. The date is 1721. Clement Downing, who was a Lieutenant aboard the frigate *Fame Gally*, wrote a book, the shortened title of which is: *A Compendious History of the Indian Wars with an Account of the Rise, Progress, Strength and Forces of Angria the Pyrate.* In it he recalled that, while anchored off Gujarat in West India:

> We lay here a fortnight before they return'd and all the while kept a good lookout; and tho' all the country round was inhabited by the Culeys, we every day diverted ourselves with playing at Cricket and other exercises, which they would come and be spectators of.

The site of these cricketing activities must have been Cambay, 250 miles north of Bombay and 30 miles west of Baroda. Unfortunately, no detailed biography of Downing exists and he died in 1737, the year the book was published.

Apart from this reference, cricket in India is not mentioned again until the last years of the century and then in Calcutta (1792), on the eastern side, followed by military references in Bombay (1797) and Seringapatam (1799). It seems likely, however, that the Calcutta Cricket Club was in existence before 1792 since, on 23 February of that year, the *Madras Courier* reported that it had recently played three matches: two against Barrackpore and one against Dum Dum.

The last quarter of the 18th century and the beginning of the 19th were years of social hardship in England. The industrial revolution and the enclosure of common land, while benefiting some people, were having dire economic and social consequences for many others. The poor rates system, which was especially prevalent in the east and south of the country, was depressing agricultural wages, while the price of grain remained high. Meanwhile ever larger numbers of people – including women and children – were working 14–16 hours a day in the new factories. At the same time, Britain was engaged in a vastly expensive war with France, for 23 years from 1792, which made heavy demands on British manpower. The perceived threat of invasion was enough on its own to justify tighter control over the people and the curbing of what we would now call political rights and civil liberties. However, the establishment was particularly concerned to prevent the ideas generated by revolutionary France from finding open and violent expression, and sparking a similar revolution in England. G.M. Trevelyan (1876–1926), the noted social historian, later wrote: 'If the French noblesse had been capable of playing cricket with their peasants, their chateaux would never have been burnt.' Whatever the attraction of such a theory, it seems likely that the social, economic and political pressures of this period had a damaging effect on cricket throughout the country.

CRICKET IN DECLINE

The Haygarth graph on page 44 shows clearly how the popularity of the game plummeted. The first volume of Haygarth's book of *Cricket Scores and Biographies* prints only two matches a year for both 1811 and 1812. Arthur Haygarth (1825–1903), who was educated at Harrow and played many matches for the MCC, collated important cricket scores and published these in 14 volumes. Most of his scores at that time came from matches in the south-east of England; but the

3

THE

MOULD

BEGINS

TO SET

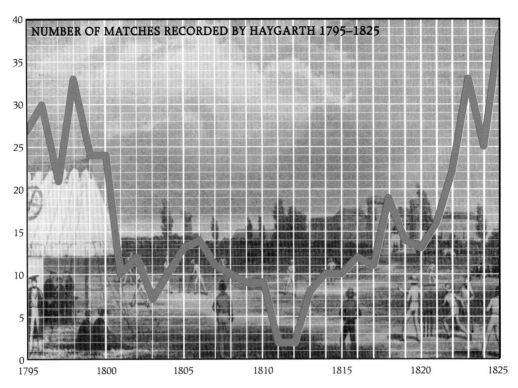

NUMBER OF MATCHES RECORDED BY HAYGARTH 1795–1825

Matches recorded by Haygarth, 1795–1825. Arthur Haygarth's 14 volumes of cricket scores from 1744 to 1878 are a major reference work and an essential tool for every student of cricket history.

Nottingham Journal, after several years of no cricket notices, adds this comment on a match in 1813: 'The manly and athletic game at cricket, for which the boys of Sherwood have been so long and so justly famed, it was thought had fallen into disuse, if not disgrace.'

Another barometer with which to measure the decline of cricket is the book trade. From 1790 to 1805 a cricket annual giving match scores was published, compiled by the MCC Scorer. The publishing of such scores then ceased and did not resume until 1823. Similarly, the first instructional cricket book ran through three editions between 1801 and 1804, and then stopped, not resuming until 1816. The original versions were by Thomas Boxall; the 1816 version by William Lambert. Lambert's book was issued 13 times, up to about 1830.

The number of matches which Haygarth publishes had risen to 38 by 1825 – an almost threefold increase on 1820 – and was to continue to rise. In 1830 the number went up to 45 and by 1840 to 84. At the same time, while the laws of the game changed little (apart from the move from under-arm to round-arm bowling), the organising, financing and social aspects moved steadily to a position which became a set pattern for the next one hundred years, and indeed from which cricket has never escaped.

THE HISTORY OF CRICKET

GENTLEMEN AND PLAYERS

Dealing with the social aspect, in 1806 the first match was played in a series destined to survive until 1962. In hindsight this series must be regarded as the most divisive of any long-running sporting events held in England.

The match was Gentlemen vs. Players at Lord's on 7, 8 and 9 July 1806 (which was followed by a second game later in the month). At the time it was first played, England was still largely split into the landed gentry and the rest, but it was a split that was rapidly being blurred by the creation of the middle classes. For the rest of the 19th century and beyond members of the middle classes had to decide whether they were Gentlemen or Players. The match itself for the first 60 years of its existence was a farce. The Players were so much better than the Gentlemen that numerous devices had to be experimented with in order to make a proper match. In one game the Gentlemen fielded 18 against the Players' 11; in another the Players had to defend larger wickets; in many others the Gentlemen had the use of one or two Players. If the MCC wished to promote such games, so be it. The Players were paid to perform and enough MCC members turned out to keep the bar receipts healthy. As with cricket in general, there was a long break in the series after the initial 1806 matches, the next meeting of the two 'classes' being in 1819.

The problems with the series began when talented middle-class cricketers were paid 'expenses' to be Gentlemen. This created the 'shamateur', a category of cricketer which was to befoul English cricket right up until the abolition of the match in 1962. The most famous of the shamateurs was W.G. Grace (1848–1915). His colossal ability put the Gentlemen on an even footing with the Players, and because of his participation and that of several other shamateurs the match developed into a fine spectacle attracting large crowds. The arrival of the socially non-segregated Australians in 1878 ought to have blown the lid off this pot, but some jiggery-pokery managed to keep the shamateur system going, as will be evident in a later chapter. The honest and straightforward payment of, and rewards for, cricketers according to their talents was not destined to arrive until the Packer row of the 1970s.

The only other country in which a strict division between Gentlemen and Players was created and a match series under that title regularly played was, surprisingly, the United States. However, a large majority of 'Players' were English professionals, many of whom had emigrated permanently. The usual reason given to explain the collapse of cricket in the States is that the game was too slow for the get-up-and-go character of 19th-century America, but this segregation was surely a contributing factor. If the American amateur sides which toured England in 1884 and 1889 had included three or four top professionals, their results would have been much better, the interest would have been greater and, perhaps, cricket would have won a popularity in the States which in fact it was never to achieve.

FINANCE IN NORTH AND SOUTH

A fundamental change in the way major matches were financed emerged in the years either side of the turn of the century. For much of the 18th century the major inter-county games were promoted by wealthy backers, one on each side, and many of the games were staged on their country estates. The move away from this system had been made by the Hambledon Club, which promoted matches involving Hampshire. With the establishment of the (Marylebone) Cricket Club at Lord's, the system of posting a subscription list in the pavilion to defray expenses for matches became the norm and would be adopted by most promoters of major county teams, specifically Sussex and Kent in the early years of the new century, and later Nottinghamshire and Yorkshire.

In the first twenty or more years of the 19th century, however, there were no major inter-county matches. Almost all the matches involving counties were a given county against a team raised by the MCC, generally entitled 'England'. It can hardly be a coincidence that the men who organised the raising of the county teams in this period had learnt their own cricket at Eton. The Etonian flavour to county cricket was another aspect of the game which was now thoroughly established and would remain in place almost to the present time.

James Lawrell (1779–1842) of Frimley was the enthusiast who kept Surrey going as a cricketing county. He employed Robert Robinson (1765–1822) – 'Three-fingered Jack' – as a gamekeeper. Robinson was the best Surrey batsman of his day; Lawrell had been a member of the famous flogged Eton XI of 1796.

Thomas Assheton Smith (1776–1858) was in the XI at Eton in 1793, played for the Bullingdon Club at Oxford in 1795 and, from 1821 to 1831, was MP for Andover. He raised the various Hampshire sides in the early years of the 19th century, using the remaining professionals of the defunct Hambledon Club. Assheton Smith himself played in the first Gentleman vs. Players match of 1806.

The Kent sides of the same era became the responsibility of Henry Tufton (1775–1849), later Earl of Thanet. He and his brother John (1773–1799) were both at Eton in the 1790s and though neither appears in the few extant Eton scores, both played for Kent and were notable performers.

Between 1795 and 1825 Surrey played 'England' or the MCC in 40 matches, Hampshire played 20 such matches and Kent six. The only other county with more than the odd game was Middlesex, but this county was largely composed of MCC members.

The one other major team of the period was The Bs – eleven cricketers whose surname began with that letter. In all The Bs challenged England 12 times and the man in charge of this unusual side was George Henry Barnett (d.1871), yet another Etonian.

The Etonians, the patrons and the MCC with their rigid class structure controlled much of cricket in the south-east; in the north (broadly north of Watford) the game was developing along totally different lines, as mentioned earlier, with artisans raising and financing their own teams. In the south cricket had begun as a youths' game and been hijacked by the landed gentry; in the north the landed gentry had brought this southern pastime to their estates and the game had spread downwards.

Although the composition of the teams in the north was entirely of artisans, with their headquarters being a local tavern, the one area often reserved for the landed gentry was umpiring. For example Sir William Charlton, the Sheriff of Nottingham, acted in that capacity for the Nottingham side and in the usual articles of agreement for a match one clause read: 'That there be two gentlemen umpires.'

In 1791, Lieutenant-Colonel Charles Churchill, stationed in Nottingham, was so impressed with the Nottingham cricketers that he sent a challenge to the MCC in 1791, backing Nottingham to beat MCC. This was the first MCC side to play a match outside London. Captained by Lord Winchilsea, the MCC won by a large margin.

When the popularity of cricket returned to Nottingham after 1813, the public subscribed sufficient funds (£40) for a second MCC visit in 1817. Nottingham won both matches, but they did field 22 players against the England XI. It was reported that 20,000 spectators watched one day's cricket. Similar crowd figures were reported for matches in Sheffield, and large crowds attended some inter-village matches throughout the Midlands.

ARRIVAL OF THE ENTREPRENEURS

The growing popularity of cricket soon galvanised speculators into exploiting its commercial possibilities. The throngs gathering at matches generally watched the game free of charge, since fixtures were staged on land which was unenclosed – the local common or racecourse were frequently used venues. Lord's was enclosed, but it was a strictly private club and virtually all the matches played there in the early years were club games.

The first 19th-century effort to harness cricket's popularity for commercial purposes was probably by George Steer of Sheffield. (London's Artillery Ground had ceased to be a public venue in the 1750s.) The bread-and-butter income to run the ground that Steer set up at Darnall, near Sheffield, came from the rent paid by local cricket clubs, from the beer sales to club members and general spectators, and from any other non-cricketing event which required an enclosed field and would attract the public. However, George Steer and his imitators had not gone into the cricket business merely to tick over financially. The really big cricket match, if it could be organised, was the one event which would bring a substantial return on the speculator's capital expenditure.

In 1822 Steer organised a match between Sheffield and Nottingham. This proved immensely successful, but also proved how inadequate were the arrangements he had made. The ground he built simply could not cope with the crowds, and the stand collapsed under the weight of spectators, resulting in a number of injuries.

Undeterred, Steer abandoned this ground and built a larger one nearby, with a grandiose two-storey pavilion and banked seating for 8,000. He opened the new ground with another successful 'local derby' – Sheffield vs. Leicester – in 1824. The following year

A view of the Cricket Ground at Darnall, near Sheffield, during the England vs. Sussex match of 1827. This was one of several grounds built about this time as commercial speculations, rather than at the specific behest of members of a cricket club.

he paid for a strong England side to come and oppose Yorkshire. It was reported that 20,000 people a day turned out for this event. In 1827 he staged the England vs. Sussex game – the first 'official' contest between under-arm and round-arm bowling.

The money rolled in, so much so that rival entrepreneurs, Messrs Wright and Hazelhurst, built a second cricket arena in Sheffield at Hyde Park. This was situated nearer to the centre of the town and by 1830 the major matches in Sheffield had moved there – perhaps Steer had made his money by then? The cost of this new ground was reported to be £4,000, so the speculators clearly thought there was plenty of money still to be made.

While this commercialisation was taking place in Sheffield, an equally enterprising gentleman was looking at the prospects in Brighton. The town already possessed an established cricket ground, which had been laid out at the request of the Prince Regent in 1791, and had been used by the Prince and his friends when they visited Brighton. It had become run-down over the past ten years and no major games had been staged since 1817. James Ireland, a draper in Brighton, took a lease on the ground and surrounding land. He

The Cricket Ground at Brighton, originally set out for the Prince of Wales in the 1790s, but shown here in 1830 after it had been expanded and renovated by James Ireland. It was the venue for the first modern County Championship match.

built a pleasure and tea garden, a fives court and renovated the cricket ground. His first major cricket speculation, organising a match between Sussex and the MCC, which came off in 1823, proved financially viable. Ireland then looked at the possibility of staging matches against Kent, but because of the absence of any organisation capable of raising a Kent side, his first attempt failed. However, in 1825 his renewed endeavours bore fruit and the first bona fide quality inter-county match, since Middlesex played Surrey in 1796, took place when Kent met Sussex home and away. Although Ireland could not have foreseen the consequences, these two games mark the seeds of the modern County Championship. The fixtures were again a success and were repeated for the next four years. The press dubbed them as being for the 'Championship Belt' – a direct reference to boxing. The two greatest cricketing counties of the day were challenging each other to decide which county was the best in England.

With the obvious financial successes of the grounds at Sheffield and Brighton, other commercially minded gentlemen decided to follow their lead. In 1825 a similar ground was laid out in Leicester; this included a bowling green, and details of the prices charged have survived. A season ticket costing one guinea entitled the holder to play cricket and bowls, the price for cricket only was ten shillings, and the price to enter the ground for the season as a spectator was 7/6d. The first major match on the Leicester ground was Leicester vs. Sheffield in 1825, and in 1826 Leicester and Sheffield combined played England there. An unusual spectacle held on the ground in 1831 was a public electors' dinner (for the Liberal Party), where it was reported 20,000 people turned out to watch 500 dine!

The great cricketing scoop for the Leicester patron, Richard Cheslyn (1797–1858), came in 1836 when the first genuine contests between the North of England and the South were staged, one at Lord's, the other at Leicester. As the North had eight Nottingham players, two from Sheffield and Fuller Pilch of Norfolk, the Nottingham public flocked to the game at Leicester. Literally hundreds walked there and then had to walk back as far as Loughborough to find a bed overnight. The South, thanks to some brilliant batting by Alfred Mynn, won by 218 runs. The Nottingham press gave much coverage to the event and especially to the fact that the game ought to have been staged in Nottingham. However, Nottingham did not have an enclosed ground, but played matches on the open racecourse.

One result of this indignation was the opening of the ground at Trent Bridge in 1838 – as another commercial speculation, the speculator being local innkeeper and captain of the Nottingham team, William Clarke (1798–1856). The present inn at the side of the Trent Bridge Ground was built in 1885, replacing the one of which Clarke was landlord.

Other commercial grounds opened around this time included one in Leeds by Robert Cadman, and several in Kent: at the White Hart, Bromley, Hodgskin's Ground in Gravesend and the ground at West Malling to which Fuller Pilch was persuaded to move in 1835.

The opportunities for making money by building arenas mainly for cricket purposes did not end in the 1830s, and for the next 20 years or so grounds continued to be built, usually attached to public houses. As towns expanded, however, the land on which the grounds stood, as Thomas Lord found earlier, was worth more to the builder for housing than as a cricket venue, and almost all these commercial grounds have long since vanished. The single famous one to survive is the Nottingham ground at Trent Bridge, where the Musters family owned land in the West Bridgford area. Because the family refused to allow much building on their land, Nottingham expanded to the north rather than the south, and Trent Bridge escaped development.

The two important off-shoots from the speculative ground building were thus the creation of the County Championship and the great annual battle between North and South. Interest in cricket was rapidly increasing, but the feeble transport system of the day meant that games between teams more than 50 miles apart took a great deal of arranging and were expensive. Reports of cricket in the press expanded with the general interest. Apart from horse-racing no other sport commanded anything like the same coverage. Most other games were confined to a few lines, while cricket could occupy a column or more.

THE HISTORY OF CRICKET

BAT AND BALL

One of the never-ending battles which cricket's legislators have fought since the game began is over how to maintain an equal balance between bat and ball. The alterations in the size of the wickets were made to give the bowler a better chance, but a more fundamental change was necessary as the run-getting increased. Tables compiled by Keith Warsop and which appear in *Cricket Quarterly*, 1966, illustrate the point. In 1786 Thomas Walker, the Hambledon Club player, averaged 47 with the bat. In 1796 Robert Robinson, the Surrey cricketer, averaged 50 and in 1803 Lord Frederick Beauclerk averaged 61. The top batsmen had clearly mastered the under-arm bowling style. Increasing the size of the wicket would not help the bowlers.

Thomas Walker had tried bowling round-arm (that is, with the arm level with the shoulder) in Hambledon Club matches in the 1790s, but the Club had enforced a ban on such deliveries. In 1807 John Willes (1778–1852) of Headcorn, Kent, employed round-arm when playing for Kent against All England at Penenden Heath and apparently other bowlers adopted the same style. The *Kentish Gazette* reported: 'The straight-arm bowling, introduced by John Willes, Esq., was generally practised in this game, in comparison to what might have been got by the straightforward bowling.' John Willes is said to have picked up round-arm bowling from his sister Christina who, having difficulty in bowling the traditional under-arm to her brother because of her voluminous skirt, began to bowl round-arm instead.

John Willes. He played for Kent from 1806 to 1822, at which date his career in important cricket ended abruptly, when he was no-balled for bowling 'round-arm'.

George Knight, the Sussex cricketer who was a powerful advocate of round-arm bowling and whose forthright opinions changed the Law to permit the new style.

Although the Laws as laid down by the (Marylebone) Cricket Club were no doubt followed in general terms at this time away from London, local umpires would have had their own ideas. Round-arm bowling was used in local Kent games, and elsewhere there are brief press comments about the use of illegal bowling in matches. The matter did not cause more than parochial comment, however, until 1822, when Willes revived the Kent team and arranged fixtures between Kent and the MCC.

When the fixture between the two sides got under way at Lord's, Willes bowled round-arm and Lord Frederick Beauclerk, the MCC captain, ordered the umpire to stop Willes continuing with this 'illegal' style. Willes is reported to have thrown down the ball, ridden out of Lord's and never played in a major cricket match again.

Although Willes gave up the struggle, it was taken up by another Kent amateur, George Knight (1795–1867) of Godmersham Park. He was a nephew of the novelist Jane Austen and had changed his name from Austen to Knight in 1812.

LORD FREDERICK BEAUCLERK

Before continuing with the progress of round-arm bowling (referred to in the contemporary press as the 'March of Intellect' style), it is necessary to insert some notes on the man who forced Willes to quit, Lord Frederick Beauclerk. As may be assumed by the way he reportedly told the umpire what to do about Willes, his lordship was the man in command at Lord's in the 1820s. A further comment relating to Beauclerk and round-arm bowling states

A typical handbill advertising cricket when its popularity resumed after the depressed years. Note the presence of Lord Frederick Beauclerk.

THE HISTORY OF CRICKET

that he allowed it so long as it was used by his bowlers and not against him as a batsman. This comment says a great deal.

Beauclerk, the fourth son of the Duke of St Albans and therefore a direct descendant of Charles II and Nell Gwyn, was born in 1773. His cricketing ability was noticed at Cambridge by Lord Winchilsea, who introduced him at Lord's. By the age of 25 Beauclerk was the outstanding amateur batsman of the day and his record apparently proves this (his average of 61 in 1803 has been noted). However, F.S. Ashley-Cooper later commented: 'Being generally captain he (Beauclerk) was able to go in at the most favourable time – a fact which should be remembered when comparing his average to those of his contemporaries.' (Many later captains have used the same ploy.)

Beauclerk himself claimed to make 600 guineas a year from betting on cricket. He grew increasingly unpleasant as his authority at Lord's grew. In effect, he succeeded Winchilsea as the power behind the MCC, but his character was the complete opposite of the urbane Winchilsea's. Beauclerk's temper was foul and his language worse. The stage was reached when no one would dare to question his authority and he was quite capable of abusing it. For example, he once persuaded the press not to publish a single wicket match, simply because he had lost. Even the infamous Daniel Dawson, who was to be hanged for horse-poisoning and was regarded as thoroughly obnoxious, refused to share a carriage with Beauclerk on account of his lordship's temper and language. Another commentator noted that it was fortunate that during Beauclerk's reign the MCC's influence did not extend far beyond Lord's, since the principal character would employ any trick, however devious, in order to win his bets.

Beauclerk's last important match was in 1825. The following year he was President of the MCC, by which time his influence was waning in favour of William Ward, though even in 1836 it is reported that he 'captained' the South of England (vs. the North) 'from the pavilion'.

Mention is made above of 'single wicket matches'. The most famous games of this type were between Alfred Mynn and Nicholas Felix for the Championship of England in the 1840s, but such games virtually died out later in the century.

A 'single wicket match', 25 August 1845

Two of Castle Howard	Runs	Runs
Etty	5	6
Lidster	0	32
	5	**38**

One of York	Runs	Runs
R. Letby	10	32
	10	**32**

The Two of Castle Howard winning by 1 run.

Returning to the bowling debate, George Knight managed to persuade the authorities to arrange three official trial matches involving the major cricketers for the season of 1827. The matches were to be between Sussex, whose two principal bowlers, James Broadbridge (1795–1843) and William Lillywhite (1792–1854), bowled round-arm, and an England side bowling under-arm. The matches would be staged at Sheffield, Lord's and Brighton.

The fierce debates and arguments raised by the issue were equal to any that have developed since. There is little evidence on the strength of feeling on major Law changes prior to 1827, but the fact that cricket was now more of a national than a regional game heightened public interest in the bowling debate. Sussex won the first two matches and some idea of the concern felt by the conservatives is shown by the following extract from William Denison's *Sketches of Players*:

> There has been considerable discussion on this point, – whether it (round-arm) could be allowed, and whether it shall be continued to be practised. The writer of this, an old cricketer, really shakes with fear of its adoption, as it certainly gives birth to the hope of gaining a wicket by chance, by a wild twist, instead of the fine steady length, as shown us in former times by Lumpy, Harris, John Wells etc. It is true these men could twist, but there was not that space taken for the chance, as at present. The general complaint of the hitting now being so much superior to the bowling, can alone justify the experiment; and it is on that account it has been brought forward. Other means have been suggested to produce more equality, and to shorten the game; such as four stumps, increased length, and narrower bats; but this has been the one adopted, and the effect is certainly imposing. Indeed it appeared in these matches, that there were only two men capable of playing against it with confidence, and to understand it, Saunders and Mr Ward, – although many runs were made by others.

In the third match between England and Sussex, George Knight bowled round-arm for England and proved successful, thus obtaining victory for his side.

Knight put a proposal to alter the law regarding the height of the bowling arm to a special MCC meeting, but William Ward, on behalf of the conservatives, spoke against Knight and carried the day. In spite of this many umpires turned a blind eye to the height of the bowler's arm and, in 1835, the Law was finally altered to legalise round-arm. This 1835 alteration to the Laws is important because, for the first time, the MCC published their suggested changes in the *Sporting Magazine* seven months before the proposed meeting to make the decisions, thus giving everyone ample time to discuss the proposals. This act of consultation was a recognition of the public interest in the matter and of the importance of gathering opinions. The actual decisions would still be taken only by members of the MCC, but its membership was increasing. In 1832 the membership was 202; in 1842, 381.

Williliam Ward, the conservative in the round-arm debate, was a most generous patron of cricket, as well as a talented batsman. His innings of 278 for the MCC vs. Norfolk in 1820 was the first double century ever made in a major match, and was to remain the highest score in a major match at Lord's until 1925, when Percy Holmes hit 315 not out for Yorkshire against Middlesex. Ward became a very wealthy man through his banking interests and cricket was fortunate that he was on hand when, in 1825, Thomas Lord proposed to build houses on a large section of his ground. Ward paid Lord £5,000 to obtain the lease, and with this money the founder of Lord's retired to West Meon in Hampshire, dying there in 1832 aged 76.

Three other cricketers whose fame in the period around the time of Waterloo deserves some notice are Edward Budd, George Osbaldeston and William Lambert. Budd's epitaph, noted by Ashley-Cooper, possibly says as much about his contemporaries as it does about Budd: 'No word of scandal was ever whispered against him, and to the end of his long life he retained the affection of his friends and the respect of all who knew him.' Budd died in Wiltshire in 1875 aged 90, but he resigned as a member of MCC in 1826, retiring to the country. He was considered the hardest hitting of all major batsmen of the day and between 1813 and 1824 was in the top three run-getters most years. He was also a brilliant fielder and good slow bowler.

George Osbaldeston's career came to an abrupt end. He had a hasty temper and, in 1818, having boasted of his cricketing ability, he was beaten in a single wicket match by Brown of Brighton. The crowd laughed at his defeat and he immediately resigned from the MCC. He soon regretted the act and tried to get re-elected, but previously he had crossed Beauclerk and the latter refused to allow him to resume his membership. He turned his attention thereafter to hunting and other sports, performing some startling deeds – killing

George Osbaldeston, one of the outstanding all-rounders of the post-Waterloo era. He was also a crack shot and famous rider, familiarly known as 'The Squire' of England.

98 pheasants in 100 shots for example. While at Eton and Oxford Osbaldeston had been considered the outstanding bowler of his time. He died in 1866 aged 79.

William Lambert's career also came to a sudden end, supposedly because in 1817 he 'sold' the England vs. Nottingham match. Edward Budd, a member of the England side, recalling the game in later years, said: 'In common with others I lost my money and was greatly disappointed at the termination. Our paid player was accused of selling and never employed after.' In the game, the odds were against Nottingham and England gained a first innings lead, but Nottingham ended by winning by 30 runs. Lambert was the first batsman to score two hundreds in the same match, a feat he achieved for Sussex at Lord's in the same year. He died in Nutfield, Surrey, in 1851.

Betting was part and parcel of cricket in the 18th and early 19th centuries. James Pycroft in *The Cricket Field* (1851) devoted an entire chapter to 'A Dark Chapter in the History of Cricket'. Newspapers reporting matches devoted almost as much space to details of the changes in the odds as the match progressed as they did to descriptions of the actual play. Contemporary accounts are unclear about the date when bookmakers were debarred from the pavilion at Lord's, but it seems to have occurred in the 1820s. The Laws of the game contained a section on betting which was retained until 1884, long after betting on matches apparently stopped.

William Lambert, the first batsman to hit a century in each innings of an important match. He was accused of 'selling' the England vs. Nottingham game in 1817 and was never again chosen for a major match at Lord's.

THE HISTORY OF CRICKET

SCHOOLS AND UNIVERSITIES

The attitude of school authorities towards pupils playing matches against other schools changed gradually. In 1821 the Eton headmaster announced a ban on a match between Eton and Harrow only a few hours before it was due to begin. In the following year the boys changed tactics and arranged for the inter-school game to take place at Lord's rather than at Eton or Harrow and, as a further precaution, in the school holidays. Dr Butler, the headmaster of Harrow, vetoed a match between his school and Winchester in 1824. Meanwhile, the Eton vs. Harrow matches at Lord's began with another contest altogether. The boys at Harrow would order a number of post-chaises (three boys per chaise) to take them to the ground and then organise a race. This continued until there was a multiple pile-up when the leading chaise crashed and those following were unable to stop. The race was forbidden from that date.

The inter-university contest made the same hesitant start as Eton vs. Harrow. In 1827 two of the leading university players were Charles Wordsworth (Oxford), later Bishop of St Andrews, and Herbert Jenner (Cambridge). They had already played cricket against each other in both 1822 and 1823, when Wordsworth appeared for Harrow and Jenner for Eton in the annual schools match at Lord's. As with the early schools games, the match did not seem to have the blessing of the university authorities. Wordsworth stated later that he had to pretend he was visiting his London dentist in order to obtain leave of absence. The Oxford side of 1827 contained six Wykehamists (Winchester), while Cambridge had six Etonians. Harrow was represented by Wordsworth and Lewis for Oxford and by Handley for Cambridge. Westminster School and Rugby each provided one player, the Rugby representative being none other than Webb Ellis, the founder of rugby football.

No game took place in 1828, but in 1829 the match, at Oxford, was just before the first university boat race. Wordsworth was in the Oxford eight as well as the cricket team. Jenner had gone down by then. A break of six years then followed before the University Match was revived in 1836, back at Lord's. The leading figure in the revival was the later cricket historian James Pycroft. Whereas Wordsworth, the nephew of the poet, had been to a great cricketing school and thus developed his ability and love of the game among his school companions; Pycroft was born in Wiltshire and had been educated at King Edward VI School in Bath. Although apparently far away from the mainstream of cricket, the Bath area clearly had enough enthusiasts to practise cricket and, together with Pycroft, to form the Landsdown Club in Bath itself. This demonstrates how the game had spread by the 1820s and early 1830s. Pycroft was clearly smitten, for in 1835, as a 22-year-old undergraduate, he published *The Principles of Scientific Batting, or Plain rules, founded on the practice of the first professors and amateurs, for the noble game of cricket*. The author is given simply as 'A Gentleman'.

The following year Pycroft organised the Oxford vs. Cambridge match, opening the batting for Oxford. In the same year he discussed with the Revd John Mitford an idea for a

University students playing cricket at Cambridge in 1842.
The annual match against Oxford was by now well established.
The colleges at Cambridge employed professional cricketers
as coaches and the game was an integral part of university life.

book, which was eventually published as *The Cricket Field*, the first popular history of the game. Pycroft left university to become a law student, but after four years left law for the church. In later life he was an influential member of the Sussex County Cricket Club Committee. The University Match was established on a sound footing by the end of the 1830s. As the university cricketers left and in numerous cases went back to teaching at public schools, this in turn helped to change the schools' attitude to cricket.

THE HISTORY OF CRICKET

THE WANDERING CLUBS

In July 1845 four Cambridge undergraduates were having supper at the Blenheim Hotel in Bond Street, London. They decided to form a new sort of cricket club, one without its own ground, the membership of which would be by invitation only. The four named their club I Zingari (Italian for The Gypsies). They wrote to 20 friends, telling them that they had been enrolled as members – as the club had no expenses, there was no need for subscriptions. These friends were selected from the Canterbury Amateur Dramatical Society, an integral part of the Canterbury Cricket Festival. The Beverley Cricket Club of Canterbury had created this mix of theatre and cricket for a week in early August, three years before.

The new club played two matches during its foundation year: at Newport Pagnell and at the country seat of J.G. Sheppard in Suffolk. In its second year I Zingari arranged nine matches, and by 1851 its importance was such that Fred Lillywhite's *Cricketers' Guide*, covering that season, ranked I Zingari second to the MCC.

In the same year that the students conceived their cricket club, William Clarke, who had laid out the Trent Bridge Ground, also dreamt of a cricket club without a ground and with an exclusive membership. His club came into being in 1846, playing three matches late in that season. In 1847 its fixture list increased to ten games and in 1851 the team, the All England Eleven, had a full fixture programme of three-day matches and filled ten pages of Lillywhite's *Guide* with its matches and averages.

Both schemes proved by the rapidity of their success and their subsequent imitators that an enormous demand existed for the type of cricket which they offered.

On the basis of the facts so far outlined the two organisations appear very similar, but in reality they could not have been much more contrasting. I Zingari – amateur to the core and playing teams drawn from the landed gentry; All England Eleven – professional and attracting the *hoi polloi*. The two sides further emphasised the division between the Gentlemen and the Players.

4

DIVERSIONS

AND

DEVELOPMENT

Rowland Hill, First Viscount (1772-1842). As Commander-in-Chief General Hill signed the Order (see below) regarding cricket grounds at barracks throughout the United Kingdom. His family were the patrons of Shropshire cricket in the early years of the 19th century.

General Order No. 551

Horse Guards, 8th March, 1841

The Master-General and Board of Ordnance being about to form Cricket Grounds for the use of the Troops at the respective Barrack Stations throughout the United Kingdom, the General Commanding-in-Chief desires that Commanding Officers of Regiments, Depôts, and Detachments, will cause these Grounds to be strictly preserved, and that no carriages or horses be suffered to enter them.

The Cricket Ground is to be considered as in the immediate charge of the Barrack Master, who, however, cannot reasonably be expected to protect it effectually, unless assisted in the execution of that duty by the support and authority of the Commanding Officer of the Station, as well as by the good feeling of the Troops, for whose amusement and recreation this liberal arrangement is made by the Public.

Lord Hill will treat as a grave offence every trespass that shall be wantonly committed by the Troops, either upon the Cricket Ground or upon its Fences.

The Troops will, moreover, be required, in every such case, to pay the estimated expense of repairs, as in the case of Barrack damages.

Special Instructions, concerning the Cricket Grounds, have been issued to the Barrack Masters by the Master-General and Board of Ordnance.

By Command of the Right Honourable
General Lord Hill, Commanding-in-Chief,
John Macdonald, Adjutant-General.

The enthusiasm which greeted the two wandering clubs took the breath out of the infant County Championship, born when James Ireland arranged his Sussex vs. Kent matches in 1825. Those two counties had been challenged by Nottinghamshire in 1835 and, in 1846, Surrey was at last organising a county team. Even so, public interest in inter-county cricket was muted, mainly because of the impact of Clarke's fixtures. One major reason for the success of the wandering teams was the expanding rail network providing, at least in comparison with stage coaches, fast and cheap travel.

I Zingari and its imitators were ideal clubs for the public school and university cricketers initially looking for some cricket in their vacations. When they had finished their education, the clubs allowed them to keep contact with their former companions. They were drawn from all parts of the British Isles and therefore as a group did not have a specific geographical home and did not want a home cricket ground.

The opponents of I Zingari came broadly from four categories: public schools, university colleges, regimental clubs and country house sides. The teams were all from their own social group, therefore, though some opposition sides contained two or three professional bowlers. The regimental clubs would appear to stem largely from the General Order issued by General Lord Hill in 1841, which stated that all Barracks throughout the United Kingdom should lay out cricket grounds and maintain those grounds to a high standard. However, military cricket was common long before 1841, the year in which the first Woolwich vs. Sandhurst match is also believed to have been played. As far back as 1798 the full scores of several military matches in Yorkshire were published, and many of the pre-1840 matches in the colonies were either inter-regimental, or military vs. civilian contests. According to an article on Army sport in the *Cavalry Journal* of 1941 (vol. XXXI), 'the years that followed Waterloo (1815) and the Peace of Paris saw the practice of cricket steadily increasing'.

Country house cricket grew more popular from the 1830s onwards. Cricket grounds had been a feature of some country houses for more than a century – the Duke of Richmond's ground at Goodwood and Mr Brodrick's ground at Peper Harow are two that have been noted already.

Now, the boys coming home from Eton and Harrow, the young men from Oxford and Cambridge, pressed their fathers to have cricket grounds laid out on their estates. The 18th-century cricket patrons had employed talented cricketers as grooms, gardeners, bailiffs and the like, making use of their talents when they raised a side. In the 19th century, the nobility and landed gentry employed professionals for the cricket season, or just for July and August, using them as net bowlers and coaches. Lord Burleigh, the Earl of Stamford, the Earl of Leicester, Captain C. Alexander of The Auberies, Captain Townley of Beaupre Hall and Mr Du Cane of Braxted Park were just a few of these employers of professionals in the 1840s and 1850s. The professionals would not normally appear in matches against such sides as I Zingari, but by agreement, the resident professional could make an occasional match appearance.

William Clarke's first professional All England Eleven game

On the Hyde Park Ground, at Sheffield, August 31 and September 1 and 2, 1846 (all 20 of Sheffield fielded)

The England Eleven	1st Innings		2nd Innings
W. Clarke, b Skelton	0	c and b Barker	5
J. Dean, c Wright b Dearman	11	not out	2
W. Dorrinton, c Smith b Bentley	33	c Dearman, b Skelton	1
F. Pilch, c Ellison b Skelton	6	c Vincent b Skelton	1
A. Mynn, Esq., b Bentley	7	b Barker	3
J. Guy, b Barker	5	b Skelton	12
W. Martingell, c Dearman b Barker	2	b Barker	3
T. Sewell, lbw b Barker	0	c Parker b Wright	38
G. Butler b Barker	2	c Skelton b Bentley	17
V.C. Smith, Esq., c Dearman b Skelton	5	run out	9
W. Hillyer, not out	0	c and b Skelton	0
Byes 2, wides 7	9	Byes 5, wides 10	15
	80		**106**

Bowlers	Balls	Runs	Wides	Bowlers	Balls	Runs	Wides
Skelton	85	27	2	Skelton	68	30	3
Bentley	60	12	2	Bentley	40	28	3
Barker	56	11	1	Barker	64	28	4
Dearman	24	24	0	Wright	52	20	0
E. Vincent	8	6	2				

The Country House Week, which was to vanish almost entirely when war broke out in 1914, developed in conjunction with I Zingari and the other wandering amateur sides. Cricketing friends of the family were invited to stay for the week and the event was an important social affair in local circles. An Edwardian example is captured in L.P. Hartley's novel *The Go-Between.* I Zingari's imitators included the Quidnuncs (1851), Harlequins (1852), Free Foresters (1856), Peripatetics (1857), Butterflies (1862), Incogniti (1862) and dozens of others, many of whom survived just a few seasons; on the other hand, some are still playing.

William Clarke's travelling professional side was aimed at an entirely different market-place. The reason he arranged his first matches right at the end of the 1846 season was in order to gather, from the start, the best cricketers in England – by then they would be free of any other professional commitments. The venues he chose for these first three matches were large industrial towns, already well known for their interest in cricket. Clarke was not taking too much of a gamble. If his scheme was going to make money it would do so with the best players and with the possibility of large local crowds. He went to Sheffield,

Twenty of Sheffield	*1st Innings*		*2nd Innings*
G. Coates, c Butler b Dean	10	b Hillyer	9
C. Parker, c Guy b Hillyer	5	b Hillyer	13
C. Wragg, c Guy b Hillyer	7	c Dorrinton b Dean	4
E. Vincent, b Hillyer	1	b Dean	0
Paul Smith, b Dean	12	b Dean	6
H. Davenport, b Hillyer	1	b Hillyer	0
H. Wright, b Dean	8	b Dean	8
G. Chatterton, c Guy b Hillyer	0	c and b Dean	9
H. Sampson, c Dorrinton b Hillyer	3	not out	16
J.P. Burbeary, Esq., c Clarke b Dean	0	not out	0
James Dearman run out	9	b Dean	11
R.F. Skelton, Esq., c Pilch b Dean	0	b Hillyer	0
Gillott b Dean	0		
J. Bentley, b Hillyer	2		
J. Vincent, jun., c Guy b Hillyer	0		
T.R. Barker, Esq., c Mynn b Dean	3	b Hillyer	2
T. Linley, b Hillyer	0	b Hillyer	4
M.J. Ellison, Esq., c Hillyer b Dean	3		
B. Wake, Esq., not out	1	st Dorrinton b Clarke	25
B. Chatterton, c Guy b Hillyer	0	b Hillyer	0
Byes 4, wides 3	7	Byes 3, wides 5	8
	72		**115**

Bowlers	*Balls*	*Runs*	*Bowlers*	*Balls*	*Runs*
Mynn	24	8	Mynn	32	11
Hillyer	172	37	Hillyer	172	45
Dean	148	27	Dean	164	38
			Clarke	38	21

Sheffield winning by five wickets.

Manchester and Leeds. What type of opposition did he have in mind? Clearly the power of his side would reduce a match against the local eleven to a farce, finished in a day. Clarke abandoned the idea of eleven-a-side cricket. He allowed the opposition up to 22 players, all to bat and field, against his eleven. If necessary he even allowed the 22 to engage one, and sometimes two or three, professional bowlers for additional reinforcement. His three matches of 1846 were a huge success in terms of attendance, and thus profit. This success encouraged him to repeat the same three fixtures for 1847 and add Birmingham, Liverpool, Stourbridge, Stockton on Tees, Newcastle upon Tyne, York and Leicester.

James Dark, who at that time owned Lord's Cricket Ground, questioned Clarke's judgement. Dark thought Clarke over-optimistic in taking cricket to such back-of-beyond places as Newcastle. Clarke proved Dark wrong. The size of crowds and the excitement generated by the first three fixtures had been puffed up by the press and everyone wanted to see Clarke's team. They were the pop stars of the day. Lithographs of the players were published and sold well, as did a team lithograph. Local businessmen saw a chance to cash in on the assembling of large crowds and therefore put up any advance fee that Clarke requested, and local cricketers fought with each other to obtain a place in the local team.

Traditionalists moaned that XI vs. XXII was not proper cricket; that the true spirit of inter-county cricket was being killed; but the public paid no heed. Within a year or two, Clarke had to seek fixtures no longer; demand was such that he turned them away. He was considered as sharp a businessman as he was a cricketer. Not everyone was comfortable with his dictatorial ways and after six years, some professionals rebelled. John Wisden, the Sussex cricketer now remembered through his *Cricketers' Almanack*, set up a rival 'United' All England Eleven. It did not matter. Clarke had his full quota of 24 three-day matches; Wisden picked up 15 such fixtures with no difficulty. The public demand continued into the 1860s and Wisden's United side itself split into two. The enthusiasm for Clarke's type of cricket gradually diminished through the 1870s, ending with a series of Clown Elevens, whose popularity was a brief craze. Until then, the ultimate ambition of any young player who wished to earn a living at the game was to obtain a place in Clarke's side. To do so was to achieve the best paid post in cricket, and therefore Clarke had little trouble in filling vacancies as older players lost form, or retired through age.

The job of 'cricket professional' in the modern sense – as a full-time job from April to September – was created during the period between 1830 and 1860. At the start of this era there were at most 20 professionals in England. The others, as shown in contemporary match scores, were simply paid a match fee for a few games a season. By the 1850s cricket professionals were numbered in hundreds – the colleges of Oxford alone employed 25 pros for the season. The number at Lord's and The Oval rose steadily; the public schools employed coaches, as did the main regiments; players engaged at country houses have been mentioned; local clubs were increasingly engaging a professional as combined bowler and groundsman, and the better-off clubs also had an assistant professional.

A by-product of the mania for cricket was the creation of sports emporia, selling mainly cricket goods, and of course the firms which manufactured the goods. Frederick Lillywhite began the publication of his *Cricketers' Guide* in 1849, and the space given to cricket in the press grew as the matches increased. The Augustan or Golden Age is the term coined by Charles Box, cricket editor of *The Times*, to describe cricket during the first 40 years of Queen Victoria's reign.

THE HISTORY OF CRICKET

The great burgeoning of cricket in mainland Britain was thus brought to full bloom by the four elements mentioned: the two types of wandering team; the advance and encouragement of the game at public school and university level; and the very positive support of the Army. In the past historians have tended to credit William Clarke's team with doing much more than any other agency to popularise cricket, but the thrust by the military authorities and in the schools pre-dates Clarke, and therefore he was building on existing enthusiasm rather than creating it himself. The following extract from the press dated 15 July 1836 is worthy of note, since it gives an idea of the standing of cricket even before the wandering clubs and the Army Order on cricket grounds:

> National amusements are emblematic of national character; they partly borrow their tone from it, and partly contribute to form it. A fiery, restless Arab delights in the tournament of the jereed; the indolent, sententious Turk strokes his beard, and with the chess board before him whiles away hours without the motion of a muscle; the revengeful, stormy-souled Spaniard gazes with savage glee on the dying struggles of the bleeding bull, and watches with a thrill of pleasure the risks and dangers encountered by the agile matador. The Englishman's game is Cricket. It is a pastime dear to the London nobleman and the Sussex peasant, to the full-blooded youthful aristocrat of Eton and the honest ploughboy of Hampshire. The players' virtues in this game are promptitude, activity, cheerfulness, and noiseless vigilance. 'Still as the breeze, dreadful as the storm' is every combatant.

This quote is not quite what it seems, for it did not appear in an English newspaper, but in one published in Toronto. It is the first paragraph of a report on the match between Toronto and Upper Canada College. It provides a suitable juncture at which to leave cricket in Britain and move across the Atlantic.

CRICKET IN NORTH AMERICA

Cricket in both Canada and the United States – or more specifically on the eastern sides of those countries, especially the New York and Toronto areas – was flourishing in the 1830s, with soundly based clubs both sides of the border. Matches between the two countries however were started by a hoax. A person calling himself Mr Phillpots came to New York in 1840 and arranged for the St George's Club in that city to travel to Toronto for a match against Toronto CC. The New Yorkers arrived to find that no one in Toronto knew of the fixture. The Canadians hurriedly gathered a side together and a match was played; St George's won by 10 wickets. In 1843 the Toronto side played a return fixture in New York, and the following season a match was advertised as United States vs. Canada. In fact it was Toronto CC with some reinforcements against the St George's Club with one or two Philadelphians. Both sides included an English professional – French for Canada and Wright for the States. North America therefore, rather than England, was the instigator of international cricket. The series of international matches continued on a fairly regular basis – 11 in 17 years – until the outbreak of the American Civil War in 1861. The match was later resumed intermittently, from 1865, and is still played.

The British Army played an important role in Canadian cricket. The regiments stationed in Canada formed their own clubs and several Army cricketers appeared in the Canadian national side, notably J.H. Denne, who later played for Kent.

Cricket in the States spread from New York to Philadelphia, so that by the outbreak of the Civil War Philadelphia could match New York. The first Philadelphian club to lay out a private ground was Union CC in 1843; while the two clubs which were to play an important role in later years, Philadelphia CC and Germantown CC, were both formed in 1854. A handful of English professionals established themselves in the States prior to 1861, but the large influx did not occur until the 1870s and 1880s.

For the general growth of cricket in the States, it was most unfortunate that the pioneering 1859 tour of English cricketers to America occurred only 18 months before the Civil War. If the war had not broken out, it is highly likely that two or three follow-up tours might have been arranged in the early 1860s, thus building on the interest created by the initial trip. As it was, the enthusiasm for cricket faded in the war years and the troops on both sides adopted the embryonic game of baseball. When English teams resumed tours to America in 1868, not only did they have to try to rekindle the enthusiasm, but in baseball they had a serious rival to contend with.

The historic 1859 English tour to North America is well documented. Fred Lillywhite, who accompanied the side as programme seller and scorer, published a full account on the team's return to England. The book, *The English Cricketers' Trip to Canada and the United States*, the first of so many tour books, has been republished in the recent past.

The idea for the tour came from W.P. Pickering (1819–1905), the Eton captain of 1837 and 1838, who emigrated to Canada in 1852 and played for Canada against the States the following year. He opened discussions for a possible tour in 1856, but financial problems meant that it was three years before the money could be raised. The English team required a guarantee of £750, which Pickering obtained through the Montreal Club. The English team comprised six members of the All England Eleven and six of the United Eleven, with George Parr as captain (Parr had taken over the All England Eleven in 1857 after William Clarke's death in August 1856).

Five matches were played, all against XXIIs, plus three exhibition games, in which the England party divided in two and added five North Americans to each team to make up eleven-a-side matches. Including travelling time the trip lasted two months and each English player (it was an all-professional side) cleared about £90.

The English side was of course exceedingly strong and won all five games – they would probably have beaten any XXII in England. There were excellent crowds for the first three matches, but the weather, it being mid-October, turned very cold and cut down attendances in the last two. It was reported that the fielders wore gloves and overcoats in the last match!

The England side, the cream of professional talent in 1859, comprised H.H. Stephenson,[3] Julius Caesar, Tom Lockyer, William Caffyn of Surrey, George Parr (captain), Jemmy Grundy, John Jackson of Nottinghamshire, Tom Hayward, Robert Carpenter, Alfred Diver of Cambridgeshire, and John Wisden and John Lillywhite (brother of Fred) of Sussex.

FRANCE

Moving from North America to England's nearest neighbour, cricket had a number of opportunities to take root in France. A press report of 1828 states: 'A Cricket Club has been formed at Paris which includes in its members sixty persons of the first families in the French capital – boxing and racing are going out of fashion here.' The Paris Cricket Club once launched continued to play matches, but it cannot be said that it flourished. Sir Robert Clifton took a club side to the French capital in 1864, played three one-day matches against the Paris Club and won all three with ease. What is just as indicative of the situation of cricket in France at the time was the fact that the whole of the Paris team (judging by their surnames) were of British descent.

During the 1820s and 1830s, a slump in the English lace trade caused a great many English families to move to the Pas-de-Calais and take up employment in the French lace manufacturing industry. The English set up several cricket clubs in the area and occasional matches were played between Calais and Dover. This spate of French cricket lasted some 30 years, but few Frenchmen seem to have been tempted to adopt the game and it died when the English left for home.

IRELAND

Across the Irish Sea, the 1656 oddity has been noted. The first match recorded in the Irish press was played in 1792, and cricket in Ireland around the turn of the century and later owes almost everything to the presence of English soldiers. The first game was styled 'The Garrison of Dublin against All Ireland'. The Garrison was captained by Colonel Lennox (the future 4th Duke of Richmond) and All Ireland by the Rt Hon. Major Hobart, Secretary for War and the Colonies. The report in the newspapers makes it clear that cricket was not a game commonly seen in the country. *Freeman's Journal* notes: 'The game of cricket is in England what that of hurling is in Ireland.'

It is perhaps worth commenting that these regional games such as hurling, knur and spell, stoolball and others were largely swept aside by the tide of cricket, except in Ireland and Scotland.

---

3   H.H. Stephenson was the first cricketer to be awarded a 'hat' for taking three wickets in consecutive balls – the origin of the hat-trick. He performed this feat for the All England Eleven against Hallam in September 1858.

In 1830 some Irishmen began to take up cricket and the Phoenix Club was formed in Dublin. John Parnell (father of Charles Stuart Parnell, leader of the Irish Home Rule Party) was an early member. The 1830s also saw cricket introduced into Dublin University, principally by Irish boys educated at English public schools.

In the 1850s the Phoenix Club engaged their first English cricket professional, Charles Lawrence (1828–1916) of Middlesex. He was a man with big ideas and formed an All Ireland eleven in imitation of Clarke's team. The major snag was that there were very few teams in Ireland to provide opposition. Lawrence did persuade Wisden's United side to visit Dublin in 1856 and Parr's All England side in 1860. Another brainwave of Lawrence was to stage an Ireland Gentlemen vs. Players match. He appears to have overlooked the fact that apart from himself there was only one professional in the country at the time, Peter Doyle (born Dublin 1831). Undaunted, Lawrence filled the Players team with nine soldiers. After 1860 he gave up and returned to England, obtaining a place in the first England side to go to Australia in 1862 – he will appear again.

THE MEDITERRANEAN

Around the shores of the Mediterranean the English, mainly through military and naval cricket, arranged matches at various towns. Gibraltar and Malta were centres of such cricket. The first mention of cricket in Corfu comes in a letter from Major H.R. Lewin of the 32nd Foot on St George's Day, 23 April 1823. Gibraltar's first reported match was a year earlier, on 6 July 1822.

A British presence in Egypt meant that there was a cricket club in Alexandria in 1851. After the opening of the Suez Canal and the purchase by Disraeli of canal shares in 1875, the amount of cricket in Egypt increased, but only among the English.

The British colony in Naples played regular if bizarre cricket – three of the World beat two of Eton there in December 1839. In Rome in May 1843 a combined Oxford and Cambridge side beat 'All the World' for a stake of 500 scudi (a scudo was worth about four shillings).

The English in Turkey managed very briefly to attract some Bulgarians, who were studying at the Armenian College in Constantinople, to cricket. One Bulgarian proved a useful bowler – he was appointed Postmaster-General when Bulgaria gained independence.

SOUTH AFRICA

In southern Africa the first reported bona fide match occurred on 5 January 1808 in the Cape of Good Hope when Officers of the Artillery Mess opposed Officers of the Colony – the Cape had been captured from the Dutch in 1795. Although not many details have survived of cricket in the first half of the 19th century, there must have been some activity and the first mention of cricket in Natal is on 24 March 1848, when the 45th Regiment was playing at Fort Napier, Maritzburg. The first full score of a match there is published in January 1852. The first reported game in Durban occurred in 1858 and the two Natal towns of Maritzburg and Durban played each other for the first time in 1860. It took three days to travel between the two towns at that time, so the match was a major occasion. In Orange Free State, the Bloemfontein Club was founded in 1855, even though the population was only about 100.

INDIA

On the Indian subcontinent the Calcutta Club at Eden Gardens remained exclusively English and was to stay aloof for many years to come. This was a deliberate policy, but elsewhere in the world, with the very odd exception, the inhabitants perhaps watched cricket and decided it was not for them. By 1850, therefore, it seemed as if cricket would remain simply the game of the English, but a small community in Bombay thought otherwise. Unlike the rest of mankind, they were apparently fascinated by cricket. They watched military matches being played near Fort George in Bombay and in 1848 formed, with little encouragement from the British, their own cricket club – the Oriental CC.

In passing it is worth just comparing this single development with England's other sporting export, soccer. The rules of soccer were set down in 1863. Fifty years later 16 countries – Argentina, Austria, Belgium, Brazil, Denmark, Finland, Germany, Hungary, Ireland, Netherlands, Norway, Portugal, Scotland, Sweden, Switzerland and Uruguay – had established domestic soccer leagues, while at least a similar number had some informal soccer teams operating. In 1848, cricket's laws had been established for 100 years, but, with the exception of the United States (where the players were generally of English descent), the Oriental CC was a single shaft of light.

The Indian community that established this club was Parsee.[4] Although this pioneering side lasted only two years, it was quickly followed by the Zoroastrian CC. Shapoorjee Sorabjee published a small booklet in 1897 describing the history of Parsee cricket and his description of its earliest roots must surely be an echo of what originally occurred in The Weald three hundred years before:

> The more they (Parsees) watched the game the intenser grew their desire to play it. And they did begin with a makeshift of cricket – quaint bats unskilfully hewn out of old logs or cut out of planks that once served as lids or bottoms of dealwood boxes, and balls as artistically turned out of materials foreign to ball-making. The height and shape of stumps were matters of absolutely no moment; any sticks that showed the points where and whence the ball was to be flung were sufficiently good for their purpose. But this state of things was ere long

---

4   Parsees (or Parsis) are descendants of Persians who fled to India in the 7th and 8th centuries to escape religious persecution, and who still retain their Zoroastrian religion.

found very unsatisfactory: something of a better cricket was felt to be wanted. In their way of beginning the game regularly and with a regular kit there were two great obstacles – the impermissibleness of their parents and want of chink. The great solicitude for the game soon overcame the punctiliousness of their sense of duty of obedience to parents, but the second obstacle proved the Stonewall Jackson. However, their yearning was to be satisfied: The sinews of war were soon to be forthcoming: A young gentleman of means stepped in to help out. He had grown too fatty not to be strongly recommended by his doctor to take open-air and vigorous exercise, and he took to cricketing.

As a result therefore of the singular efforts of this Parsee community, cricket at last divested itself of its Anglo-Saxon exclusiveness. Within a few years the one Parsee club was joined by several others, and on 14 April 1870, one of the newer clubs, Mars CC, opposed an English side for the first time – the 95th Regiment led by Captain Cotton. Although the regiment won the game easily, the remarkable development of Parsee cricket was set on a steep upward path.

Elsewhere on and near the Indian mainland cricket was extensively played wherever the British established bases. Military cricket is first reported in Rangoon, Burma, in 1824, and in Ceylon the 97th Regiment played cricket in November 1832.

THE FAR EAST

Continuing eastwards, there is a mention of cricket in Singapore in the 1830s and a club was established there, playing Straits Settlements for the first time in October 1852. This must have been a very short encounter, since the Settlements made 11 and 1, Singapore 14 and 12.

Hong Kong Cricket Club was formed in 1851 and the famous match series between that colony and Shanghai began in 1866. As noted, the local population ignored this strange game, but at least one foreigner was later impressed. A German warship, with Prince Henry of Prussia aboard, was touring the European enclaves on the Chinese coast and inspecting the defences. At Kiaw Chow Prince Henry noted thousands of coolies erecting fortifications; at Port Arthur he saw the same activity. When he came to Wei-hai-wei all he saw were two British officers laying out a cricket pitch. He commented to a British bystander, 'The world is yours.'

AUSTRALIA

In Australia the first settlers, under the command of Arthur Philip, arrived in what is now New South Wales in 1787. If this landing was similar to others elsewhere it was no doubt not long before cricket was being played, but only when a newspaper was published did any written evidence of the game appear. The first extant score in 1804 was a match between

THE HISTORY OF CRICKET

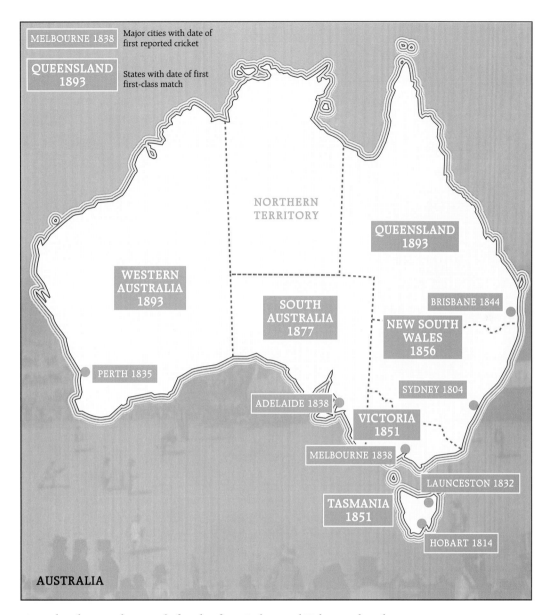

NORTHERN TERRITORY

QUEENSLAND 1893

WESTERN AUSTRALIA 1893

SOUTH AUSTRALIA 1877

BRISBANE 1844

NEW SOUTH WALES 1856

PERTH 1835

ADELAIDE 1838

SYDNEY 1804

VICTORIA 1851

MELBOURNE 1838

LAUNCESTON 1832

TASMANIA 1851

HOBART 1814

AUSTRALIA

Australia, showing the spread of cricket from Sydney and Hobart to the other major centres.

the 57th Regiment and Civilians. Two years later it was reported that a match in Sydney between two regiments attracted a crowd of 2,000.

After New South Wales, the second colony was founded in Van Diemen's Land (renamed Tasmania in 1856). The first recorded official match was Free Settlers against the Garrison in Hobart in 1825. Hobart Cricket Club was established in October 1832 and its rival, Launceston CC, in 1843.

New South Wales playing Victoria at Sydney for the first time. In the previous season the two sides had met at Melbourne.

Settlers from Van Diemen's Land moved to what is now Victoria in 1834. Here the population grew rapidly and within four years there were 30,000 Europeans living in or around the new town of Melbourne. Melbourne Cricket Club was founded in November 1838. The colony of Victoria was formed in its own right in August 1850 and as part of the celebrations, a cricket match was arranged against Van Diemen's Land. This, the initial inter-colonial contest in Australia, was played in Launceston in February 1851 and was considered a great success.

In 1856 the Melbourne Club, acting for Victoria, put out a challenge to play any club in Australia for £500. A group of businessmen in Sydney accepted the challenge, but refused to play for money. The press report commented: 'Of late years cricket, like chess, has been invariably a game of love, money being a thing unmentionable. The stake is now for the supremacy of local play respectively, and the broader grounds upon which the contest is placed are decidedly more calculated to produce the better sport.'

The match duly took place in March 1856 – Victoria beating New South Wales in a very low-scoring game by three wickets – and these matches superseded Victoria vs. Van Diemen's Land as the premier contests in Australia.

THE HISTORY OF CRICKET

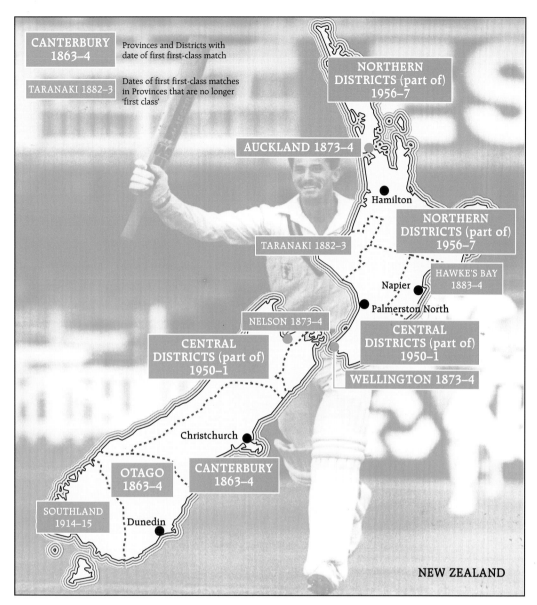

The following labels appear on the map:

CANTERBURY 1863–4 Provinces and Districts with date of first first-class match

TARANAKI 1882–3 Dates of first first-class matches in Provinces that are no longer 'first class'

NORTHERN DISTRICTS (part of) 1956–7

AUCKLAND 1873–4

Hamilton

NORTHERN DISTRICTS (part of) 1956–7

TARANAKI 1882–3

HAWKE'S BAY 1883–4

Napier

Palmerston North

NELSON 1873–4

CENTRAL DISTRICTS (part of) 1950–1

CENTRAL DISTRICTS (part of) 1950–1

WELLINGTON 1873–4

Christchurch

OTAGO 1863–4

CANTERBURY 1863–4

SOUTHLAND 1914–15

Dunedin

NEW ZEALAND

The first inter-provincial match in New Zealand took place in Dunedin in January 1864.
The map shows the initial dates for inter-provincial first-class games by the various teams.

NEW ZEALAND

In New Zealand the arrival of settlers meant the arrival of cricket. The original settlements began in 1840 and cricket was reported as being played in Auckland and Wellington within two years. Canterbury was founded in 1850 with cricket in progress the same year. Otago Cricket Club was founded in December 1848, and cricket was being played in both Hawke's Bay and Nelson in the 1850s. The opening up of the goldfields in Otago brought in a great influx of prospectors from Australia.

The first inter-provincial match was in March 1860 between Wellington and Auckland, but this and some subsequent games were only one-day matches. Wellington also opposed Nelson in one-day games in the 1860s. The first major inter-provincial contest was a three-day affair between Otago and Canterbury in January 1864, and this fixture, which continued on an annual basis, is considered the start of first-class cricket in New Zealand.

NOTABLE CRICKETERS

The Cricketers of My Time, written by Cowden Clarke from the recollections of John Nyren and published in 1833, gives an evocative word picture of the players of the Hambledon era, but the assessment of them is obviously very subjective. Apart from occasional quotes it was not until 1846 that descriptions of players emerged in any quantity, making it possible to get a true idea of the standing of individuals. The author was William Denison and the publication, *Sketches of Players*. In the preface he claims to have begun the work 20 years earlier. Thirty-seven players are described, all but one being professionals. The biographies run to some 76 pages and should be read as they stand by anyone interested in this epoch. Here, however, are some brief notes on the most illustrious of those players.

Of Fuller Pilch, whose career extended from 1820 (when he was 17) to 1854, Denison comments:

> There has been no man, having played as many matches, who has approached him in effectiveness and safety of style, or in the number of runs he has obtained. His vast length of reach and powers of smothering a ball by his forward play, the brilliancy of his cuts on either side of the point and into the slips, and the severity of the punishment he administers to the leg, have all and each, over and over again, caused a spontaneous ebullition of applause to burst forth.

Fred Lillywhite's *Cricketers' Guide* for 1855 simply states: 'His style of play needs but little comment, having for years carried the sway as the most scientific bat in England.' Fuller Pilch's actual bat is currently housed at Trent Bridge.

The commentators are unanimous in their opinion that Pilch for 20 years from 1826 was the best batsman in England, the reason being that he was the player who thoroughly mastered the new round-arm bowling. Pilch is also of historical interest because he was paid to leave his native Norfolk, for whom he played very successfully, and move to Kent, in order to raise the standard of cricket in that county (he appeared for Norfolk from 1820 to 1836 and for Kent from 1836 to 1854). So even in this very early stage of modern county cricket, a player was being induced by larger financial rewards to switch counties. The move was highly successful for Kent, but spelt the collapse of Norfolk as a major cricketing county. The present county club dates from 1876.

THE HISTORY OF CRICKET

Fuller Pilch (1803-1870), the outstanding batsman of his day, initially for his native Norfolk and then, from 1836 to 1854, for Kent. (Lithograph by G.F. Watts, c.1840.)

Felix: self-portrait. Nicholas Wanostrocht, who played cricket under the name of 'Felix', apart from being a leading batsman of his day, was the author of an innovative book on cricket technique, illustrated by lithographs showing the correct and incorrect methods of batting.

The second player of the same generation as Pilch was a Kent man through and through. Alfred Mynn was the son of a gentleman farmer living near Maidstone (see plate section). Denison states:

> Strictly the sketch of Mr Mynn ought not to appear in this collection; because it was intended to contain a memoir only of those who are recognised as professional players, and who are regularly paid for their assistance. But as Mr Mynn is one of the brilliant wonders of his day in the game, the author could scarcely have felt justified in sending this work to the world without having devoted a few of its pages to a gentleman who has been so great an instrument in the illustration of the science, and so important a feature in all our matches from the day of his advent.

Haygarth commented: 'It was considered one of the grandest sights at cricket to see Mynn advance and deliver the ball.' Mynn played for Kent from 1834 to 1859 and was the best fast round-arm bowler of his day, as well as a very powerful batsman. He excelled at single wicket matches, a form of cricket which attracted great crowds during most of his career. Mynn was one of the few 'amateur' members of Clarke's All England Eleven, but was clearly paid for his services at the same rate as the professionals: an early example of the difficulty of the sharp divide between the two classes.

Although Nicholas Felix (being an amateur) is not included in Denison's work, he ranks only a place or two below Pilch and Mynn. Felix (the name he used as a cricketer in place of Wanostrocht – his ancestors were Flemish) was another 'paid' amateur and member of Clarke's team. His career, chiefly with Kent, lasted from 1834 to 1852. A schoolmaster and talented artist, he resided in Blackheath. Haygarth wrote: 'Was a left-handed batsman, and possessed the most brilliant cut to the off (from the shoulder) ever seen. His drives and forward play were also very good . . . He is what is called a late player, that is to say, he did not begin to distinguish himself much, in the great matches, till he was about 30 years of age, he then however ran a most brilliant career for several seasons.'

These three – Pilch, Mynn and Felix – were largely responsible for the superiority of the Kent side in the 1830s and 1840s. Nottinghamshire's greatest players in those decades were William Clarke, Thomas Barker and Samuel Redgate. Clarke's effectiveness as a slow under-arm bowler came to the fore in the 1830s, when most bowlers used the round-arm style. Denison's comment is: 'Of late years, he has become distinguished and, it may with truth be added, notorious as about the most awkward bowler with whom a batsman has to deal in the present age.'

Barker is described as follows: 'His delivery is far from graceful, for it always appeared – so violent was the style in which he ran up to the crease and propelled his instrument of attack – as though his head would follow the ball.' Barker broke a leg in 1843 and afterwards was mainly played as a batsman.

Redgate's style of fast bowling was clearly quite different from Barker's: 'His pace was extremely rapid, his delivery beautiful and unexceptionable as to fairness, whilst its length was excellent and its rise quick and very effective.'

Redgate played for Nottinghamshire from 1830 to 1845; Barker from 1826 to 1845; and Clarke's career spanned 1826 to 1855, with most of the last ten years being for his All England Eleven. A fourth Nottinghamshire player who ranks highly is George Parr. His career commenced in 1845 and continued until 1870. Parr's rise to fame was too late to feature in Denison's book, but he succeeded Pilch as the best batsman in England.

The two great Sussex bowlers, William Lillywhite (father of Fred and John) and Jem Broadbridge, have been previously noted when dealing with the rise of round-arm bowling. Lillywhite played for Sussex from 1825 to 1853 and, like Clarke, came to the peak of his career much later than is common. Broadbridge played for the county from 1815 to 1840. The famous Surrey cricketers who made up the great county side around 1860 were H.H. Stephenson, George Griffith, William Caffyn, Tom Lockyer and Julius Caesar.

GEORGE PARR

By 1860 the professional wandering elevens had been established for more than a decade. Professional cricket outside London was effectively in the hands of two men, the dominant one being William Clarke's successor, George Parr (see right). In bald terms Parr controlled 104 of the 403 'money' matches staged in the British Isles during the five-year period 1858–1862. In reality, however, his influence stretched beyond that 25 per cent of the market, since at least another 25 per cent of the matches were pale shadows of what they ought to have been unless Parr agreed to release his contracted players. Fixtures such as North vs. South, Gentlemen vs. Players and Yorkshire vs. Surrey needed several of Parr's men to acquire the representative teams that would attract the public.

Parr was not merely the controller of the best professional side in England; he had also succeeded Fuller Pilch as the outstanding batsman. His position was not appreciated by everyone in the cricket world, as the following pen-picture, written in 1865, reveals:

> Parr, George, born at Ratcliffe, Notts, May 22, 1826. Has been a splendid bat – a brilliant leg-hitter. His time is now devoted to other purposes far from promoting the game of cricket. He is *so clever* that he stands umpire against Twenty-twos, and *makes the matches himself.* His cricketing abilities, no doubt, were owing to his well-known good temper, easy and quiet disposition, void of jealousy, and never interfering with other people's business. He appears to be manager of the United, as well as the All England Elevens, who will shortly follow 'Deerfoot'.[5] Was the able manager (when out of his bedroom) in America, and took an eleven to Australia, fortunately after he had received a benefit at Lord's Ground – receipts not known. Collector to the Cricketers' Fund Society, without five per cent commission, having now Box and Wisden to work with him.

5   That is, become extinct, like the Native Americans.

5

CLUBS

COUNTIES

AND TESTS

1860–1890

This apparently libellous description was published by Fred Lillywhite in his *Cricketers'*
Guide, in the midst of the humdrum 'Playfair-type' Who's Who of professional players. The
reference to the United Eleven is to Parr's rival professional team, run by John Wisden. In
the same five-year period it played 67 matches. Parr and Wisden were business partners in
setting up a ground in Leamington.

It was all a question of who controlled 'money' matches, and how the fixture lists for
these games should be arranged. Parr had the best professionals contracted to him, because
he paid the best wages. He planned his list of All England matches without any regard to
other fixtures, although, according to Lillywhite, he co-operated with Wisden on the
United matches. The authorities at Lord's and The Oval were therefore forced either to
work their major matches around Parr, or play them without using Parr's cricketers. *Baily's*
monthly magazine in 1867 illustrates the point: 'The Gentlemen and Players matches were
shorn of much of their ancient attractions. In fact there is nothing left of them now but the
name, for the context is between a picked eleven of gentlemen and a chance eleven of
players.'

That summer the five top professionals – Hayward, Tarrant, Jackson, E. Stephenson
and of course Parr himself – were all playing in an All England odds match at Hull, when
Gentlemen vs. Players was staged at Lord's.[6]

OVER-ARM BOWLING

In 1863 the idea of a cricket parliament was the subject of letters to the press. The idea fell
by the wayside, not because it was a stupid plan, but because it upset both Parr and his
followers and the Marylebone Cricket Club, whose Committee wished to remain in control
of the Laws. The parliament was intended to be a body representing the county clubs. The
fixture list was one problem that required resolution; the other was the adjustment of the
Laws to permit over-arm bowling.

Perhaps because of the threat of the cricket parliament, the MCC acted relatively
promptly in changing the Law to permit over-arm bowling (in comparison with the drawn-
out battle over the switch from under-arm to round-arm). The matter had come to a head in
1862 when Ned Willsher, the Kent bowler, had been no-balled six times in succession at The
Oval, for bowling over-arm. By a strange coincidence the umpire was John Lillywhite, whose
father had been one of the Sussex pioneers of round-arm bowling. After discussions and
letters to the press, the MCC voted by 27 to 20 on 10 June 1864 to change the Law. Charles
Marsham (1829–1901), an Oxford blue in 1851, proposed the change, which was seconded
by Henry Perkins (1832–1916), a Cambridge blue of 1854 and later MCC Secretary. The
reason for the switch from round-arm to over-arm was precisely the same as the switch from
under-arm: the bowlers were having problems dismissing batsmen.

---

6 Odds matches were those in which one team had more players than the other, to balance up the sides.

THE DECLINE OF THE WANDERING CLUBS

The fixtures problem was not so easily sorted. The atmosphere if anything seems to have got worse, as the following comment from *Baily's* magazine of September 1867 shows: 'Very sensibly men (i.e., amateurs) prefer to go about when and where they feel inclined, among their own friends, and to matches where the loser is as happy as the winner, where officious committee men supervise not and the grumblings of surly professionals are unheard.'

The committee men are those at Lord's and The Oval; the surly professionals are those under the thumbs of Parr and Wisden. The situation was further confused when seven professionals from the southern counties broke with Wisden's United Eleven in the autumn of 1864, and a third major professional side began operations in 1865 – the United South of England Eleven. Ned Willsher was the secretary and captain. The demand for fixtures involving the professional sides, though, still remained high. In 1865 Parr's side played 31 matches, Wisden's 9 and the new United South 15. It seemed that Wisden's side was losing out to the United South, but the following year a flood of fixtures was arranged. Parr had 30 matches, Wisden 22 and Willsher 17. However, 1866 was to prove the high point and Wisden's United side went into decline, owing to lack of initiative on the part of its promoters, and played its last match in 1869. This did not leave the expected duopoly of the All England Eleven and the United South, since yet another rival emerged from the remnants of Wisden's side – United North of England under Roger Iddison of Yorkshire.

The 1870s therefore began with three professional wandering sides; it seemed as if the old order would continue to flourish. Parr retired as a player in 1871, leaving the paperwork for organising All England matches largely in the hands of yet another Nottinghamshire batsman, Richard Daft (1835–1900), who was more interested in running his Nottingham sports emporium. James Lillywhite (1842–1929, a cousin of Fred and John) ran the United South, but judging by his later financial dealings had little head for monetary matters; while the United North, following an initial burst, never really captured the public's imagination. By 1880, the professional wandering sides, except for the United South who recruited W.G. Grace, were dead as far as major cricket was concerned. Public interest in odds matches dwindled, except when Grace played, so promoters could not secure the best players. With the exception of England-Australia tours, the era when the players themselves controlled cricket had ceased. This did not result in fewer top-class matches in Britain, since the decline of one type of cricket was matched by the rise in another: county cricket, or as George Parr aptly named it, 'Committee Cricket'.

COUNTY CRICKET

In 1840, county cricket of any substance had comprised Kent, Sussex and Nottinghamshire. At that time only Sussex possessed a genuine county club which selected and financed the county team. The Kent side was the product of the organisation

at West Malling under Fuller Pilch, and the Nottinghamshire side was raised by William Clarke. During the rest of the 19th century virtually every county in England and Wales, and many counties in both Scotland and Ireland, found themselves with a county club of some description. These county clubs can be broadly divided into two classes: 'professional' and 'amateur'. The former comprised what later became the 'first-class' counties, and emerged in one of three ways.

Sussex, Nottinghamshire and Yorkshire, for example, began with county teams supported through subscription lists. Two individuals acted as Secretary and Treasurer and persuaded their cricketing friends to subscribe whatever sum they could afford to a fund that paid the expenses of a county team for home and away matches against one, two or three opponents in a given year. This group of subscribers, after a period of time, formed themselves into a club with a formal committee, which ran the finances of the club, picked the county side and issued members' tickets, allowing subscribers free admission to matches – in other words, the basic structure of today's county club.

Surrey and Lancashire took another route. A group of cricket enthusiasts in each case formed a cricket club, established themselves at a ground and built up a fixture list against other local clubs, at the same time employing several professional bowlers for their club. Part of their remit as a club was to raise representative county sides to play other counties. For historians, particularly in Surrey's case, this on occasion causes confusion, because it is difficult to distinguish between 'Surrey Club' matches and 'Surrey County Club' games – especially when Surrey opposed non-county sides.

The third method was a hybrid of the two, which sometimes caused much heartache at the time. One set of individuals would be raising a county side via the subscription method, while a second would be using an established club. Kent is a prime example, with the cricketing base of the Canterbury Club and the looser organisation at Maidstone.

Running parallel to these 'professional' clubs was the growth in amateur county clubs, normally under the title of 'Gentlemen of Blankshire'. The casualty rate among these county Gentlemen's Clubs was high, some clearly relying on a single individual. Most of the counties with 'professional' teams also had County Gentlemen's sides, in some cases based at the same county ground, in others totally independent. Rowland Bowen seems to have been the first person to attempt a systematic search of the founding dates of every county club. His efforts were published in *The Cricketer* in 1962 and *Cricket Quarterly* in 1963. His results demonstrate how much more research is needed on the lesser counties, research which can only achieve its ends by a time-consuming trawl through 19th-century local newspapers.

The amateur county clubs acted in the same was as any 'friendly' cricket club in their method of gathering a fixture list. Each Secretary assessed the possible opposition and by contacting the appropriate Secretary arranged mutually convenient dates. It was not necessarily county opposition: I Zingari, the Free Foresters and regimental sides often featured on the lists.

THE HISTORY OF CRICKET

From the 1820s the sporting press were interested in which was the 'Champion' county club. Until the 1860s only Kent, Sussex, Surrey and Nottinghamshire had any pretensions in that direction and it was relatively simple to decide which of the four merited the accolade 'Champion County'. The award was not an annual event, but depended on what fixtures were made; these were increasingly irregular in the 1850s because of the competition from the wandering professional elevens. Surrey were the only one of the four to arrange a sensible fixture programme and on more than one occasion paid the opposing county's expenses to get a match arranged. In broad terms the 'crown' remained with a county until another county beat the holders. Boxing was already run on the same lines with its 'Championship Belt'.

In the 1860s Yorkshire, Middlesex and Lancashire formed viable county clubs of a strength equal to the original four. As all seven top-class counties did not play each other, it became more difficult to make a decision on the Champion county. Counties did not have a full-time staff of cricketers, and, in the case of professionals, had to persuade the local club who employed the player to release him for a county game. Meanwhile, the press proclaimed a county 'Champion' and tried to rank the others in some kind of order, which in turn created a table of results. If the table had been confined to the seven counties it would have made a relatively neat compilation, but several other counties also had aspirations – Hampshire, Cambridgeshire, Derbyshire, Gloucestershire, Buckinghamshire and Somerset. Of these only the claims of Gloucestershire were consistently justified. The western county possessed in the Grace brothers such a talent that they were the equal of any county. Cambridgeshire also had some brilliant players, but the county organisation was confused and lacked direction. Hampshire were cricket's answer to Bruce and the spider, trying to reach the required standard again and again. Buckinghamshire shone briefly in the 1860s. Derbyshire were tenacious but lacked quality. Somerset's efforts fell between those of Hampshire and Derbyshire.

By 1875 the press were in basic agreement as to which counties, in any one season, ranked as 'first class', and thus the results of matches between the first-class counties determined their relative positions in the table. The actual term 'first class' had come into use, not in order to grade teams, but to compile batting averages. Fred Lillywhite from the 1840s tried to rank the best batsmen and, as bowling analyses were more frequently kept, bowlers as well. He used performances in certain matches to compose his tables, and had separate tables for the wandering elevens in matches against odds. The matches he used were then termed 'first-class' matches, and teams involved became 'first-class' teams.

As the County Championship system was being accepted and generally recognised by the public, as well as by the county committees, the first problem which arose was the need for a rule on how players qualified to represent a given county. It had been a tradition from the 18th century that players could represent the county of their birth or the county in which they resided. Some players were taking advantage of this by playing in the same year for both the county of birth and that of residence. Furthermore, some of the landed gentry often had at least two possible places of residence, in addition to a claim elsewhere if they resided at a public school or university.[7]

Who was going to sort out this potentially contentious point? The move to form a cricket parliament had been stamped on in 1864. MCC's interest in county cricket was slight; no county matches were staged at Lord's, and Middlesex did not move there until 1877. Coincidentally, the greatest sports administrator, perhaps of all time, had been appointed Secretary to Surrey CCC in 1872. Charles William Alcock was born in Sunderland in 1842. Educated at Harrow, he was, as an active player, better known on the soccer field than as a cricketer. He was appointed Secretary of the Football Association in 1867 and had captained the winning side in the FA Cup, which was his brainchild, in 1872. He also led England against Scotland.

After various discussions and press comments over the qualification question, a meeting of county representatives approved a set of rules at The Oval on 9 June 1873.[8] The counties represented were Surrey (in the chair), Middlesex, Sussex, Kent, Gloucestershire, Yorkshire and Nottinghamshire. The basis of the rules was that no one could play for more than one county in a year and each player had to be qualified by birth or two-year residence. The MCC were asked to act as adjudicators if any disputes arose.

Alcock himself writes that Frederick Burbidge (1832–1892), a former Surrey captain, took the first steps in sorting out the qualification rule, but the initial meeting of county representatives was held at the residence of another Surrey Committee member, Dr E.B. Jones, with Alcock acting as Secretary to the meeting. Whoever the front man was, Alcock was at his elbow.

Two years later it was at The Oval that the county representatives met to discuss, for the first time, the planning of the county fixture list. Again Alcock's hand guided the officials. The fixture meeting was held at The Oval for two years, then Lord's adopted it.

The one brainwave which did come from Lord's was the 1873 scheme for an inter-county knock-out cup – all matches to be played at Lord's. As has been pointed out, no county cricket took place on the ground at that time. Only Kent and Sussex agreed to the plan; one match was played, Kent winning by 52 runs, and the idea was abandoned. The two reasons why the scheme failed were that most counties were happy with their fixture lists and did not want an extra game; and the professionals liked to know when all the county fixtures were at the start of summer – clearly impossible with a knock-out competition.

With the fixture list and qualifications solved, the awarding of the title 'County Champion' was still left to the press. Alcock, with another hat on, was the founding editor

---

7   G.B. Buckley explains in more detail how players qualified to play for counties in the 18th century. (See his book *Fresh Light on Pre-Victorian Cricket*, pages 218-220.)

8   The Kennington Oval had been laid out in 1845 and was from its establishment the headquarters of Surrey County Cricket Club.

THE HISTORY OF CRICKET

in 1872 of James Lillywhite's *Cricketers' Annual* (also known as *Red Lilly*). As well as writing extensively for the newspapers, Alcock compiled the basic County Championship league table and published it in *Red Lilly*. The 1872 table is worthy of reproduction.

Results of the matches played by all the counties, 1872

	Matches	*Won*	*Drawn*	*Lost*
Surrey	15	8	2	5
Nottinghamshire	7	2	5	0
Yorkshire	10	2	1	7
Middlesex	5	1	1	3
Gloucestershire	7	3	3	1
Sussex	7	4	1	2
Lancashire	4	4	0	0
Kent	6	1	0	5
Derbyshire	3	0	1	2
Staffordshire	1	0	0	1
Worcestershire	3	2	0	1
Shropshire	2	0	0	2

A detailed analytical essay in *Red Lilly* explains that Nottinghamshire are Champions, Gloucestershire and Sussex joint second, and Yorkshire and Surrey joint fourth, followed by Lancashire and then Kent. This might seem rather cruel (looking at the table) on Lancashire, but their wins were two against Derbyshire and two against the weak Yorkshire side. On the other hand, Nottinghamshire played the stronger counties and finished unbeaten. It is interesting to see Staffordshire, Worcestershire and Shropshire in the list. Alcock was soon to chop out the lesser counties and include them in a separate section – 'Minor Counties'. Worcestershire were promoted to first-class status in 1899, while Staffordshire and Shropshire remain Minor Counties to this day.

This example for 1872 gives a flavour of the way the press handled the Championship question until the late 1880s. The subject is an intriguing one, but this is not the place to go into a season-by-season discussion of the counties' merits.

The ordinary cricket follower was probably conscious of the gradual decline in interest in the wandering professional sides and the steady, if equally slow, rise in the number of major inter-county matches. In addition, membership tickets for county clubs allowed a subscriber to bring his wife to the matches free of charge; there was a separate section for ladies on major grounds. Meanwhile, not only the ordinary cricket follower but almost anyone in touch with day-to-day affairs in England was very quickly aware of the emergence of cricket's greatest genius to date – William Gilbert Grace.

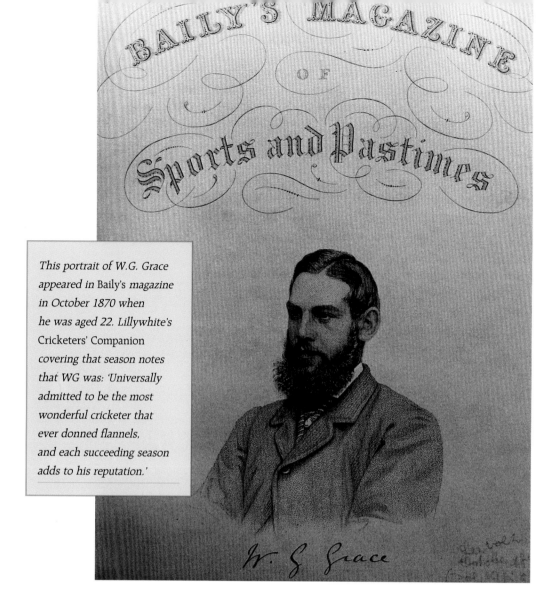

This portrait of W.G. Grace appeared in Baily's magazine in October 1870 when he was aged 22. Lillywhite's Cricketers' Companion covering that season notes that WG was: 'Universally admitted to be the most wonderful cricketer that ever donned flannels, and each succeeding season adds to his reputation.'

W.G. GRACE

At the age of 21, Grace is described as follows in John Lillywhite's *Cricketers' Companion*: 'W.G. Grace, Gloucestershire and MCC. Generally admitted to be the most wonderful cricketer that ever handled a bat. The reviews in preceding pages tell much relating to his performances; suffice it here to state that his average of 57.9 for 23 innings in the great matches of the season has never been equalled; a certain scorer off any bowling and the quickest run-getter in England; very successful as a medium pace bowler; a magnificent field any where; plays for Gentlemen v Players.'

Two years later, the same source begins a similar brief biographical note with: 'Acknowledged by all to be the best cricketer that ever stepped on to the cricket field, and is, in fact, unapproached and unapproachable.'

THE HISTORY OF CRICKET

And five years later, in a review of 1876: 'Is familiarly styled "the Champion", and fully merits the title. Undoubtedly the most wonderful cricketer that ever donned flannels, and his batting in 1876 has been more extraordinary than ever. He is at once the largest scorer, the safest bat, and the quickest run-getter off first class bowling that has ever defended a wicket.'

At the present time, Brian Lara has broken long-standing records and been accorded great praise. He has a brilliant reputation among cricket fans, but on a wider canvas he must compete as an outstanding sportsman with footballers, golfers, athletes and tennis players. Then whoever is judged the greatest sportsman of the time must compete with TV, cinema and pop idols. The competition for centre stage as the 'greatest entertainer' is fierce.

In the 1860s and 1870s, there were no footballers, golfers, athletes or tennis players of national importance, and no TV and pop idols. Cricket stood alone as the one national ball game; horse-racing and boxing were the only other sports to which the newspapers gave much space. As 'The Champion' of the greatest English game, W.G. Grace was the outstanding sporting personality. The cliché, a legend in his own lifetime, is inadequate. Because of the number of competing sports and entertainments today no one can reach the heights of national acclaim achieved by Grace. The only two personalities who were on the same plane as the cricketer were Queen Victoria herself and Gladstone. Some wag even suggested that Grace and Gladstone were one and the same person (with and without beard).

W.G. Grace was born in Downend near Bristol in 1848, a doctor's son. He had three older brothers, Henry, Alfred and Edward (E.M.) and a younger one, G.F. (Fred). A maternal uncle, Alfred Pocock, was their earliest cricket mentor, though the boys' mother Martha was also a cricket enthusiast. Of the boys, Edward was the first to make a national name for himself. He was to remain a formidable force in Gloucestershire cricket, but on the national stage his feats were soon eclipsed by 'WG'.

Into the equation of financial viability for the two competing types of 'professional' cricket (inter-county and wandering elevens) came the exceedingly viable W.G. Grace . His appearance on the cricket field was a guarantee of a good attendance. However, the first matches to benefit from Grace's presence did not fit into either of these two categories, but were the Gentlemen vs. Players fixtures. The combination of brother Edward and himself (WG made his debut aged 16 in 1865) ended the long professional domination of the series and meant that the contest became a worthwhile game. In 1868, just before his 20th birthday, WG hit a century (134 not out) and took ten wickets for the Gentlemen at Lord's; his side won by 8 wickets. Grace was to achieve this feat 15 times in first-class cricket. No one else in the English game to the present day has managed half that number.

In 1866 WG was brought into a professional wandering side for the first time, the newly founded United South of England Eleven. This eleven, as noted earlier, survived the general slump in the fortunes of the professional wanderers, and in the 1870s the Grace family more or less controlled the side. W.R. Gilbert, WG's cousin, was the Team Secretary

Colonel James Fellowes (1841-1916). Serving in the Royal Engineers, Colonel Fellowes was one of the Army's outstanding cricketers and administrators, once hitting three successive deliveries from W.G. Grace out of the Bat and Ball ground at Gravesend. When stationed in Southampton he acted as co-Secretary to Hampshire CCC, and founded both the Hampshire Hogs and the Devon Dumplings. When stationed at Woolwich, he played for Kent.

from 1879. In 1869, WG was elected a member of the MCC, and in 1871 the Grace family almost single-handedly created the present Gloucestershire County Cricket Club, WG's father being the first Treasurer. WG was therefore able to appear in first-class inter-county matches, in matches involving the MCC and in the odds matches of the United South. On occasions when he had to choose between them, the crowds followed him. The advent of this enormously popular figure took the game to its peak. Cricket now had a truly great national figurehead.

C.L.R. James, the West Indian writer, begins his essay on W.G. Grace with:

A famous Liberal historian (G.M. Trevelyan) can write the social history of England in the nineteenth century, and two Socialists, Raymond Postgate and G.D.H. Cole, can write what they declared to be the history of the common people of England, and between them never once mention the man who was the best-known Englishman of his time. I can no longer accept the system of values which could not find in these books a place for W.G. Grace.

THE HISTORY OF CRICKET

TOURS ABROAD

If it seemed possible that the public might one day tire of cricket with its continuing round of county and odds matches – and in the 1860s there was no evidence of it – that remote danger was soon to be removed by the exchange of touring teams to and from Australia. While the Civil War was raging in the States, the English cricketers made two trips to the Antipodes, in 1861–62 and 1863–64. George Parr and his cronies declined to go on the pioneering visit, because the financial rewards were insufficient, but they soon learnt that there was money to be made and happily joined the second expedition, which also took in games in New Zealand. Both English sides found the opposition as weak as in the States, but in 1862 one of the side, Charles Lawrence (last remembered as an Irish cricketer) stayed in Australia, and in 1864 William Caffyn, the leading Surrey all-rounder, did not make the return journey either. Both acted as coaches in Australia. Lawrence helped to develop cricket

Three of the Aborigines' team which toured England in 1988, 120 years after the previous side came on their pioneering visit. The players shown are John McGuire, captain (centre), Jean Appoo (left) and Mark Ella, manager (right).

among the Aborigines, and in 1868 brought his pupils to England. The tour was relatively successful, but more from a curiosity angle: spear-throwing and boomerang demonstrations were part of each match programme. The Aborigines were not good enough to take on first-class county sides. In the same season the English professionals resumed their tours to the States and found the baseball bug beginning to bite. At the top level, however, there was a definite improvement in the standard of American cricket and XXII of Philadelphia came close to beating the England side.

The next venture abroad was again to America, but by an amateur side organised by MCC Secretary R.A. Fitzgerald. If W.G. Grace had not been included, the matches would have been close contests. The averages give an idea of the situation. Grace averaged 49 with the bat; the next best average was 16. His bowling average was 7 runs per wicket – again the best.

Fitzgerald published his account of the tour, *Wickets in the West*, in 1873 and sums up the American attitude towards cricket and baseball as follows:

> Cricket has to contend against the business habits of Americans. They will not give the time necessary for the game. They will snatch a few moments from the counter for base-ball, and they would do the same for cricket; but the same two men may be in at the one game the whole time they can devote to leisure, and they are not charmed with monotony, even if it be High Art. Whereas, at the other game, they may see several sides out in the same time. We believe this to be the true social position of cricket in the States. Time is money here, and there is no denying that much of that valuable commodity is egregiously cut into ribbons at cricket. Americans might learn much, if they chose, from our noble game: if it inculcates one thing, it preaches and practises patience, it enforces self-control, it eliminates the irascible, it displays the excellence of discipline, it is more eloquent than Father Mathew on temperance and sobriety. With all respect for base-ball and its disciples, we believe that it principally encourages the two leading failings of American character – ultra-rapidity, quicksilver-sosity or whatever else of lightning proclivity you like to call it, and ardent speculation.[9]

The cricket tours to and from England from their inception in 1859 to the close of the 19th century fall into two basic categories. The first was simply a business venture, the promoters organising the trip to line their own pockets. The second category, which involved amateur players, was a holiday with cricket matches. In some cases the nature of the touring party meant that the two were, to an extent, merged. Almost all the England-Australia exchanges were business ventures; after the early professional trips to the States, most other tours there fell into the holiday category.

By far the most important of the touring interchanges, from the public's point of view, were those between England and Australia. Mention has been made of the two English visits to Australia in the 1860s and the Aborigines' visit to England. The first venture of the next decade came in 1873–4, when the Melbourne Club agreed terms with W.G. Grace that he should bring a side out. Several leading English professionals refused the offer of £170 and the side comprised five amateurs and seven professionals. (A study of the scores of the

---

9   One is reminded of Lord Mancroft's definition of cricket over 100 years later: 'A game which the English, not being a spiritual people, have invented in order to give themselves some conception of eternity.'

touring sides at this time reveals that they managed very well with only 12 men, and it was unusual to have to co-opt a stranger to make up the side because of injury.)

The pattern of Grace's tour was one that was to be followed in broad terms by its successors; it is therefore worth giving a brief outline. The team left England on 23 October, arrived in Australia after a voyage lasting 7½ weeks, played 15 three-day matches, finishing at the end of March, and returned to Southampton on 17 May – a total of nearly seven months. All the games were against odds, since cricket in Australia, though improving through the efforts of William Caffyn, was not equal to the standard of Grace's side. This particular trip was a messy embarrassment, because the five amateurs lodged in first-class hotels and the professionals in lesser establishments. The financial controllers of the venture did not help either, as this contemporary description shows:

> It was most unfortunate for the team that they should have fallen into the hands of twelve speculators, all of whom were in business of some sort or another, and, I am sorry to say, knew really nothing of cricket. To prove this, I may say that they actually wanted us once to commence at two o'clock on the third day; and on another occasion proposed that all the twenty-two should bat, but only eleven field! The trip, on the whole, was an enjoyable one, as far as seeing the Colonies and meeting good friends; but in a cricket point of view it was not a good one. We were met in a bad spirit, as if contending cricketers were great enemies. (From John Lillywhite's *Cricketers' Companion*, 1875, page 18, written by 'One of the Twelve'.)

Lessons were learnt from this tour, so that when James Lillywhite, who had been on the Grace visit, was invited to bring another party over in 1876–7, he chose only professionals. In complete contrast to the arrangements for Grace's tour, he offered his professionals first-class hotels and travel, which included first-class berths on the voyage to and from Australia. Alfred Shaw (in his book *Alfred Shaw: Cricketer*, written with the help of A.W. Pullin) gives a vivid account of this tour. Conditions on the New Zealand part of the visit were of the pioneering variety, but the cricket overall was a huge success. Australian skills had made a great leap forward and for the first time an Australian representative side played an eleven-a-side match against the English tourists. This confrontation is now regarded as the inaugural Test Match. It was played in Melbourne on 15, 16, 17 and 19 March 1877 and amid great jubilation was won by the home side by 45 runs. The victory caused a return fixture to be hastily arranged. The English side proved victorious by four wickets. Shaw comments: 'Cricket education was not as highly developed in the Colonies then as now. Consequently it was not surprising to find that we were accused of "kidding" by losing the first match in order to obtain another game and gate.'

Betting on cricket in England by the 1870s was rare, but in Australia it held centre stage, and since the Australian team for the second match had co-opted their greatest bowler, Fred Spofforth, who had had to miss the first game, the odds were heavily on

James Lillywhite's team to Australia, 1876–7. The side opposed Australia in the inaugural Test Matches in Melbourne in March 1877.

another Australian victory. A lot of people lost a lot of money. A number of the English players were tempted into side bets throughout the tour – Ted Pooley (1838–1907) the wicketkeeper missed the two 'Test' matches because of some betting arrangement turning sour – and this was a feature which marred one or two subsequent visits.

The overall interest in the tour, and the Australian win, persuaded John Conway, who had arranged the English fixtures in Australia for James Lillywhite, that the time was ripe for an Australian tour to England. In contrast to the way in which Lillywhite had financed his tour, each Australian cricketer picked by Conway was asked to speculate £50; the profits

THE HISTORY OF CRICKET

from the tour would then be divided between the 12 cricketers. Some Australian journalists thought it a risky venture, but clearly the players were of a contrary opinion and about the best possible team was assembled. Lillywhite, back in England, arranged the fixture list.

The Australians landed at Liverpool on 13 May 1878. Twenty odds matches, mostly against XXIIs, and 17 eleven-a-side matches were played, though none against a fully representative England side. The team got off to a bad start, being beaten by Nottinghamshire, but the next three games brought wins over the MCC, Yorkshire and Surrey. The crowds flocked to watch the matches. The twelve Australians each made at least £750 out of the venture – a very substantial sum. Conway, as manager, made a good deal more. The outstanding player of the trip was Fred Spofforth, the demon bowler. He took 97 first-class wickets at 11 runs each. Appropriately, the leading batsman was Charles Bannerman, who had enabled Australia to win the 1877 Melbourne 'Test' by scoring 165 (the first Test century). The upshot of this lucrative tour was that an Australian side returned to England every other season until 1890 – seven trips in 13 years.

If money promoted these frequent tours, it also had its down side. The English cricketing hierarchy debated whether the Australians were Gentlemen or Players. It had already been necessary to perform contortions on the status of W.G. Grace and his immediate Gloucestershire colleagues; they received twice as much in 'expenses' as the genuine professional received in wages. The Australians were receiving on average £20 per match, as against the English professionals' £5–£7. The MCC agreed to treat the Australians as honorary amateurs.

Billy Midwinter (1851-1890), who was the only cricketer to play for England against Australia in Australia and for Australia against England in England. He was born at St Briavels, Gloucestershire, but emigrated to Australia.

PAY AND POWER

The pay differential between the Australian tourists and the English professionals (when appearing in the same matches) was a major irritant. The matter came to a head at the beginning of September 1878, when the Surrey Club arranged a match which was intended to be similar to the two Test Matches in Melbourne in 1877. A representative English professional team was to oppose the Australians. The English professionals decided to demand the same pay that the Australians had received from Lillywhite's team in Australia (and roughly what the Australians would receive in this match at The Oval, i.e., £20 per man).

The following English professionals wrote a letter to the press explaining their request: William Oscroft, John Selby, Fred Morley, Arthur Shrewsbury, Alfred Shaw, William Barnes, Harry Jupp, Ted Pooley and Wilfred Flowers. Jupp and Pooley were Surrey players, the other seven came from Nottinghamshire. In addition, the Yorkshire county players concurred *en bloc*. The Australians and the Surrey management ignored the request. The match went ahead with a third-rate side, all of whom were happy to receive £10. Due to some exceptional bowling by Edward Barratt of Surrey, the tourists just scraped home by eight runs. The crowds were vast – about 23,000 over two days – and to stoke the fires of discontent, the players who turned out were given an extra £10, making a total of £20 each.

Whereas in George Parr's day the top professionals had clout, now, it would appear, management and County Committees were in control. This was to be proved beyond doubt in 1881. Six of the Nottinghamshire signatories to the letter above, plus William Scotton, put a series of demands to the Nottinghamshire County Committee. They wanted to be guaranteed a given number of matches in a season, also a benefit match after a number of years' service, etc. When their demands were refused, the seven went on strike. The Committee would not bow to this pressure and fielded what was in effect a Second Eleven. As it happened Nottinghamshire were so strong in the 1880s that even the improvised team fared quite well. One by one, as the season dragged on, the strikers came to heel, save for Alfred Shaw and Arthur Shrewsbury, the ring-leaders. The autocratic Honorary Secretary of Nottinghamshire CCC, Captain Henry Holden, was subsequently 'retired' and Shaw and Shrewsbury resumed their county careers.

There were a few other instances of single players, or small groups, making demands of the County Committees, but it became increasingly obvious that the days of professional power had gone. Cricket in England at first-class level was run by the County Committees, and the contracted players were little more than domestic servants. They travelled third class, stayed in third-rate hotels, used separate dressing rooms to the 'Gentlemen' and, in the case of Lord's, walked out on to the ground through separate doors: a real 'upstairs-downstairs' scenario. In other walks of life at the time the division was commonplace, but in general those other walks did not have the shamateurs, who became more numerous as the first-class matches multiplied. Fewer cricketers could afford to play as genuine amateurs, but equally they did not relish going 'downstairs'.

The one avenue of financial exploitation left to top English professionals was touring Australia, and in 1881–2 the two Nottinghamshire professionals, Shaw and Shrewsbury, combined with James Lillywhite to organise the greatest of all tours: across the Atlantic, playing on both sides of North America, and across the Pacific, playing in New Zealand and Australia. The North American section of the tour, especially St Louis and San Francisco, proved a financial flop, but New Zealand and Australia made up for it. No less than four 'Test Matches' were arranged, each lasting four days. Betting was still a big feature of the matches and rumour had it that two of the English side were paid £100 to throw a match. In another game, when the odds were 30 to 1 against the English side winning, most of the tourists put

£1 on England. England turned the game round and won. Apart from the betting, though, the tour went well and each player made about £300.

The same organisers, cutting out the North American leg, went back to Australia in 1884–5 and 1886–7 and, like the Australians in England, did very nicely. They decided to go again in 1887–8, but found a rival England team being organised, sponsored by the Melbourne Club. Each party continued with their independent plans, hoping the other would withdraw. Both were a financial disaster. Lillywhite, Shaw and Shrewsbury claimed they lost all the profit made from the previous visits. In order to recoup the losses, Shrewsbury remained in Australia and managed the first English rugby football tour; but rugby was only popular in New Zealand, and in Australia the side had to try to play Victorian Rules football – another financial failure.

What had started with William Clarke in 1846 therefore came to an end in Australia in 1888. The days of English professionals in command of their own cricketing destinies were no more.

The Lillywhite, Shaw and Shrewsbury combination, while they held the purse strings, were as hard on the Australian home players as the Australian manager had been on the English professionals in England. In 1884–5 for example, Billy Murdoch, the Australian captain, demanded that the 'Test Match' profits be split 50/50. The English side offered 30 per cent, then £20 per man; but Murdoch refused to lessen his demands and withdrew his men. England beat Australia, so-called, by ten wickets.

Unlike today's sides, none of these touring teams to and from Australia was selected by a group carefully chosen from the countries' Boards of Control. The person, or persons, who raised the necessary capital and managed the team, picked the personnel. The record books contain a neat list of 'Test Matches' dating from the great 1877 Melbourne game and involving all the touring teams both ways up to 1890, apart from the 1878 Australians. However, none of the English teams travelling overseas was truly representative of England's full strength. The Australians were more so, but only because the managers had a pool of just 20 or 30 players from which to pick their 12 (having only three major teams – Victoria, New South Wales and South Australia). Either way, being a friend of the manager helped!

AUSTRALIAN ADMINISTRATION

In Australia cricket administration was split in two. Sydney and Melbourne, the great cricketing centres, were usually locked in deadly combat. Each, however, was likewise split in two. The New South Wales Association (formed in 1857) set itself three tasks: to select a representative NSW side, to arrange matches for the side and to find a suitable home venue. In reality the only sensible home venue was the Sydney Cricket Ground, run by a group of trustees, with minds of their own. The Association therefore had to grovel to the trustees to obtain the best terms they could to play inter-colonial matches.

Alfred Shaw, who bowled the first ball in the first Test Match. He was considered the most accurate bowler of his day, and captained both Nottinghamshire and England.

A similar set-up prevailed in Victoria, except that the Victorian Cricket Association was a feeble body and the Melbourne Cricket Club, which ran the ground, was the most powerful cricketing body in Australia (the equivalent of the MCC).

The organisation in Adelaide and South Australia was much better balanced, but without the pull of the other two. The attempt to gather these diverse, not to say warring, parties into a 'Board of Control' for Australian cricket, was not going to be easy.

EARLY TEST MATCHES

A brief outline of the early 'Tests' and 'Ashes' series needs to be added here, although these games did not stand out in quite the way they now do. As a simple illustration, when the journalists began to create 'Test' records in the 1890s, the initial list of Test Matches to date in the Australian press did not agree with the matches included as Tests in the English press.[10] Many years later, one or two players were very surprised to find their names in the list of Test Cricketers, having been unaware at the time that they were taking part in a Test Match! The very first Test should be the one staged at Trent Bridge in 1899, which was the first time an official English group of Test Selectors chose an England team. I do not however advocate crossing the first 59 'official' Test Matches off the list.

After the first two Tests in Melbourne in 1877, the next game on today's list was also in Melbourne, in January 1879, when a very moderate touring side, mainly amateurs led by Lord Harris, was beaten by Australia by ten wickets.

10　The phrase 'Test Match' was coined in Australia before 1877. It was used by the press to describe major matches on the 1861-2 English tour of Australia. (See Hammersley's *Victorian Cricketer's Guide*, Sands and McDougall, Melbourne 1862, page 159.)

Left to right: Fred Spofforth, Tom Horan, John Blackham and Harry Boyle – four notable Australian Test players of the 1880s.

In 1880 C.W. Alcock, the Surrey Secretary, made another of his pioneering moves by organising an England team, under Lord Harris, to play the Australian tourists in a hastily arranged fixture on 6, 7 and 8 September at The Oval. This is now considered the first Test in England and the home side proved victorious by five wickets – W.G. Grace made 152. As has been pointed out before, the 1881–2 English team in Australia played four 'Tests'. In 1882 C.W. Alcock repeated his fixture at The Oval. Spofforth took 14 wickets, Grace for once failed and Australia won, giving rise next day to the famous obituary notice in the *Sporting Times* about the death of English cricket: 'In Affectionate Remembrance of English cricket, which died at The Oval on 29th August, 1882, deeply lamented by a large circle of sorrowing friends and acquaintances. R.I.P. N.B. – The body will be cremated and the ashes taken to Australia.' The composer of the 'obituary' was Reginald Brooks, a London journalist.

The Lillywhite, Shaw and Shrewsbury side which toured Australia in 1884–5 under the captaincy of Arthur Shrewsbury, winning the Test series by three matches to two.

The Melbourne Club were keen to cash in on the kind of money made by the Lillywhite, Shaw and Shrewsbury trip of 1881–2, and arranged and paid for an England side of eight amateurs and four professionals to come to Australia in 1882–3 (the initial agreement was that the professionals would travel second class, but they refused and the decision was rescinded). Among the fixtures planned were three against the Australian team currently touring England. Since Australia had won at The Oval, these games were awaited with great interest. England, under the Hon. Ivo Bligh, won two matches and Australia one. Bligh was presented with the legendary urn and some ashes. A fourth match was arranged, which Australia won; so who won the 1882–3 series remains a moot point.

The Lillywhite, Shaw and Shrewsbury combination played five Tests on their 1884–5 trip, winning the series three matches to two. Their next visit, in 1886–7, was far more complex. Two separate series of games were played against 'Australia'. In the first, the Englishmen faced the team of Australians who had toured England in 1886; this team was selected exclusively by the Melbourne Club, who had promoted the 1886 tour. The English won this three-match series, gaining two victories with one match drawn.

Later in the same season the Englishmen were, in theory, faced by the best possible Australian team. The first match was against a very strong home side, and England won by the narrow margin of 13 runs. All the Victorian players, bar one, boycotted the second match, and England won with ease. Because of the boycott, the third match was cancelled and substituted with a game between Smokers and Non-Smokers, in which both sides were a mixture of English tourists and Australians. The Non-Smokers created a new record total for first-class cricket of 803, Arthur Shrewsbury scoring 236, and the game ended on a farcical note when William Scotton faced the last ball, stopped it with a dead bat and picked it up to keep as a souvenir. He was given out 'handled ball'. Only the first two games of this second series, and none of the first, were classed as Test Matches. As the tourists discovered, Australian cricket during the 1886–7 season was a battleground between the leading players and the organisers of the Victorian and New South Wales teams.

Finally, the season of 1887–8 saw the two rival English touring parties going to Australia. The only game ranked as a Test was when the two sides combined, winning easily, but both sides played 'Australia' individually.

NOTABLE CRICKETERS

Among the principal personalities of this early Test era, for England W.G. Grace stood out far beyond the rest. He did not, however, take part in any Test tours to Australia between 1877 and 1890, his two tours being in 1873–4 and 1891–2.

Arthur Shrewsbury dominated the professional batting. Making his debut for his native Nottinghamshire in 1875, he was the model for all the modern professionals dedicated to their craft, that is, achieving the skill required to score runs and not lose your wicket. Charles Fry wrote in 1899:

Arthur Shrewsbury, second only to W.G. Grace as a batsman. Shrewsbury was the first cricketer to reach 1,000 Test runs.

To the generation of cricketers to come Arthur Shrewsbury will go down as the greatest professional batsman of our day. Late on results scored in black print will have a great weight, and by results Arthur Shrewsbury must be put first among his brethren. It has been said of him that he is a marvellously skilful batsman who has reduced the game to an absolute science – almost to a certainty; and that the secret of his great success is his perfect judgment of the length and pace of every ball bowled to him ... The pre-eminent trait in Shrewsbury's play is his absolute mastery of the back stroke.

Shrewsbury topped the first-class batting averages in England for the last time in 1902. In May 1903, aged 47, he committed suicide, partly it is believed because ill-health meant that his cricket career could continue no longer.

THE HISTORY OF CRICKET

Shrewsbury's colleague in the Nottinghamshire side and business partner was Alfred Shaw, whose first-class career stretched from 1864 to 1897. Ashley-Cooper wrote:

> That Shaw must be reckoned the greatest of all medium-paced bowlers is acknowledged everywhere. His extreme accuracy of pitch and a deceptive flight combined to credit him with hundreds of wickets. He always bowled with his head, and many a batsman, when opposed to him, ran out to hit his slow half volley, only to find themselves struggling with a good length ball ... The off theory he regarded as more or less a waste of time, and he always preferred to bowl on the wicket and trust to variation of pace and elevation to beat the batsman.

For Australia, the four outstanding figures are Spofforth, Murdoch, Blackham and Giffen. R.H. Lyttelton wrote:

> I regard him (Spofforth) on the whole as the greatest bowler the world has ever seen. He has tried and succeeded in all paces, except, perhaps, the very slow; and has bowled in two hemispheres on every variety of wicket, and against the leading batsmen of the world.

Of Billy Murdoch, who led Australia on the tours of 1880, 1882, 1884 and 1890 and then settled in England to captain Sussex, W.G. Grace said that he was the best batsman Australia had produced.

John Blackham is described by W.G. Grace:

> It can be said of him as of no other Australian, that he is without a rival in his own particular branch of the game. Blackham has a genius for wicket-keeping, but it is a genius that has been built up by stern hard work and pluck ... Before he had been a month in England in 1878 his quickness with the gloves was the admiration of all cricketers; to-day (1890) he has still no equal behind the wickets.

George Giffen's obituary, published in *The Cricketer* in 1928, commented:

> At his best he was an excellent all-round performer, to be feared with both bat and ball, although in this country he was probably more successful as a bowler than as batsman. Possessed of a strong defence and having many strokes, he often scored heavily whatever the conditions, while his bowling – medium-paced with skilful variation in pace and flight – brought him hundreds of wickets. As he was also a good field, it will be realised that his worth to any side was most pronounced, and until M.A. Noble reached the height of his powers, he fully merited the title, 'The W.G. of Australia', which was bestowed on him by his admirers.

Behind those few outstanding cricketers were a mass of talented players, all of whom had some brilliant seasons and match performances.

BAT AND BALL

The bowlers meanwhile were fighting a losing battle in an effort to stem run-getting. The change in the law which permitted over-arm bowling had proved only a temporary respite. The lawnmower had been invented in Stroud, Gloucestershire, by Edwin Budding in 1830 and was in widespread use by the middle of the century, except at Lord's, where sheep were still used. In the 1870s the heavy roller arrived, covering of pitches was happening to a limited extent and pitches were growing blander, especially at The Oval, Trent Bridge and Hove. Ned Willsher (1868), Alfred Shaw (1875, 1879 and 1880) and A.G. Steel (1878) captured more than 100 wickets in a season at less than 10 runs each: this type of economy was never to be repeated. The run glut became so bad that some sides found themselves simply throwing away their wickets in order to complete the game inside three days. This unwholesome practice led in 1889 to the introduction of the declaration law: 'The batting side is allowed to declare its innings closed at any time on the last day of the match.'

The excessive use of the pads to defend the stumps, a feature of Nottinghamshire's batting, began to be seen in the 1880s. There were calls for a change in the lbw law, but all that happened was that the MCC put out a statement in 1888 saying that the deliberate use of pads to defend the wicket was against the spirit of the game. The advantage to the batsman was destined to continue.

WISDEN AND LILLYWHITE

In 1864 John Wisden, the Sussex cricketer and proprietor of a sports goods firm, published *The Cricketers' Almanack*. This annual, known now simply as *Wisden*, has been the principal English cricket publication over the past hundred years.

In the 19th century, however, it was in competition with three other annuals, all published by members of the Lillywhite family: Fred Lillywhite's *Cricketers' Guide* (published 1849–66); John Lillywhite's *Cricketers' Companion* (1865–85); and James Lillywhite's *Cricketers' Annual* (1872–1900). These three are familiarly known as *Fred's Guide*, *Green Lilly* and *Red Lilly*. The family name lives on in the famous Lillywhite's sports store in Piccadilly Circus and other branches outside the capital.

The publication of three rival national cricket annuals between 1872 and 1885, plus the founding of a weekly magazine in 1882 (*Cricket*), demonstrates the increase in cricket's popularity at this time. The editor of *Cricket* was none other than C.W. Alcock.

It has been a habit among cricket statisticians and others to make comparisons between top-class cricketers of separate generations. In reality such comparisons are problematic because the conditions under which the game is played changes too much to enable true parallels to be drawn. Nevertheless, if one assumes that the top-class professional of 1860 was more or less as good as his counterpart in 1890, then one thing is clear: there was a measurable improvement in cricket at the highest amateur level in England between these two dates. The measuring stick to prove this point is the annual Oxford vs. Cambridge University Match.

OXFORD AND CAMBRIDGE

In 1860 neither Oxford nor Cambridge was capable of playing the top-class counties on level terms. For example, both universities were allowed 16 men when they played Surrey. In the same year, playing eleven-a-side, Oxford were beaten by an innings by Oxfordshire and Cambridge lost by 115 runs to the Quidnuncs, a club of present and former Cambridge University cricketers.

Compare those facts with 1890. Cambridge beat Yorkshire by nine wickets and Sussex by 425 runs; Oxford beat Lancashire by eleven wickets (twelve-a-side) and Sussex by 86 runs.

The 1890 University Match contained no less than 16 cricketers who went on to play first-class inter-county cricket, including such notables as Stanley Jackson, Sammy Woods and Lionel Palairet. Furthermore, the days had not yet arrived when counties were often led by amateurs who hardly reached the required first-class standard; so the 16 were good-quality performers. The 1860 University Match did contain 11 who played for first-class counties, but only two or three who made more than a few appearances and no one who could be called outstanding.

6

THE

AMATEUR

GAME

1860-1890

THE PUBLIC SCHOOLS

In the 1890s the two universities were employing roughly the same number and quality of professional bowlers and coaches as they had done in the 1850s. So the standard of coaching at the university colleges can only have been marginally responsible for the vast improvement. The principal reason, in fact, was the quality of coaching and enthusiasm for cricket in an increasing number of public schools. In the 1850s, a player who gained a place in the side at Eton, Harrow or Winchester would almost certainly go on to the university side. At least half if not three-quarters of the blues of the first half of the 19th century hailed from those three schools. In 1890 only six of the 22 blues came from Eton, Harrow or Winchester and no less than 11 other schools provided the 16 other participants. H.H. Stephenson, the Surrey professional, went to coach at Uppingham in 1872 and his obituary comments:

> He found that there was very much to be done, if the school, from a cricket viewpoint, was to take its place among the other great schools. He set to work with determination, and helped by masters and boys alike, he very soon began to make headway. Then came the famous succession of cricketers who made Uppingham famous.

The school sides of 1890 contained such cricketers as Archie MacLaren, Pelham Warner and Charles Fry, all destined to have flourishing Test careers. During the second half of the 19th century two of the great social occasions at Lord's were the University Match and Eton vs. Harrow. The stuttering, almost illicit beginnings of these two matches were forgotten, as fashionable London came to view one other and occasionally view the cricket.

Baily's magazine, a monthly sporting publication founded in 1860, opens its report on the 1861 University Match with: 'The company was brilliant in the extreme; such an assemblage of beauty, rank, fashion, and learning was never before clustered on a cricket ground.' Its cricket report for the August 1865 edition reveals the true standing of the Eton vs. Harrow game. It begins with Gentlemen vs. Players; notes 'other great matches' as Nottinghamshire vs. Surrey and Yorkshire vs. Surrey; then follows with:

> But the Public School Match, is, after all, the great event of the season; and this year proved no exception in point of the numbers who thronged to this 'cricket Derby'. Really, by this time, the meeting deserves that name; for you have (proportionably) the same concourse, not only of pedestrians, but drags and carriages of every sort, all duly Fortnum and Mason-ed to make a day of it. How else, but as of a Derby Day, should we speak of twelve thousand people in the space of Lord's.

Thomas Arnold, who had been appointed to the mastership of Rugby in 1828, steadily transformed the way the school was run and by 1840 had effectively created the basis of the

Cambridge University, 1878. Of this outstanding side, Lillywhite's Cricketers' Companion *noted:* 'The Cantabs won every match they played, achieving a series of triumphs such as has never previously been chronicled in University annals.'

Tonbridge School about 1850. The enthusiasm for cricket at the principal public schools and the game's encouragement by the school authorities from the 1840s onwards had a great deal to do with raising the standard of cricket throughout the British Isles.

public school image which was to remain intact until the 1950s. The rest of the public schools followed his lead. Part of Arnold's ethos was the organisation of athletic pursuits: a healthy body and a healthy mind, muscular Christianity. Cricket was the only team sport with a nationally agreed set of rules in the middle of the 19th century (soccer's rules were not nationally in force until the late 1870s). It was well established in the great public schools and was therefore ideal for Arnold and his disciples. The Introduction to Nyren's book sets the pattern in 1833:

> Of all the English athletic games, none, perhaps, presents so fine a scope for bringing into full and constant play the qualities both of the mind and body as that of Cricket. A man who is essentially stupid will not make a fine cricketer; neither will he who is not essentially active. He must be active in all his faculties – he must be active in mind to prepare for every advantage, and active in eye and limb, to avail himself of those advantages. He must be cool-tempered, and, in the best sense of the term, MANLY; for he must be able to endure fatigue, and to make light of pain; since, like all athletic sports, Cricket is not unattended with danger, resulting from inattention or inexperience.

In 1851, the Revd James Pycroft opens his book *The Cricket Field* with:

> The game of cricket, philosophically considered, is a standing panegyric on the English character: none but an orderly and sensible race of people would so amuse themselves. It calls into requisition all the cardinal virtues, some moralist would say.

These two short extracts set the tone for a deluge of similar literary outpourings, both factual and fictional. The famous cricket scene from *Tom Brown's Schooldays*, published in 1857, includes the following passage:

> 'Come, none of your irony, Brown,' answers the master. 'I'm beginning to understand the game scientifically. What a noble game it is too.'
> 'Isn't it? But it's more than a game. It's an institution,' said Tom.
> 'Yes,' said Arthur, 'the birthright of British boys old and young, as habeas corpus and trial by jury are of British men.'
> 'The discipline and reliance on one another which it teaches is so valuable, I think,' went on the master, 'it ought to be such an unselfish game. It merges the individual in the eleven; he doesn't play that he may win, but that his side may.'

Sir Henry Newbolt's well-known poem 'Vitaï lampada' was published in 1897, taking this attitude to its ultimate chauvinistic conclusion (Play up! play up! and play the game!).

In the short and medium term this turning of the common game of cricket into a public school quasi-religion further boosted the development of cricket throughout the British

Empire, but in the long term its appeal among the population of the British Isles as a whole lost out to soccer.

The growth in cricket in public schools produced a secondary branch – Old Boys' cricket clubs. Eton Ramblers were founded in 1862, Uppingham Rovers in 1863, Harrow Wanderers in 1870 and Marlborough Blues in 1882. Every school of any note had its club. They usually played a week of matches at their alma mater and then toured for a week, adding to the number of wandering sides.

LOCAL CRICKET

Village cricket remained much the same as it had been in the earlier years of the century. In towns tradesmen's clubs were established, and the churches ran their own clubs in competition with the long-established ones based on public houses, thus reversing their 17th- and 18th-century attitude to cricket. Some of the earliest knock-out cup competitions took place between church sides. The public parks became a network of cricket pitches for the use of local urban sides, sparking another set of competitions – again knock-out – between all the clubs playing on a given public park. The cricket was played on half-closing day and Saturday afternoons; no Sunday cricket was acknowledged, although some 'social' games were played on the Sabbath. Perhaps Nottingham was slightly more enthusiastic about cricket than other county towns, but in 1888 there were 23 cricket clubs belonging to the Cricket Association for clubs playing on the Forest Recreation Ground. A complaint from a cricketer about the administration brought the following comment from the Association's Secretary, in 1885: 'In six months I have written 168 letters, spent 1,092 hours in the Association's service, walked 532 miles and used 15 quires of notepaper.'

SCOTLAND

The enormous popularity of cricket in England at last had its effect north of the Cheviots. The first *Scottish Cricketers' Annual* appeared in 1870–1 and its initial note, 'To Our Readers', states: 'Year by year the game of cricket has grown in importance in Scotland till there is not a town of any note which does not possess at least one club, and at the several seats of industry and commerce the players are numbered by hundreds and thousands.' Twenty-six professionals are listed as being currently engaged by Scottish clubs. An article in the *Annual* urges the formation of the Royal Caledonian Cricket Club to run the affairs of Scottish cricket. The first Scottish Cricket Union in fact came about in 1879, but collapsed in 1883. The Scottish enthusiasm for soccer, no doubt aided by the colder climate, was pushing cricket into the background except at the Scottish public schools. The present Scottish Cricket Union was formed in 1908.

In Ireland there had been some growth in cricket clubs through the country as a whole. John Lawrence published an Irish cricket handbook, starting in 1865, and urged landlords to encourage cricket among their tenants, labourers and servants. His was a lone voice, though, in the face of the Irish Land League and even those rural clubs that existed largely disappeared as prices dropped and the agitators for land reform took over. Cricket was therefore confined to Dublin and a few of the larger county towns. In view of this it is perhaps surprising that an Irish team was invited by the St George's Club of New York to tour America in 1879, and the Irish side – all amateur players, but with a professional as umpire – visited Philadelphia and Canada in addition to New York. Irish sides returned to the States in 1888, 1892 and 1909.

In 1880 the Australian side touring England came to Ireland and played two matches, one in Belfast against XVIII of the North of Ireland CC, and a second in Dublin, against XVIII of Dublin University. It was the university which was destined to become the stronghold of cricket in Ireland.

The industrial developments of the 19th century in South Wales saw a great increase in the population and with it the founding of cricket clubs in the major towns. In 1855 William Clarke's side visited Wales for the first time, opposing XXII of South Wales in Cardiff. In 1859 South Wales CC was formed, based in Newport, Monmouthshire, and in 1879 a South Wales knock-out competition was inaugurated. From these beginnings the present Glamorgan County Cricket Club emerged in 1888.

Before leaving the British Isles, a note is necessary concerning the development of Army cricket. The Royal Artillery Club at Woolwich, which was long established in 1860, was joined in 1862 by the Royal Engineers of Chatham, and these two Corps played each other on a regular basis from 1864. Lord Hill's Order of 1841 meant that regiments throughout Britain were organising matches and had established fixture lists. The Lillywhite *Annuals* of the 1870s devoted several pages to results and averages of such clubs as the Royal Engineers, Household Brigade, and Army and Navy at Portsmouth.

AUSTRALIA

During the first half of the 19th century club cricket in Australia grew in a haphazard manner. Victoria had a few powerful clubs by 1850, but their fixtures were not yet organised into leagues. This situation began to change in about 1858, when George Coppin presented a Challenge Cup for clubs in the Melbourne area. An initial match was played for the Cup by the two most powerful sides, Melbourne CC and Richmond. The Cup matches attracted popular attention and crowds of 5,000 or more turned out. Richmond won the first match, then the newly formed East Melbourne Club challenged and took the crown. Unfortunately a return match between East Melbourne and Richmond ended in dispute and the Cup went into permanent abeyance! In 1870–1 a second Challenge Cup was inaugurated and this was to boost club competition in the Melbourne area until the 1890s.

In New South Wales, club cricket was also not yet organised into leagues. The top clubs in Sydney in the 1860s were the Albert Club, founded in 1852, and the Warwick Club, which had persuaded William Caffyn to remain in Australia as a coach after the 1863–4 England tour. Other clubs included the National, Belvedere and Carlton. As in Victoria, league cricket was not destined to start until the 1890s.

In South Australia, the 1860s saw the South Australian Club as the premier cricket organisation. When the South Australian Cricket Association was formed in 1871, the constituent clubs were South Australian, Kent, North Adelaide, Norwood, Register, Stepney, South Adelaide and Hindmarsh. A club competition was inaugurated in 1873–4. In the 24 seasons of this competition's life, Norwood won 16 times.

The three major cricket colonies in Australia – New South Wales, Victoria and South Australia – were therefore moving towards the establishment, in the 1890s, of the club competitions that still exist today, but it was progress fraught with disputes and muddle.

SOUTH AFRICA

The first major competition in South Africa began in 1876 when the Municipality of Port Elizabeth presented a 'Champion Bat' for competition between the towns of Cape Colony. Cape Town, Port Elizabeth, Grahamstown and King William's Town took part in this initial contest, which King William's Town won. The same town won the second contest in 1880, but after this the populations of both Cape Town and Port Elizabeth rapidly outgrew that of King William's Town, whose cricket nursery was Dale College, so that the trophy holders had no chance of retaining their title.

In Orange Free State cricket enthusiasts received a great boost when, in 1880, a tournament was held in Boshef, involving the local club and sides from Kimberley and Bloemfontein. Kimberley were invited to take part in the Champion Bat Competition of 1884, when Port Elizabeth won the title, and were themselves the winners three years later. In that same season a touring side from Kimberley, the Stray Klips, went on a seven-match tour of Cape Colony.

In Natal the two principal cricket centres were Durban and Pietermaritzburg, but after an initial game between the two towns in 1860, no similar contest took place until 1888. Despite this Natal was a hotbed of cricket and in 1885 the *Natal Cricketers' Annual* was launched. Unlike many such ventures it flourished and after four issues evolved into the *South African Cricket Annual*, which lasted until 1907.

Until the goldfields opened there were relatively few English people living in Transvaal, but from 1886, when Johannesburg mushroomed from a few houses into a metropolis within a few years, cricket boomed. In 1888 a competition was held in Pretoria between the local team, Johannesburg, Barberton and Potchefstroom.

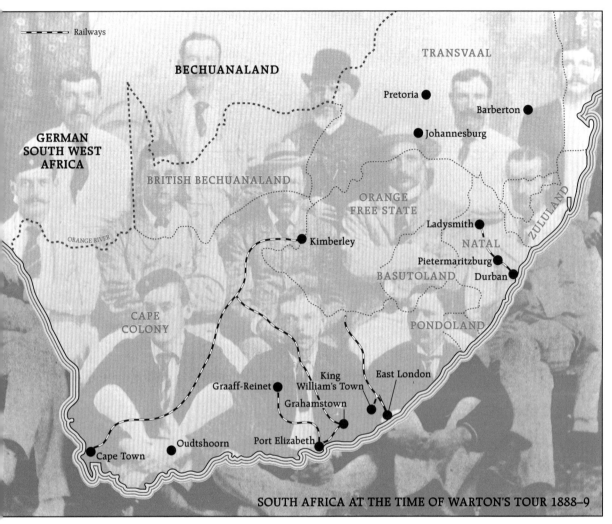

Railways

GERMAN
SOUTH WEST
AFRICA

ORANGE RIVER

BECHUANALAND

BRITISH BECHUANALAND

CAPE
COLONY

Cape Town
Oudtshoorn
Graaff-Reinet
Port Elizabeth
Grahamstown
King
William's Town
East London

TRANSVAAL

Pretoria
Barberton
Johannesburg

ORANGE
FREE STATE

Kimberley

Ladysmith
NATAL
Pietermaritzburg
BASUTOLAND   Durban

ZULULAND

PONDOLAND

SOUTH AFRICA AT THE TIME OF WARTON'S TOUR 1888–9

South Africa, showing the towns visited by Major Warton's English side in 1888–9. One result of the tour was the introduction of the Currie Cup for competition among the major sides in South Africa.

It required some unifying act to draw together these separate cricketing strands and this duly occurred in 1888–9, when Major R.G. Warton, who had spent five years stationed in South Africa, decided to gather an English side together and arrange a tour of the country. Until then English sides had only toured Australia, New Zealand and North America. Warton was materially assisted by Sir Donald Currie MP, founder of the Castle Shipping Line, and by the Western Province Cricket Club. (This club, founded in 1864 and playing on Southey's Field, Cape Town, considered itself the Marylebone Club of South Africa.)

Before the touring party left England (captained by C. Aubrey Smith, the Sussex player and later film star), Sir Donald Currie announced that he would present a Cup to whichever

THE HISTORY OF CRICKET

The first English team to South Africa, 1888–9. The tourists opposed the home side in the first two England vs. South Africa Test Matches. England were led in the first by C. Aubrey Smith who, 50 years later, was a well-known Hollywood film actor.

of the following – Cape Colony, Natal, Transvaal, and Griqualand West – performed best against the tourists. The English side played 19 matches, winning 13 and losing 4. All matches were against the odds except the 17th and 19th fixtures, which were eleven-a-side against Combined South Africa. These two games are now considered 'Test Matches', but the weak England touring party (perhaps just about first-class county standard) won both by large margins. Kimberley (Griqualand West) beat the tourists by ten wickets and were awarded the Currie Cup.

INDIA

In India, the Parsee cricketers were making progress, so much so that in the autumn of 1877 they arranged a programme of matches for a tour of England between June and September 1878. For financial reasons this was postponed until 1879 and then abandoned. Internal squabbles among the sponsors led to a libel suit and it was not until 1886 that B.B. Baria managed to heal the wounds and arrange another trip. The Parsees paid for Robert Henderson, the Surrey cricketer, to travel to Bombay to coach the touring party before it left home. The programme of matches was against what in today's terms might be described as first-class county 2nd XIs. Only one match out of the 28 ended in victory. The Parsees were not disappointed: the whole idea of the tour was to improve the standard of their cricket. The venture was entirely amateur and very little money was taken from the 'gate'. Two years later the Parsees came a second time. They won 8 out of 31 matches and had found an outstanding bowler in M.E. Pavri, who took 170 wickets at 11 runs each. As in 1886 the opponents were below first-class standard and the tour did not attract much public attention.

In the autumn of 1889, a team of English amateurs under the management of George Vernon, the Middlesex cricketer, embarked on the first English tour to India. The team possessed only three cricketers who had played county cricket regularly in 1889, and it was not as strong as the Warton team to South Africa. Thirteen matches were played, all against Englishmen stationed or based in India and Ceylon, except for a fixture against the Parsees in Bombay. This last game proved to be the visiting team's only defeat. M.E. Pavri described the event:

> No cricket match in India created greater interest amongst all classes than this. Additional zest was lent to the encounter by the fact that the English Team had an unbeaten record in their eastern tour (ie, Calcutta, etc) and only a week before they had scored a decisive victory over the Bombay Gymkhana (full strength of the English in Bombay) . . . The city went mad on the game. Business was quite at a standstill, while the match was in progress, for two days. The variegated oriental crowd, numbering close upon 12,000, was early on the ground to see, in the words of Captain Trevor,[11] 'the most famous match ever played in India'. The Maiden, the scene of many international contests, presented a most animated and picturesque sight; almost all the varied nationalities of the great city were represented there.

Pavri goes on to draw a parallel between Australia's victory over England in that first Test at Melbourne in 1877 and the Parsee victory over Vernon's team. He states in addition:

> To my mind the three great bonds of Empire are not so much conquest, strength and prestige, as one great Empire with community of interests, a literature teaching equality and fraternity, and last but not least, the grand national game of old England. Among the many links that bind us together cricket is one, and it is for the first time I learn (according to Capt Trevor) that it is likely to loosen the bonds of Empire if the best side wins. Far from it; on the contrary it has always strengthened them.

---

11   Captain Philip Trevor (1863-1932), later Colonel, was stationed in India in the 1880s and 1890s. He was successively a sports journalist on *The Sportsman*, *The Daily Mail* and *The Daily Telegraph*. He managed the 1907–8 MCC team to Australia.

As the small Parsee community celebrated their great victory, some progress towards cricket was being made by the Hindus and Muslims. The Hindu CC was formed in 1877 and the first Mahomedan CC in 1883, but they were not up to Parsee standard until the turn of the century. These were of course in Bombay; Indian cricket in Calcutta made very little progress. In Madras, the other centre, it was not until 1898–9 that the Indians played against the Europeans, and then an easy victory was obtained by the latter.

One exclusive cricket outlet for Indians, however, was established in 1870 with the opening of Rajkumar College at Rajkot, for the sons of princes. The college principal was Chester Macnaghten, educated at Trinity College, Cambridge. He was determined to build up Rajkumar as a model English public school and athletic pursuits, including cricket, were very much encouraged. At first the sons of the princes arrived with vast retinues of retainers, but Macnaghten managed to reduce the retinue to one servant per pupil. In 1880 a very young 'Ranjitsinhji of Nawanagar' was enrolled. At the age of 16 he was the outstanding cricketer in the school and that year, 1888, he was chosen to go to England with two fellow pupils to further his education. Effectively he walked out of Indian cricket and into the English club and county scene. Ranjitsinhji was therefore lost to Indian cricket, but a number of other Rajkumar students remained and as they left the college and returned to their homes, they were to encourage the spread of cricket in many of the native states.

CEYLON

Vernon's team had played two matches in Ceylon, prior to going to the mainland of India. Both matches comprised only Europeans and in both the local side was overwhelmed. There was however some cricket among non-Europeans. In 1872 the Malay Cricket Club had been formed in Colombo, and the Ceylonese formed the Colts Cricket Club in the following season. In 1887 the Colts side challenged the English Colombo Club and this match developed along the lines of the Parsees vs. Bombay Europeans series, becoming the country's major domestic match.

NEW ZEALAND

In cricketing terms Ceylon was to India what New Zealand was to Australia. George Parr's side to Australia in 1863–4 had travelled to New Zealand for four matches and a make-up exhibition game.[12] Three of the games (all against XXIIs) were easy wins, but there had been an even draw against a combined Canterbury-Otago XXII at Dunedin, although this was largely due to Thomas Wills, the Victoria cricketer, who was co-opted into the local side. Wills, though born in New South Wales, was educated at Rugby. He gained a blue at Cambridge in 1856, without ever being in residence, and returned to Australia later the same

---

12 A game in which the 12 tourists divided into two sides which were then 'made up' with local players.

year. The fact that Parr's side actually visited New Zealand at all was due to the enterprise of Shadrach Jones of Dunedin, a local businessman.

The second English side to travel to New Zealand was Lillywhite's team of 1876–7. Eight matches (all vs. XXIIs) produced six wins and two draws. Given the size of the population tremendous crowds watched the main contests – at least 10,000 attending the Christchurch game. The following year an Australian side (en route for England via the Pacific) came to New Zealand and were beaten by XV of Canterbury. E.T.A. Fuller, Canterbury's 'express' bowler, took 8 for 35 in Australia's second innings. Canterbury were the undoubted Champions of New Zealand and in 1878–9 decided on a tour of Victoria. Unfortunately their visit coincided with the England touring side and very little attention was paid to the seven Canterbury games, all against local club sides. The tourists took no money, and funds had to be sent from Christchurch in order to pay for the team's homeward journey.

The English tourists to Australia in 1881–2 and 1887–8 also visited New Zealand, both returning undefeated, as did the Australian teams to England of 1880 and 1886. These matches drew the crowds, but a far better measure of the standard of cricket in New Zealand was the performance against the first Tasmanian touring side in 1883–4. The Tasmanians, playing eleven-a-side games, were beaten twice by Canterbury and once by Otago. It was a different story, however, when New South Wales despatched a powerful side to New Zealand in 1889–90. The provincial sides fielded elevens and were easily beaten. All this activity kept enthusiasm for cricket very much alive in what might have been a backwater. There would be a great stride forward in the last decade of the century.

NORTH AMERICA

After the end of the American Civil War in 1865, interest in cricket revived, together with the possibility of visits from English sides. In 1868, a professional team under the leadership of the Kent cricketer Ned Willsher played six games, all against XXIIs, winning five and drawing one. Four years later W.G. Grace led the first all-amateur team across the Atlantic, where they achieved results similar to Willsher's. The teams were guaranteed against loss by their hosts. These visits, which included games in both the States and Canada, at least prevented cricket from being totally swamped by baseball, and in 1874 an initiative by Captain N.W. Wallace – stationed in Halifax, Nova Scotia – was to lead to a governing body for cricket in the States.

Wallace, educated at Rugby, had played for Gloucestershire under the captaincy of W.G. Grace in 1871 and, on moving to Canada, had been the prime mover behind the touring side going to North America under WG. He now proposed a series of matches between America, Canada and England to be played in Halifax in August 1874. He sent an invitation to the United States cricketers. Adverts were placed in various American papers to publicise the event, but the only response was from Philadelphian cricket clubs, and the American side which travelled to Nova Scotia thus consisted only of players from that city. The England

Colonel N.W. Wallace. Described
in 1874 as 'a gallant captain in the
60th Royal Rifles quartered in the
Citadel at Halifax, Nova Scotia',
Wallace organised the great cricket
tournament in Halifax that year.
When in England he played for both
Gloucestershire and Hampshire.

The Halifax team of 1874 which took
part in the tournament in Halifax,
Nova Scotia, that season.

team in Nova Scotia was drawn from English troops stationed in Canada. The American side won the tournament and was presented with the Halifax Cup. A return tournament was held in Philadelphia in 1875, again won by America.

In June 1877 the weekly magazine *American Cricketer* began publication. It estimated that there were 300 cricket clubs in the States and published the addresses and details of 81 of them. The magazine wanted a national cricket organisation to be set up. In May 1878 'The Cricketers' Association of the United States' was founded, with an executive committee to select representative national teams: it duly picked the side which opposed the Australians who had toured England in 1878 and were passing through the States on their way home.

The Americans were therefore becoming organised, even if in cricketing terms the United States meant little more than the city of Philadelphia. It was however the Canadians, rather than the Americans, who were the first to send a cricket team to England (an American baseball team had toured in 1874 and played seven cricket matches of minor importance). Unfortunately the 1880 Canadian side to England more or less collapsed when it was discovered that the captain of the tourists was a deserter from the British Army, playing under an assumed name. He was arrested and imprisoned. In mid-July the team ran out of money, cancelled the rest of their fixtures and returned home.

Four years later the Philadelphian clubs raised $8,000 and organised an 18-match tour of the British Isles. The American side was made up entirely of amateurs and fixtures were against county amateur sides for the most part. The Americans beat an amateur Gloucestershire team which included W.G. Grace and in all logged eight victories. A repeat visit was made in 1889, when the Americans won three of twelve matches. Three more tours were to take place prior to 1914.

In Philadelphia, the major clubs joined a competitive league using the Halifax Cup as their trophy. The competition commenced in 1880 and was to continue until 1926. At school and university level, an inter-collegiate competition began in 1881 which soon became just a three-horse race between the University of Pennsylvania, Haverford College and Harvard. After Harvard dropped out in 1905, there were a few years of cricket enthusiasm (1904–11) from Cornell. The competition finally lapsed in 1924. Baseball had won.

Across the border in Canada the principal inter-collegiate match, which began in 1867, was Trinity College School (Port Hope) vs. Upper Canada College (Toronto). The matches between Canada and the United States resumed in 1879 after a lapse of 14 years as a result of the efforts of the Toronto and Hamilton Clubs.

THE WEST INDIES

Cricket in the British West Indies in the 1860s was largely a pursuit of the English administrators, plantation owners and military personnel resident in the various colonies. The two colonies which first made an attempt to play cricket on an organised basis were Barbados and Demerara, now part of Guyana. The latter had a well-established club,

Georgetown CC, and in February 1865 chose a representative colonial team to travel to Barbados to oppose that colony's eleven. The match was played on the Garrison Savannah in Bridgetown and resulted in victory for the home side. A return game took place in September of the same year on the Parade Ground in Georgetown. After the match a boating trip was arranged for the players which ended in disaster when there was an accident on the treacherous Essequibo river. Seven lives were lost including those of two of the Demerara cricketers, R.D. Stewart and H.S. Beresford. In January 1869, the Demerara side went to Port of Spain and played two matches against Trinidad, whose team included Pelham Warner's eldest brother. Each side won a match. Matches between these three colonies continued spasmodically through the 1870s and 1880s.

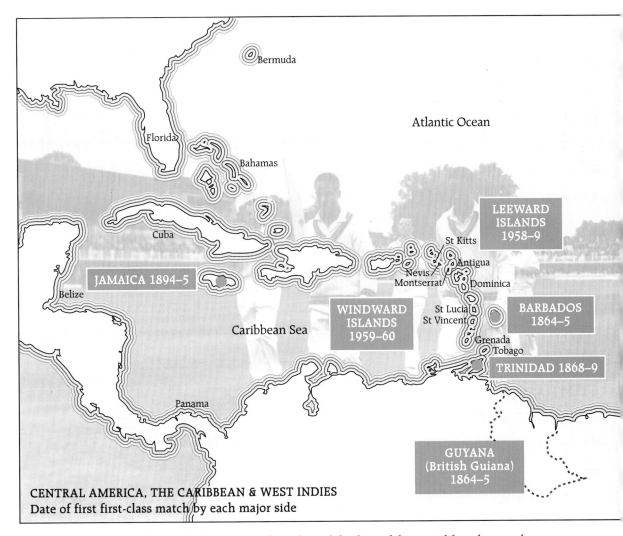

The British West Indies, showing the first-class cricket sides and the dates of their initial first-class match.

Through the enterprise of G. Wyatt, a member of the Georgetown Club, West Indian cricket broke new ground in 1886. Wyatt organised a West Indian tour to the States and Canada, playing 13 matches of which six were won. His report on the tour read:

> The attempt of a West Indian team visiting Canada and the United States was sneered and laughed at by many more than most people imagine, as rather a farce – it has been done, though not so successfully as the players themselves could have wished, but looking at the team that actually represented the West Indians as compared to one that might have done so, the result may be considered fairly satisfactory. The ball has been set a-rolling now, and if the result of our recent tour gives us many visits in the West Indies from our Canadian and American friends, and wakes up our Island neighbours and our own Colony to move about amongst each other and farther afield, in the interest of the noble game, something tangible and well worth having will have been gained, and the writer fully and well recompensed for what trouble he has taken in the matter.

Wyatt was immediately rewarded, for in the season of 1887–8 a side from the United States played 11 matches in the West Indies, visiting Jamaica, Demerara, Trinidad, Barbados, St Kitts and Grenada. The tourists won six of their games. At this stage the teams representing the West Indies were all white, but in Trinidad in particular black players were emerging, as Pelham Warner noted in his autobiography.

SOUTH AND CENTRAL AMERICA

In South America, the cricket club in Buenos Aires (first established in 1831) was revived in 1858 and grew quickly as the British colony expanded. In 1868 the Club visited Montevideo, playing a two-day game against the local side, while in 1888, a Brazilian team came to Argentina. The Rio de Janeiro Club had been founded in 1872 and was encouraged by the Brazilian Emperor, Dom Pedro II, who had a special stand built on the Club's ground and reportedly watched some of the matches there with his family. In Chile, the first match between Valparaiso and Santiago was staged in the 1870s. Mexico City had a club as early as 1838 and was joined by other clubs later. Cricket in Latin America (aside from British Guiana) was destined to remain a game played exclusively by the British community, and its ups and downs reflect the ebb and flow of Britons in the various countries.

THE PACIFIC AND EAST AFRICA

Most of the British possessions in the Pacific can claim some cricket in the 19th century, the one in which the game was most firmly established being Fiji. It became a British Colony in 1874 and a cricket club was formed in the then capital, Levuka, the same year. The Fijians took to cricket and in 1894–5 a Fijian side, comprising seven British residents and six Fijian chiefs, toured New Zealand, playing eight matches and winning four. The chiefs, who wore native dress, were somewhat baffled by slow bowling, since all bowling in Fiji was fast. The opposition were the main provincial sides and six of the fixtures are considered 'first class'. The leading promoter of Fijian cricket was the Hon. John S. Udal, the Attorney-General. He had been educated at Bromsgrove and Oxford, and played first-class cricket in England for the MCC and county matches for Somerset.

In the Sandwich Islands, discovered by Captain Cook in 1778, a cricket club existed as early as 1852 and their ruler King Kalakaua, visited both Lord's and The Oval when he came to England in 1881. The islands were annexed by the United States in 1894 and became the State of Hawaii in 1959.

In Samoa cricket was introduced in 1884. According to reports the local population invented their own variation, with matches involving whole villages and games lasting weeks. All other interests were abandoned, including work, so much so that the King had to issue the following proclamation:

THE LAW REGARDING CRICKET

To All The Districts of Samoa, Notice

1. It is strictly prohibited for a village to travel and play cricket
with another village.

2. It is strictly prohibited for two villages to play cricket together.

3. It is also prohibited for a village to play cricket among themselves.

4. Should any village or district fail to keep this law in any respect,
they will be fined a sum not exceeding forty-five dollars,
or in default be sent to jail for three months with hard labour.

MALIETOA, THE KING OF SAMOA
RESIDENCE OF THE KING, APIA
JUNE 20, 1890.

The Kent cricketer, the Rt Revd Cecil Wilson, was Bishop of Melanesia from 1894 to 1917, and did much to promote the game in the Pacific.

The long series of matches between Hong Kong and Shanghai began in February 1866 in Hong Kong. A return game took place in Shanghai the following year, although there was then a break until November 1889. It was in 1892 that the entire Hong Kong team was drowned during a storm on the voyage back from Shanghai. The series was to continue until the Second World War.

CONTINENTAL EUROPE

On the continent of Europe two countries were developing a love of cricket. As early as the 1780s, the English traveller Samuel Jackson Pratt, while visiting the Dutch port of Scheveningen, was 'curious to observe' the local people playing a number of different games, including cricket (and the Anglophile Mr Hope, who was brought up in Holland, was painted playing cricket in Rome in the 1790s). The first report of an actual cricket club in Holland is in Utrecht in 1855, when some students from the Cape of Good Hope were at the university, but this club was short-lived. The real beginning of the present game was at Daventer in 1875, when Mr Romiju, a former Consul in Britain, set up a club. In September 1883 the Nederlandsche Cricket-Bond was formed. In 1888 James Lillywhite's *Cricketers' Annual* notes: 'It often happened last year that English travellers passing through Holland were astonished to see their national game played there. As there are by this time many Dutch Clubs, it will be useful to give the addresses of those now in existence.' This was followed by details of the Cricket-Bond and of 18 clubs with a total membership of about 300 players. Cricketers in Holland, apart from the occasional English coach, were all amateurs.

Between 1881 and 1889 ten club sides from England played matches in Holland and the first tour in reverse came in 1892 when the Gentlemen of Holland played five matches in England. The standard of the Gentlemen was up to club level; the five matches were all played in Yorkshire, against such sides as Scarborough and Hull Town. The Dutch were mainly students aged between 18 and 26. Apart from J.S. Harrison, who was captain of the Johannesburg Club in South Africa, they were all Dutch-born.

In Denmark the first club was formed in 1861 and was much encouraged by the British engineers working on the laying of the Danish railway system. It is believed that there were 70 Danish cricket clubs in existence before 1900, but information on these is sparse and cricket on a serious scale did not really develop until after the First World War.

A brief note from Portugal ends this chapter on the amateur game between 1860 and 1890. An extract from an article on 'Cricket in Portugal', translated from a Lisbon newspaper, was published in *Punch* on 7 June 1862:

> An active, running, driving, jumping game, which can only be played by a person having a good pair of legs, and in a climate where warmed punch is found insufficient to keep up animal heat . . . Sometimes the ball tumbles into a thicket and the players take hours before they can get hold of it, and all this time the player does not cease running from post to post and marking points . . . At other times the projectile sent with a vigorous arm cannot be stopped and breaks the leg of the party who awaits it. The arrangements for the cricket match include a sumptuous dinner in a marquee for fifty persons, an indispensable accompaniment to every cricket match.

Cricket in Portugal remained an English game with clubs in Oporto and Lisbon. A strong English side played two two-day matches there in 1895.

A ccording to the modern Test Match list, England teams had been involved in 32 Tests by the beginning of the 1890 season. By 1890, too, the County Championship had been a regular feature of cricket annuals for at least 25 years. Nevertheless, in contrast to soccer (whose Football Association had been founded in 1863), no national administrative body existed yet for cricket. The MCC arbitrated on the Laws and had reluctantly taken on board the county qualification rules of 1873; and Lord's was used for a meeting of county secretaries each December to settle county fixtures for the following season.

Meanwhile, it was clearly unsatisfactory that teams representing England should be picked either, at home, by the committee whose ground England proposed to use, or, abroad, by the promoters, or agents, of the touring parties. It was equally unsatisfactory that the county 'league' published in the press should use methods devised by journalists to decide the position of each county, without any reference to the counties themselves.

As has been noted, the cricket parliament mooted in 1863 was still-born; the inter-county knock-out cup set up in 1873 by the MCC collapsed after one match. The need for a central authority was obvious, but the county committees were very independent. The issue came to a head in 1885, when the press, using a system of 'least matches lost', announced that Nottinghamshire were County Champions. Nottinghamshire had lost only one match, but won just six out of 12; whereas Surrey had won 12 out of 20, and Kent and Lancashire had both won 6 out of 11. The following year, in the view of the Surrey supporters, was even more unfair. The Champions, Nottinghamshire again, were undefeated, but had won only 7 out of 14; Surrey had won 12 out of 16.

To overcome the prejudicial parochialism of the counties required a blunt, hard-headed individual. Such a man was the captain of Kent, Lord Harris. At the December 1886 fixtures meeting, he proposed the setting up of a County Cricket Council. A sub-committee was established to look into the

7

THE

GOLDEN

AGE?

Lord Harris, the most influential figure in English cricket from the 1880s to his death in 1932. The prime mover in stamping out the 'throwing' epidemic in the 1880s. County cricket might have taken a different course in the 1890s if Harris had not been absent in India as Governor of Bombay.

idea and its proposals were laid before a meeting of the counties. Rules were agreed and the Council launched, but the northern counties were suspicious and lukewarm in their support. They feared that Harris was acting in the interests of improving the standards of Kent cricket by changing the qualification rules. Undeterred by opposition, the Council discussed and resolved several knotty problems during 1887 and 1888.

At the same time as Harris was galvanising the reluctant counties, an energetic young journalist had been appointed to revive the lacklustre Wisden's *Cricketers' Almanack*. The new editor, Charles Pardon, wrote a strong editorial in the second edition (1888) under his control. He announced that the almanack would operate a new league points system for counties in 1888 and he pressed the County Cricket Council to investigate the possibility of a league containing two or three divisions with promotion and relegation.

When the 1888 season ended he printed the county results as two leagues: first-class with eight counties (Surrey won), second-class with ten (Leicestershire won). He repeated this system for 1889, but embarrassingly for him the first-class league of eight counties under his system ended with a triple tie (Lancashire, Nottinghamshire and Surrey). Nottingham supporters ignored Pardon and the Nottingham papers printed their own league table with their county as outright Champions (Nottinghamshire had lost the least matches); but the Pardon outcome is the one which remains in the record books.

When the County Cricket Council held their meeting of 9 December 1889, the matter of the County Championship was discussed and Lord Harris set up a sub-committee to investigate and report back during 1890. Harris had been appointed Governor of Bombay and would be leaving England in the spring to take up his new post. In his closing speech to the Council he said that he would not take the liberty of offering advice, because he was sure they would be very careful to watch that the thin end of the wedge of 'prize' was not inserted into county cricket, and he hoped that the counties would discourage as far as they possibly could prize-giving for any cricket matches whatsoever. County cricket was the one form of athletic sports at the present moment which was absolutely pure, and there was nothing beyond the honour of the game. He could not help remarking that if honour and glory were enough for county cricketers, he did not see why anything else should be required by cricketers in the lower social classes.

After the fixtures meeting the next day, the eight first-class counties and the eight top second-class counties agreed among themselves a points system for the 1890 season: losses were to be deducted from wins and draws ignored.

The County Cricket Council's sub-committee duly reported on their recommendations: three divisions of eight counties each with promotion and relegation. When the Council met in full session in December 1890 to discuss and decide on the recommendations, the meeting disintegrated into a shambles (without the strong voice of Lord Harris they had no pilot). The Council never met again. As for the results of the inter-county matches of 1890, Surrey won the title for the first-class counties and Sussex ended at the foot with 11 losses from 12 games. Somerset won eight out of eight matches in the lower division and then arranged fixtures with the first-class counties for 1891 and moved up. Sussex did not move down. The sad process of expanding the first-class division had begun and would continue for ever, producing the muddle and misery we have today.[13] In 1895, the first-class division increased to 14 (with Derbyshire, Essex, Hampshire, Leicestershire and Warwickshire) and in 1899 to 15 (with Worcestershire). The weaker sides had little hope against the most powerful; the merit of performances by the players in the stronger counties against the weak was of little value and in turn devalued the first-class averages. No one watched the weak counties, who were financially propped up by a few wealthy patrons. The increase in taxes in the 1940s removed the remaining patrons.

As far as further rules were concerned, the MCC, under instruction from the counties, laid down the following stipulations in October 1894: the counties shall be divided into first-class or not, and there shall be no limit to the number of first-class counties. The non-first-class counties were left to their own devices and for 1895 formed the Minor Counties Cricket Association, running their own league, which now in 1996 has 20 counties competing.

Soon after the number of first-class counties had risen to 16 (with Northamptonshire in 1905), the top counties realised the error of their ways and tried to reduce the number, but like the County Cricket Council scheme, the idea just fell by the wayside.

In the early years of the new century the MCC was persuaded to propose alterations in the lbw law and in the size of the wicket. Both these motions failed and in January 1904 the

---

13 By contrast, the West Indies and Australia each have first-class leagues of six teams; India created the Duleep Trophy of five teams; and South Africa have two divisions, the first having eight teams.

Sydney Barnes who, in the years immediately prior to the First World War, was England's greatest bowler. He was, however, a difficult character to deal with and had no time for first-class county cricket. He played for Staffordshire from 1904 to 1935.

MCC Secretary wrote to the counties suggesting the formation of an Advisory County Cricket Committee to liaise with the MCC and avoid any further embarrassing votes. This Committee was duly set up and comprised a representative of each first-class county, with a member of the MCC as chairman. All its meetings were held at Lord's, and it continued effectively to control first-class county cricket until 1969.

On the international stage, a Board of Control to regulate future home Test Matches was set up in 1898 and took up its duties in time for the five Tests against Australia in 1899. The Board comprised six members of the MCC, plus six county representatives; the chairman was the MCC President. The Board also chose the panel of England Test Selectors.

The final piece of the legislation jigsaw involved England teams travelling overseas. After the muddle of the twin tours to Australia in 1887–8, the next attempt to take a team to the Antipodes was in 1891–2 when Lord Sheffield, the patron of Sussex cricket, was persuaded to finance a tour. He agreed, but only if W.G. Grace would captain the side. Grace complied. From the cricketing viewpoint the tour was a success, but the cost of Grace and his wife and their expenses was so great that Lord Sheffield lost £2,000.

Three seasons later Sydney and Melbourne combined (for the first time) and promoted a tour to Australia under Andrew Stoddart, the Middlesex amateur. There were five Tests (England won 3–2) and a profit of £7,000.

In 1897–8 Sydney and Melbourne repeated their speculation, again with Stoddart as England's captain. Australia won the series. The MCC made a first attempt to organise an Australian tour in 1901, but backed out when several players refused to go. Archie MacLaren, the Lancashire captain, was asked to take a side and, without five of the country's best players, led a second-rate team to defeat. The one discovery was Sydney Barnes, a little known Staffordshire player, who topped the bowling averages. The tour to Australia in 1903–4 was a reverse of

THE HISTORY OF CRICKET

the previous venture. MacLaren was asked to organise it, but declined when Barnes and William Lockwood refused to go; the MCC then came in and sent a team under the Middlesex amateur, Pelham Warner. England won the Ashes, but the MCC lost £1,500.

This tour established a precedent and all major 'Test' tours from 1903–4 onwards involving England were under the auspices of the MCC until 1977, when the Test and County Cricket Board suggested that Test-playing tours should be titled 'England' instead of 'MCC'. The first such tour was to Australia in 1977–8.

By the middle of the Edwardian period, therefore, the MCC had effectively acquired control of English Test and County Cricket, in addition to their ancient command of the Laws.[14] No one can be praised or blamed for this state of affairs which, as has been shown, simply evolved through 'natural causes'.

The same can be said of the world governing body of cricket – the present 'International Cricket Conference'.

In 1907 the South Africans came to England for their first Test tour. The visitors possessed a formidable attack, headed by three 'googly' bowlers: Schwarz, Vogler and Faulkner.[15] Although they lost the Test series by one match to nil with two draws, they won 17 of 27 tour matches and surprised critics by their talent. The principal patron of South African cricket was Abe Bailey. In the autumn after the 1907 tour, he suggested a triangular Test tournament for the 1909 season between England, Australia and South Africa. The English authorities had already invited the Australians to tour that summer. After meetings of the Advisory County Cricket Committee and a mass of newspaper comment the idea fell down because the Australians opposed the scheme, since they would have lost out financially. In December 1908 the MCC Secretary, Francis Lacey, announced that the triangular contest idea would be looked at again during 1909, when it was hoped that representatives of England, Australia and South Africa could hold a meeting.

The first Imperial Cricket Conference, as it was then styled, was held at Lord's on 15 June 1909. The Earl of Chesterfield (President of the MCC) was in the chair; Lord Harris and the Earl of Lichfield represented the MCC; Dr Leslie Poidevin, Australia; and Henry Leveson-Gower and George Hillyard, South Africa; Francis Lacey completed the members present. Among other matters it was agreed to hold a triangular Test tournament in 1912 in England. The ICC was duly launched. The fact that Lord Harris was present at the first meeting gives some idea of his standing at Lord's. He had returned from being Governor of Bombay in 1895 and was to remain the most influential single voice in cricket until his death in 1932. Francis Lacey, the MCC Secretary from 1898 to 1926, had played for Cambridge and

---

14   The county representatives were almost always guided by the MCC Chairman and Secretary in decisions reached by the Advisory County Cricket Committee – the word 'Advisory' means what it says!

15   The 'googly' is a delivery from a slow bowler which from his action seems to be going to turn in from leg, but in fact turns the other way. It was first perfected by B.J.T. Bosanquet of Oxford University, Middlesex and England. In Australia the googly is called the 'Bosie', after the inventor.

Hampshire. A barrister, Lacey was regarded as cold with a strong sense of the rule of law and order. His manner contrasted with the fiery outbursts of Harris, but they formed a duo whom few cared to cross.

A third figure in the administration of English cricket, whose career ran parallel to Lord Harris's, was Lord Hawke. Educated at Eton and Cambridge, he was appointed captain of Yorkshire in 1883. He first set about transforming that county's cricket and cricketers. He brought discipline to what had been a very unruly professional crew. More than one famous player was dismissed from the county side purely for his behaviour, but those who abided by Hawke's rules benefited. He is credited with introducing winter pay, for example. It was due to Hawke that Yorkshire's true cricketing potential was realised and his efforts bore fruit especially during the inter-war period, as well as 1893–1908. He succeeded Lord Harris as Treasurer of the MCC and died in 1938.

THE EDWARDIAN CRICKETER

What type of cricketer was being administered to by Lords Harris and Hawke in the Edwardian period? It was the heyday of the public school man. Success on the cricket field was an essential element of school life, and had not yet become a 'bore'. (Evelyn Waugh and Robert Graves were two public school boys who later took delight in having digs at the ethos of cricket.) Taxation levels were still low enough to allow fathers to indulge their sons: a generous allowance or a sinecure in the family business, or both, allowed sons a few seasons of county cricket. Taking 1907 as a typical year, 50 per cent of the players in the County Championship that summer were amateurs, the vast majority of whom came from the leading public schools. Put another way, half the cricketers the public came to watch were drawn from about 2 per cent of the total population. At Test level in 1907, five of the 12 who represented England in the three Tests against South Africa were amateurs, as were 11 of the first 14 in *Wisden's* first-class batting averages for that summer. It is true to say, though, that amateurs were very scarce in the bowling tables. Bowlers were considered the 'workhorses' of the game and therefore tended to be professional rather than amateur.

The upper middle class had hijacked cricket at the highest level. The sport was drifting away from the lower strata of society and the magnet of the soccer field was attracting the workers. The average attendance at a soccer league game when the Football League began in 1888 was about 4,000; ten years on, the First Division games were being watched by closer to 10,000, and in a further ten years the number approached 15,000. No figures exist for spectators at county cricket matches. The great bank holiday games drew full houses, as did the Test Matches. The social events such as Eton vs. Harrow, the University Match and the Festival games (end of season 'celebrations' at Scarborough and Hastings when an England team played the touring side in holiday mood) had excellent attendances, but the run of the mill inter-county game of 1907 was of little interest. Total gate receipts at The Oval for a day's play against the less attractive counties averaged £50.

CLUBS IN THE NORTH AND SOUTH

At club level during the 1890 to 1914 period the divide between the north of England and the Home Counties in the south was sharpened. League mania spread from the soccer world. The first cricket league in England is believed to be the Birmingham & District League, which began operating in 1889, followed by the Bolton & District League in 1889–90. The Lancashire League (founded as the North-East Lancashire League) was established in 1890, as was the North Staffordshire and District; the Central Lancashire League (originally South-East Lancashire League) and the Huddersfield and District first operated in 1892; the Durham Senior League, 1902; the Bradford League, 1903; and the Bassetlaw & District League, 1904. These nine are the main ones to have survived from the period before 1905, but there were others which came and went and still more which are operating today and began a little later. Most of the leading clubs from Warwickshire northwards became 'league' clubs. Again, most of them were basically 'working men's clubs' on a par with the parallel soccer development: the 12 original Football League clubs were all based in the north and midlands of England.

In the Home Counties there were some small local leagues, but the leading clubs had no interest in such competitions and the first organisation to encompass the top sides did not appear until 1915, when the Club Cricket Conference was established. Club cricket was a much posher affair than in the north, with club tours to the West Country, or some superior watering hole, a feature of the fixture list. The lower classes had much less to do with cricket in the Home Counties. The banks based in the City built sumptuous sports pavilions in the suburbs, and an ability to play cricket helped young men with promotion prospects. All sorts of weird teams sprang up, the oddest group being the Artists CC, the Authors/Allahakbarries CC, and various Publishers' XIs. The Artists were run by Edwin Abbey, an American, who laid out his own private ground in Gloucestershire. J.M. Barrie and Conan Doyle were two leading author-cricketers, whose sides included such young writers as P.G. Wodehouse. Fictional cricketing stories – E.W. Hornung's *The Amateur Cracksman*, featuring Raffles, came out in 1899, as did *Willow the King*, by J.C. Snaith – were all the vogue and especially those aimed at schoolboys. A strange relationship developed between the 'Gentlemen' cricket clubs and the village clubs, particularly in the south-east of England. It is difficult to tell whether the fictional village cricketers were based on actual village teams, or whether real village teams assumed the role ascribed to them by the writers of fiction.

NOTABLE CRICKETERS

W.G. Grace's personality towered over all other English cricket in the first 25 years of the modern game, i.e., after over-arm bowling was legalised in 1864. He was still a force to be reckoned with in the 1890s and in 1895, aged 47, had his Indian summer, scoring 2,346 runs (average 51.00) and creating yet another milestone record by reaching 1,000 runs during the month of May. Only two other batsmen have ever repeated this feat: Walter Hammond in 1927 and Charlie Hallows in 1928. His career was to take a strange turn in 1899. He started the year as captain of Gloucestershire and England, but had accepted the post of captain and manager of the commercially established London County Cricket Club, set up at Crystal Palace. By the end of 1899 he had finished in Test cricket and the County Championship, and the *Blue Book* comments in its pen-picture of him: 'Tragedy or comedy – which was it? – the severance of his long connection with Gloucestershire cricket, and his appearance as a "showman" at the Palace? May his burly form long remain an institution in the cricket field.'[16]

While Grace had been a Victorian cricketer out on his own, the Edwardian era produced five great amateurs who could also draw the crowds.

Prince Ranjitsinhji, who had come from India to play for Cambridge University, Sussex and England, is described in the *Blue Book*: 'As Prince of Cricket, Ranji has a style of his own – graceful, sinuous and charming. Not content with showing us how to play our own national game, he has added to it new strokes hitherto not considered possible – one of them his famous glance to leg.'

Gilbert Jessop (Gloucestershire) is described thus in the *Blue Book*:

> . . . the popular idol Ranji even taking second place in the public estimation. One of the biggest hitters ever seen in the cricket field – a rival to such mighty sloggers as Bonnor, Massie and McDonnell, the Australians and C.I. Thornton, Bates and Ulyett among Englishmen – it is safe to say that his position as the most brilliant and daring batsman of the dashing school will remain unchallenged for all time.'

Charles Fry, who won fame at all the major sports in which he participated – holding the world long jump record and playing soccer for England – played for Sussex and later Hampshire. The *Blue Book* notes: 'His is not the elegance of Palairet, the snake-like suppleness of Ranji, or the brilliance of Jessop, but the combination, in a less degree, of the essential characteristics of all three – a self-made batsman, overcoming natural deficiencies; the true type of Englishman.'

Of Lionel Palairet (Somerset), the *Blue Book* comments: 'The stylist. Recognised as the most graceful batsman of the period, in a class almost by himself. His off drives are real gems, achieved with scarcely any effort, while his cutting – late and square – is beautiful and convincing.'

Archie MacLaren (Lancashire) is reported as: 'Has been well described as "the skipper of skippers". Undoubtedly one of the finest captains who ever donned flannels. A feature of his generalship is the manner in which he sets his field to a batsman with a particular "shot". Trumper, the Australian, was the only man for whom he could not set a field.'

---

16 The *Blue Book*, edited by H.V. Dorey, was published from 1908 to 1913 and was an excellent 'Who's Who' of cricket players.

THE HISTORY OF CRICKET

W.L. Murdoch of Australia and W.G. Grace. These two rival Test cricketers ended their first-class playing days in partnership at the Crystal Palace, representing the London County Cricket Club. Curiously both led their counties (Sussex and Gloucestershire) in the 1890s and both resigned their captaincy in 1899.

K.S. Ranjitsinhji, the first Indian cricketer to achieve worldwide fame – but for England rather than his native country.

The *Blue Book* is not so detailed on professionals, although the outstanding bowlers of the era were nearly all paid players. Sydney Barnes, who is noted as finding first-class cricket 'distasteful',[17] is singled out as outstanding, as are John Hearne (Middlesex) and the Australian all-rounders Frank Tarrant and Albert Trott, both of whom played for Middlesex. However, at the top of the professional tree was George Hirst (Yorkshire), who is noted as: 'One of the finest all-round cricketers produced in this or any other country, he challenges comparison with Dr W.G. Grace at his best.' Hirst created the unique all-round record of 2,000 runs and 200 wickets in 1906. Yorkshire's other notable professionals were Schofield Haigh and Wilfred Rhodes; and Yorkshire won the Championship nine times and were runners-up four times between 1890 and 1914.

Public interest in England vs. Australia Test Matches remained high through the 1890 to 1914 period and the balance of power between the two countries changed hands fairly frequently, neither country winning more than three series in succession. There was the usual crop of internal quarrels on both sides (e.g., players refusing to tour because of real or imagined grievances and the so-called bias of selectors). The idea of Australian players coming to England to earn a full-time living from cricket caught on. Tarrant and Trott have been mentioned; the famous Australian captain Billy Murdoch led Sussex from 1893 to 1899, then finished his playing days with Grace at Crystal Palace.

AUSTRALIAN ADMINISTRATION

In Australia itself the inter-colonial matches were put on a more formal footing with the institution of the Sheffield Shield in 1892–3 (named after Lord Sheffield, the Sussex President, who had financed the 1891–2 England tour of Australia). It was to be a triangular contest – between New South Wales, South Australia and Victoria – until Queensland joined in 1926. The Australasian Cricket Council was set up in 1891–2 to administer the country's cricket, but was little more than a talking shop, the real power still residing in Melbourne and Sydney.

In 1903 the Victorian Cricket Association proposed a conference of the three major Associations to discuss the idea of forming a body to choose official Australian teams. The subsequent story was on a par with that of the County Cricket Council in England. South Australia refused to attend the first official meeting of the Board of Control which the conference set up. New South Wales and Victoria simply ignored South Australia and asked Queensland to come instead. In the middle of these squabbles, the 1905 Australian team to England needed to be selected. The new Board ought to have financed the trip, but the Melbourne Club and the players decided to join together, ignoring the Associations, and ran the tour. The arguments continued and a proposed England tour to Australia in 1906–7 had

---

17 Barnes played four matches for Warwickshire and 46 for Lancashire, but from 1904 to 1935 he represented his native Staffordshire in the Minor Counties Championship.

THE HISTORY OF CRICKET

to be cancelled simply because the Australians were unable to sort out their differences.

W.P. McElhone, who became the Board of Control's Secretary, managed to knock heads together. He was described as being 'as tenacious as a terrier after a rat, and as slippery as an eel or as evasive as a bird in controversy'. The Australian Board selected the players for the 1907–8 series against England and for the 1909 tour to England. The players themselves were not happy with the actions of the Board and when, in 1909, the Board appointed Peter McAlister, a Victorian batsman of the second rank, as tour vice-captain and Treasurer, the players chose Frank Laver as tour manager. Laver and McAlister were not the best of friends. The smouldering row between the Board and the players did not explode until the selectors met to pick the Australian side for the Fourth Test of the 1911–12 series. Clem Hill, Peter McAlister and Frank Iredale were the three selectors. McAlister called Hill the worst captain Australia had ever had, Hill punched McAlister in the face and in the brawl which followed the pair were only prevented from falling out of the window into the street 30 feet below by the action of the Secretary, who dragged them back into the room.

The rows escalated and the upshot was that the 1912 Australian team to England, for the triangular series involving South Africa, was virtually a second eleven because the major players had fallen out with the Board. The ill-feeling was still rumbling on when the First World War began.

Of the Australian stars who were centre stage through all the administrative mess, Victor Trumper (New South Wales) was the greatest. Again I refer to the *Blue Book*: 'As elegant as Palairet, as versatile as Ranjitsinhji, he is one of the prettiest players to watch – his only failing – if failing it can be called – being his aptitude to sacrifice accuracy for brightness.'

Clem Hill (South Australia) had a record similar to Trumper's and owed much to his very solid defence. Monty Noble (New South Wales) was four years older than Trumper and Hill, being born in 1873. He was a fine batsman as well as a very useful bowler. Noble led Australia in 15 Tests; Hill was captain in 10. Another all-rounder who led Australia was Warwick Armstrong. By 1909 he was considered the best all-rounder in the world.

P.A. McAlister. Player-Treasurer of the 1909 Australian team to England, McAlister fell out with many of his fellow players and the rows which followed finally blew up in February 1912 when Clem Hill, the Australian captain, was involved in a punch-up with him during a Test Selectors' meeting.

Looking at domestic club cricket in Australia, the major Associations all established some type of league system for clubs during the 1890s. South Australia had the least turbulent development, with electoral cricket commencing in 1897. Grade cricket in New South Wales began in 1893–4.[18] A Victorian Cricket League was formed in 1895 by the Victoria Cricket Association, but the VCA inaugural pennant competition did not get under way until 1906–7. Eight clubs competed in the first Queensland electoral competition of 1897–8. In Tasmania there were two controlling bodies for North and South: 'District' cricket in Hobart began in 1906–7 and the following season in Launceston. In Western Australia electoral cricket began in 1898.

In 1912 Leslie Poidevin, the New South Wales and Lancashire batsman, wrote:

> The second great factor[19] in the sum of Australian cricket excellence is the splendid organisation of club cricket. It must be obvious that minor (i.e., non-first-class) cricket plays a most important part in the making of the Australian cricketer, and also in maintaining his standard of play, for he can do neither in the pursuit of first-class cricket alone in Australia. As a matter of fact, club cricket is the real foundation of Australia's cricket excellence and the real secret of its successful operation is its organisation ... suffice it to state that every self-respecting club seeks affiliation to the (state) association and every cricketer or would-be cricketer on his part desires membership of an affiliated club. Hence the association has direct control of all the principal grounds and all the players in the State. The competitions are carried through on a local, district, or electoral basis, and the qualification is a residential one.

This helps to explain why Australia, with a fraction of the number of cricketers that England possessed, was able to compete on equal terms: club cricket in Australia was strictly competitive throughout, whereas much English cricket was more of a social event.

THE SOUTH AFRICANS

In South Africa the political problems between the Boers of Transvaal and Orange Free State and the English settlers developed into a full-scale war in 1899. One would expect this major catastrophe to have pushed cricket into the background.[20] It is surprising to look at the record and see that, in the middle of the war, South Africa brought a touring side to England. This tour was financed by the Hon. J.D. Logan of Matjesfontein, the leading patron of South African cricket at that time. Logan had paid for the Surrey bowler George Lohmann

---

18 Both 'electoral' and 'grade' are terms for league cricket.

19 The first factor was the frequent interchange of visits between England and Australia.

20 A match of historic interest was played in Colombo, Ceylon, on 5 and 6 July 1901 between Boer prisoners of war and the premier club in Colombo, Colts CC. Colts won by 141 runs.

THE HISTORY OF CRICKET

to come out as a coach to South Africa in the early 1890s, when the latter was suffering ill-health. Lohmann had made a sufficient recovery to resume his Test career with England. The recovery proved unhappily of a temporary nature. He went back to South Africa and then toured England as Assistant Manager of this 1901 trip, but died of tuberculosis soon after the tourists returned home.

The tour got off to a rocky start when Conan Doyle wrote to the press stating that the South African cricketers ought to have stayed at home and fought the Boers. The visit however went as planned. No Tests were played; 13 out of 25 matches ended in victory. It was unfortunate that most of the defeats came early on in the tour and thus public interest was slight. The trip did, however, show how much South Africa had improved since their initial tour of 1894, when they had played no first-class matches (although they did play some of the major counties). It is worth noting that while both sides comprised entirely white South Africans, A. Hendriks, a Cape Coloured fast bowler, was on the 1894 shortlist of candidates, but according to M.W. Luckin's official history: 'The Committee after due consideration decided that it would be impolite to include him in the team. His non-appearance however caused some disappointment in England among a certain section of the cricketing public.' A forerunner of the Basil d'Oliveira affair.

The third South African tour to England took place, financed by Abe Bailey, in 1904. Again there were no Tests, but the visitors beat a strong England XI, which included Ranji and Jessop, at Lord's by 189 runs. This led on to the 1907 and 1912 Test tours, which have been mentioned in connection with the formation of the ICC. There were also regular visits by English sides to South Africa following Warton's first tour, and by the outbreak of the First World War seven English sides in all had made the trip. In addition, the 1902 Australians to England stopped off in South Africa on the voyage home, playing six matches including three Tests (Australia won two and drew one).

In 1910–11, South Africa toured Australia for the first time. The Australians had insisted on this visit as a precondition for Australian participation in the Triangular Tournament the following year. The home side won the Test series four matches to one, but the South Africans did make a favourable impression. Aubrey Faulkner was their outstanding batsman, and their captain, Percy Sherwell, made nine stumpings in the series, a Test record.

The driving force behind South African cricket was Abe Bailey. He was a wealthy businessman (the 1904 England tour cost him £2,000) and had been co-founder of the Transvaal Cricket Union (established in 1891). As a player he had represented Transvaal in 1894. Bailey himself attributed the improvement in South African cricket to the work of George Lohmann as a coach in the 1890s, but no less than 20 English county cricketers went out to coach in South Africa during the Edwardian period. The Union of South Africa was established in 1910. Abe Bailey, writing shortly after the disappointing 1912 Triangular Tournament in England (because of the very wet summer and a second-rate Australian team), commented:

The three Test captains –
F. Mitchell (South Africa),
C.B. Fry (England) and
S.E. Gregory (Australia) –
during the 1912 Triangular
Test Tournament. The
brainchild of Sir Abe Bailey,
the competition was ruined
by the rain and the second-
rate Australian team.

After all, the cricket result (of the Tournament) should be a secondary consideration to all lovers of Empire. That a spirit of true national comradeship will be produced must be the desire of every cricketer throughout the King's Dominions. Other Colonies will be as deeply interested in the matches as those immediately concerned, and if the strengthening of the bonds of Union within the Empire is one of the many outcomes of the great Tournament, I am hopeful that contemporary cricketers, and those who figure in Empire cricket in the days that are to come, will agree that the Triangular Tests of 1912 were not held in vain.

F.S. Ashley-Cooper, the leading cricket historian and statistician of his day, whose books on the game are still considered standard works of reference and whose articles in the cricket press reached a high level of accuracy.

By 1914 therefore Test cricket was firmly established in England, Australia and South Africa. All three countries had created national authorities to govern their domestic first-class and international affairs. The little world of cricket records for Test and first-class cricket had been created, mainly by two of a new breed of men – 'cricket statisticians' – the two being F.S. Ashley-Cooper and J.N. Pentelow. *Wisden's Cricketers' Almanack* had become the cricketers' bible and its record section ran to 40 pages. The pocket book on the game was the *Athletic News Cricket Annual*, price 3d (*Wisden* was 1s 6d (7½p)). These annuals and the daily press built up public awareness of 'records' and the pinnacle was reached in 1899, when a schoolboy, A.E.J. Collins, scored 628 not out in a junior house match at Clifton College. The newspapers made quite a fuss, and the weekly magazine *Cricket* ends its report with: 'It is hardly necessary to say that Collins has been interviewed, and that the interviewer has elicited the information that the boy is fond of cricket.' Collins joined the Army from school and played in military matches. He was killed in the First World War.

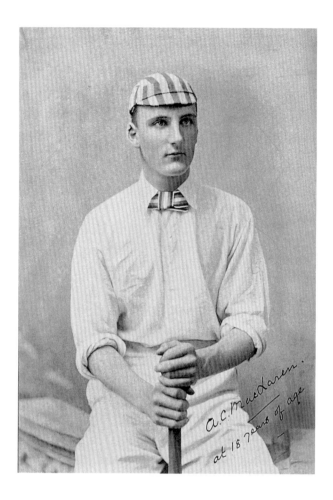

Archie MacLaren. This photograph was taken in his final year at Harrow. Five years later he created a new County Championship record by scoring 424 for Lancashire against Somerset. As a captain of England he was considered the most astute tactician. He confounded critics at the end of his long career by picking a team which beat the all-conquering 1921 Australians.

A month before Collins's feat, a comprehensive *Cricket Records* book had been published and was thus out of date as it hit the bookstalls. The book had, however, come out in time to record the first team total over 1,000: 1,094 by Melbourne University vs. Essendon at Melbourne in 1898. The opposition scored 76! In first-class cricket the Lancashire batsman Archie MacLaren had scored 424 for his county against Somerset in 1895, a County Championship record which was to remain unbroken for 99 years, until Brian Lara scored 501 for Warwickshire against Durham.

It was Charles Box of *The Times* who had described the period around 1860 as 'The Golden Age'. Between the wars writers began labelling the Edwardian era (c.1901–10) as 'The Golden Age' instead. It was certainly the Golden Age of the English amateur upper-middle-class cricketer.

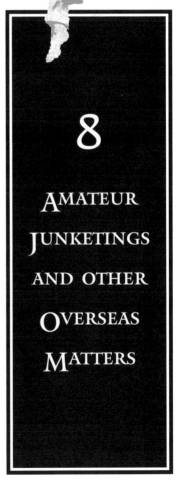

While the MCC had, albeit reluctantly, brought order out of confusion in the matter of 'official' England cricket teams travelling to Australia and South Africa, English tours to other countries remained largely in the hands of individuals. If you were an amateur of independent means in the Edwardian era and felt like a cricketing holiday abroad, the best person to know was the Yorkshire captain, Lord Hawke. He visited India and North America twice and made single trips to Argentina (under the MCC), New Zealand and the West Indies. He had also visited South Africa twice, prior to the MCC taking charge.

Lord Hawke, who turned the hard-drinking individualistic Yorkshire side of the 1880s into a coordinated team which was capable of winning the Championship. His lordship was a useful man to know if a young amateur cricketer fancied an overseas cricketing holiday.

8

AMATEUR JUNKETINGS AND OTHER OVERSEAS MATTERS

Pelham Warner, the England and Middlesex captain, who later managed the famous England team during the Bodyline tour.

One or two of the sides, especially latterly to the West Indies, included a professional or two, but the majority of players were public school men, who often paid their own passage and out-of-pocket expenses. Some of the tours were almost akin to country house cricket, with the team being put up by local bigwigs. Pelham Warner describes five of these tours in his book *Cricket in Many Climes*. He comments on arriving on the West Indian island of Grenada in 1897: 'The administrator had very kindly invited 'the Shrimp' (Leveson-Gower of Surrey) and myself to stay with him at Government House. In the afternoon we went to the races, while in the evening a capital dance was given in the Courthouse.'

The cricket itself was not the cut-throat affair associated with present-day England sides and their opponents, but there is no doubt that the tours gave a great boost to cricket, very much so in the West Indies, New Zealand and India, if not so much in North America. Lord Hawke noted regarding the last: 'At best it (cricket) is an exotic flourishing, even in Philadelphia, merely as a "side-track" to baseball … Still if the quality hardly reached that of test trials, it has furnished our amateur combinations with good games and the very best of times.'

INDIA

The first English tour to India took place in 1889–90; Lord Harris took up his post as Governor of Bombay a few months later. Both these events naturally increased the local enthusiasm for cricket and in 1892 the atmosphere was conducive to representative matches being arranged between the Bombay Europeans and the Parsees. The first game was washed out, but the return match in Poona brought victory for the Parsees, who claimed 'the Championship of India'. Later in the same season Lord Hawke arrived with his English side. The most important matches of his tour were the two against the Parsees – one win each. The English team also met a Native XI in Madras and so-called 'All India' (eight Europeans and three Parsees) in Allahabad. In contrast to the aloof attitude of the British in Calcutta, cricket was developing among the Indians in Madras and a tournament similar to Bombay's Parsees vs. Europeans evolved. This annual game was eventually arranged to coincide with the Tamil New Year.

With cricket becoming increasingly popular among the Hindus and Muslims of Bombay, the original tournament between Europeans and Parsees was expanded in 1907-8 to include Hindus, and in 1912–13 the Muslims also joined. This Bombay tournament was considered the major event in Indian domestic cricket and remained so until it ceased in 1947-8, following independence and partition.

When Lord Harris returned to Britain he set about trying to arrange fixtures for an All-India team to visit England. He talked to the English counties about a guarantee against loss for the Indian side and it seemed that the visit would take place in 1898, but, for a variety of reasons, the scheme came to nothing.

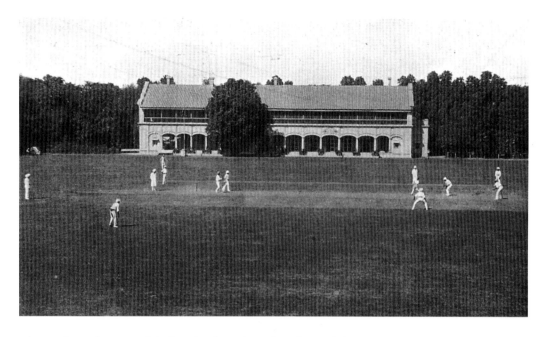

The Patiala Cricket Ground, laid out by the Maharajah and one of the main centres of Indian cricket in the early years of the 20th century.

In recent years there has been a tendency among writers to belittle the efforts Lord Harris made on behalf of Indian cricket. The theory has been put forward that Harris only encouraged the tournament in Bombay in order to cause more rivalry between the various religious groups, the English plan being to divide and rule.

Writing in 1901, M.E. Pavri, the Parsee cricketer, states however:

> It goes without saying that in Lord Harris the Parsee cricketers have their best patron and friend. Before Lord Harris came to Bombay as Governor, the Parsees had made fair progress in the game, but it was his personal example that gave great impetus to sports of all kinds in Bombay. What is more, the leading members of the varied communities of Bombay came forward to a man for the first time to give their support to the athletic movement in Bombay after his shining example. Besides, Lord Harris, as a sage statesman, at once saw that much of the friction between the Europeans and the Natives of India could be got rid of by bringing the rulers and the ruled together by means of sports.

Between Lord Hawke's trip and the next visit to India by English cricketers there was a ten-year gap: in 1902–3 the Oxford University Authentics put together a side which was just about 'first class' by English standards. The Authentics were (and indeed are) a wandering club comprising Oxford University students, founded about 1883 by Everard Britten

Holmes. He it was, with the Secretary of the Calcutta Club, who arranged this tour. The tourists were beaten by both the Europeans in Bombay and the Parsees, but otherwise fared well. Their travels took them all over the subcontinent and, compared with the tourists to North America and the West Indies, they had an arduous time: the train journey between Trichinopoly and Calcutta, for example, took five days, when floods washed away the line.

At the same time as cricket was making great strides among the various communities of Bombay, the teaching of the game at the colleges for the sons of Indian princes was having its effect. Ranjitsinhji's education at Rajkumar College in the 1880s has been noted; Sir Rajendra Singh, the Maharaja of Patiala, was the same age as Ranji, but had succeeded to his inheritance at the age of 3. In the 1890s the Maharaja laid out a fine ground at Patiala and engaged two England Test cricketers, William Brockwell (Surrey) and John Hearne (Middlesex), to act as both coaches and players. In all Hearne went out to Patiala for six winters. The Maharaja then gave Ranjitsinhji a sinecure in his army, thus adding Ranji to his now formidable cricket team. Several of the best Parsee cricketers were also engaged. The Maharaja was a keen polo player and, unfortunately, died in 1900 aged 28 as the result of a fall from a horse. He was succeeded by his nine-year-old son, whose enthusiasm for cricket exceeded even his father's. In 1909, the young Maharaja engaged the great Australian and Middlesex all-rounder, Frank Tarrant. Tarrant was to remain devoted to India and lived there on and off for the next 30 years. The Maharaja had captained the XI at Aitchison College, Lahore, and was chosen to captain the first All-India team on its tour of England in 1911. The side did not contain any Europeans, but was selected by Captain John Greig, a leading Hampshire batsman, stationed in India.

Unlike the earlier Parsee sides to England, the All-India team was granted first-class status, but it could only achieve two wins against first-class opposition. Even if English public interest in the tour was slight, it at least placed Indian cricket on level pegging with the West Indies and not too far below South Africa. Had K.M. Mistry, the best batsman on the tour, been available to play in more than three out of 14 matches, it would have made a great difference. The Maharaja also only appeared in three first-class games, giving credence to the theory that his main reason for visiting England was political, rather than cricketal. Mihir Bose is not an admirer of the Maharaja and quotes in his history, among other unflattering comments, the story: 'Englishmen start the day with bacon and eggs, Frenchmen with coffee and rolls, the Maharaja with a virgin.'

NEW ZEALAND

New Zealand preceded India with the idea of importing English professionals as coaches. In fact the official New Zealand history marks 1890 as the start of modern cricket in the country, because that was when Otago signed a coach from England for the first time. Joe Lawton (Warwickshire) came on a four-year contract. Auckland followed the Otago lead and engaged Albert Relf (Sussex); Frank Shacklock (Nottinghamshire) succeeded Lawton, and at various times such distinguished Australian cricketers as Jock Saunders, Charles Macartney and Sammy Jones acted as coaches in New Zealand.

In December 1894, the various provincial Associations formed the New Zealand Cricket Council to run the game at national level. The need for such a body had become apparent during the previous season, when a New Zealand team was picked to play against a touring New South Wales side. The Council had no sooner been formed than the country had an unusual cricketing invasion – the Fijian team whose tour is noted on pages 116–17.

The New Zealand Council financed the first English tour to the country in 1902–3. It was intended that Lord Hawke, who picked the side, should captain the tourists, but owing to his mother's illness, he did not travel. Pelham Warner acted as captain instead. Two professionals accompanied the party, which played 18 games in New Zealand, including two against a full New Zealand team. All matches ended in wins for the tourists, but the New Zealanders took a great deal of interest in the visit and good attendances meant a small profit for the Council. A second English tour under the MCC in 1906–7 lost a considerable sum for the Council. Both Canterbury and New Zealand did achieve a victory against the visitors, who comprised solely amateurs led by Edward Wynyard of Hampshire.

Percy May, the Surrey cricketer, who went on the tour, explains the defeat they suffered at the hands of New Zealand:

> It is usually argued that a touring side have a considerable advantage in that they are used to playing together, whereas the home side are only a scratch lot in representative matches. This advantage, I think, is far out-weighted by the arduous toil of travelling continuously, not to mention the wearing effect of the inevitable (and delightful) junketings for which one comes in. At the beginning of our campaign we were taken to task by a well-known Australian, who ought to have known better, for a supposed intention of enjoying ourselves, as well as playing cricket, in New Zealand. We certainly did enjoy ourselves most thoroughly, despite the hardships of the journeying to and fro, and we are not at all ashamed of it. Is it reasonable to expect a party of pure amateurs to give up six months for the tour if it is not to be a pleasure trip? It must be remembered that only bare expenses are paid (tickets and hotel bills, not including drinks or smokes, etc.), which means that every member of the team is necessarily very much out of pocket over it, apart from what income he might have earned at home during the half-year.

The visit gave a boost to domestic cricket in New Zealand, since it spurred Lord Plunket, the Governor-General, into presenting a Challenge Shield for competition among the major Associations. Canterbury were awarded the Shield for this first year, mainly because of their victory over the tourists. The other major Associations at this time were Auckland, Hawke's Bay, Otago and Wellington.

There were no further English tours to the country before the First World War and no New Zealand side came to England. However, four more Australian teams of varying quality made visits, and one New Zealand side crossed the Tasman Sea between 1900 and 1914. T.W. Reese, in his history of New Zealand Cricket up to 1915, poses the question why New Zealand cricket had not reached the same standard as New Zealand rugby football, and answers by saying that the cricketers did not practise enough, that grounds were not good enough and that the English coaches were engaged because they were good cricketers, but not good coaches. He notes: 'Truly, cricket is not only a game, but it is also an integral part in the everyday life of the young manhood of the Empire.'

THE WEST INDIES

At the beginning of the 1890s Barbados was the leading cricket colony in the Caribbean. The first triangular tournament between Demerara, Trinidad and Barbados was staged in 1891–2, resulting in victory for Barbados. The official inter-colonial tournament commenced the following season, again with Barbados victorious. In fact, domestic cricket was well organised there. In 1892–3 a club league was formed in which the seven clubs on the island each played home and away matches against the others. Pickwick CC was easily the strongest of the clubs, winning all the early competitions: in 1894–5 they won every one of their 12 games. The league included the two major schools on the island, Harrison College and Lodge School. Professionals were banned from the competition.

In Demerara, Georgetown Cricket Club remained the major centre of cricket. In Trinidad, the Queen's Park Cricket Club in Port of Spain was founded in 1891, and the present Queen's Park Test Ground was laid out in 1896. Because Jamaica was nine or ten days' sailing time from the other three cricketing colonies, it remained very much an isolated community in cricketing terms.

The first English side to tour the Caribbean visited in 1894–5. Dr R.B. Anderson, the leading inspiration in the West Indies, arranged the fixtures, while Lord Stamford and Lord Hawke gathered the team together. Lord Hawke had to decline the captaincy and the side was led by R. Slade Lucas, the Middlesex batsman. The all-amateur team was just about up to English first-class standard and of its six major games, three were won and three lost. Two years later, as the result of some crossed wires, two English sides arranged to tour the West Indies, one under Lord Hawke and the second led by Arthur Priestley (MP for Grantham from 1900 to 1918 and a keen amateur club cricketer). The two organisers met before leaving England but neither would back down. Fortunately, unlike the dual trips to Australia nearly ten years earlier, both parties were entirely composed of amateurs on cricketing holidays, so no money was lost.

In 1900, the first West Indian side travelled to England. W.C. Nock, the Secretary of the Queen's Park Club in Trinidad, acted as manager and Aucher Warner, brother of the Middlesex batsman, led the team. The side comprised 15 players, two of whom were black professionals: 'Float' Woods and W.J. Burton. These two took nearly three-quarters of all the

wickets on the tour. Of the rest, the white cricketers paid their own way, but it was difficult for the middle class black or coloured players to afford to go. One such was 'Cons' Constantine (father of the great Learie Constantine). He was the best batsman in Trinidad at the time, and it was only by means of a public subscription that he was a member of the side. The complex relationship between white, coloured and black people in the West Indies at this time is explained fully in C.L.R. James's *Beyond A Boundary*.

The 1900 West Indians struggled to come to terms with English conditions. The MCC did not grant their matches first-class status and the games attracted very little public attention. That status was granted to the second West Indian team in 1906, but again, attendances at matches were poor and results modest.

The popularity of cricket in the West Indian colonies and among all races in those colonies boomed in the early years of the century. The captain of the English team which toured the islands in 1910–11, A.W.F. Somerset, commented:

> The characteristic of West Indian cricket is, in the first place, extraordinary keenness. The spectators are in a state of excitement unknown in England. Every scoring stroke is applauded and is mentioned in the newspapers, and a good ball stopped is greeted with shouts of, 'Played!' all round the ground. A yorker chopped evokes a yell which is not given for a ball hit over the ropes in England. When that comes off, some of the spectators spring over the ropes, throw their hats and umbrellas in the air, perform fantastic dances, and occasionally some of them are arrested by the police and held until they promise to quiet down.

Both on the MCC-run 1910–11 tour and in 1912–13, which was the last before the First World War, the English team played a combined West Indies side. The tourists won both games on both trips, though in 1912–13 Barbados slaughtered the English side twice, each time by an innings. Arrangements for a West Indian side to visit England in 1915 or 1916 had to be cancelled because of the war.

BERMUDA

Bermuda, which is, in both cricketing and geographical terms, totally separate from the West Indies, relied largely on tours to and from the United States for its contact with the outside world. In 1891 Philadelphia Zingari toured the colony, playing three matches; and in 1905, Hamilton CC, the principal club in Bermuda, toured the States, winning just one game. The Philadelphian side which toured Bermuda in 1907 contained some of the best American players of the day. They won their games against the local sides with ease, then met All Bermuda and were beaten by 47 runs. T.St G. Gilbert for Bermuda took all 10 wickets for 17 runs in the second innings – the greatest feat ever recorded in Bermudan cricket history. Further frequent tours followed, and up to 1914 the results of matches between All Bermuda and Philadelphian touring teams were: Bermuda five wins, Philadelphia two.

Moving north to Philadelphia, the 25 years between 1890 and 1914 saw cricket bloom like some exotic flower and the petals droop and the whole plant wither away. John Lester in his book *A Century of Philadelphia Cricket* points to the match between the Germantown Club of Philadelphia and the 1913 Australian tourists as the end of first-class cricket in the United States. The Germantown Club won the match, their star player being Percy Clark, who was celebrating his 40th birthday. He made the highest score in the game and his second innings bowling figures of 6 for 38 were the best on either side.

Going back to 1890, the Halifax Cup (Philadelphia's cricket league) was flourishing and in 1891, when Philadelphia played an English side under Lord Hawke, Lester notes: 'Large

Philadelphians vs. P.F. Warner's XI at the Oval, 1903. The Philadelphians were capable of playing first-class cricket against county teams on three tours to England: 1897, 1903 and 1908.

J. Barton King (1873-1965) toured England with all three Philadelphian sides, crowning his career with 87 wickets (average 11.01) on the final tour of 1908, when he topped the first-class bowling table.

crowds gathered about the offices of the city newspapers, where bulletins were issued at the fall of each wicket.' Philadelphia won by eight wickets. When the Australians came to Philadelphia in 1893, Philadelphia hit 525 against a side of Test Match standard and won the game by an innings and 68 runs. In 1895 a central authority for cricket in Philadelphia was set up – Associated Cricket Clubs of Philadelphia – and this handled tours to and from Philadelphia. Through this organisation the first first-class tour by Philadelphia to England took place in 1897. The captain of the touring team, George Patterson, was interviewed while in England. He pointed out that although cricket was played in New York, Chicago and Boston, the players in those cities were almost entirely Englishmen resident there; only in Philadelphia were there many American-born cricketers.

In 1897 Philadelphia had ten English professionals engaged by the local clubs. The Philadelphian team itself, however, was entirely amateur. This was ·a great disadvantage compared with England, since the amateur cricketers in Philadelphia all had to work for a living, whereas in England this was not always the case. Philadelphian players therefore normally retired early from active cricket. The 1897 team won two out of their 15 first-class games in England. In 1903, on their next visit, they won seven out of 17; and on their third and last first-class tour they again won seven. The irony of this final tour was that Bart King, the principal Philadelphian bowler, ended the season at the top of the English first-class averages. John Barton King (1873–1965) was born in Philadelphia and was undoubtedly the greatest player produced by the United States. His first-class career lasted from 1893 to 1912.

The annual match between Canada and the United States (by now really Philadelphia) finished in 1912. It was revived after the Second World War. The Halifax Cup competition dribbled on to 1926, by which time the three centres of education which had played cricket – Harvard, Haverford College and Pennsylvania University – had also more or less ceased to play the game.

THE HISTORY OF CRICKET

CANADA

The Canadians never attained the standard briefly reached by Philadelphia. When Lord Hawke's side of 1891 played in Canada, the tourists won both matches by an innings, and the 1893 Australians also beat Canada by an innings, in contrast to the defeats both touring sides suffered in Philadelphia.

After the poor results of the Canadian sides to England in 1880 and 1887, no Canadian team visited England again until the Toronto Zingari came in 1910. They won nine out of 16 games, but these were fair club standard only. In 1913 the Australian side, which has been mentioned as being beaten by Germantown, played no less than 31 matches in Canada, beginning their tour in Victoria, British Columbia. This initial match had scores of: Victoria 57 and 76; Australians 222. The Australian side could be described as that country's 2nd XI. Most of the other matches produced similar results and of the 31, 30 ended in victory, the other being drawn. Although the standard of the Canadian teams was low, the matches attracted public attention. Charles Macartney, the Australian all-rounder, gives a good account of the tour in his autobiography. He scored over 2,000 runs and took about 200 wickets on the trip.

SOUTH AMERICA

Apart from British Guiana (now Guyana), which in cricketing terms is considered part of the West Indies, the major cricket in South America was played in Argentina. The main centre of cricket in the country was Buenos Aires, but in the 1890s the railway terminal at Tucuman had a flourishing cricket side. It was from Tucuman that the idea of an annual fixture between the North of Argentina and the South originated. The first game was played in 1891 and it became established as the principal domestic fixture. A league championship for clubs in the Buenos Aires area was started in 1898, although it collapsed after one season. The logistical problems were quickly resolved and in 1900 a two-divisional championship was being played.

The principal source of cricketers had initially been the large number of Englishmen employed on the construction of the railways, and in the years just prior to the First World War, more and more English people came out as cattle farmers.

In 1911 the Argentine Cricket Association invited the MCC to tour. This side, under Lord Hawke, arrived in February 1912. There were three 'Tests', of which Argentina won the first, but lost the other two. The touring side, though entirely amateur, was certainly of first-class standard. Lord Hawke noted: 'Our visit aroused much interest, but I am doubtful of cricket ever taking serious root there on an important scale. They prefer to play soccer with enthusiasm and rugger with vigour.' It is interesting to mention that at a banquet for the team, moving film of the matches was shown while the meal was in progress.

Lord Hawke's MCC XI in Argentina, 1912.
The matches played against Argentina
on this tour were the first to be ranked
as first-class in that country. Lord Hawke
is sitting third from right.

The first team to visit Argentina was not the MCC, but Brazil as early as 1888. There was a reciprocal tour in 1890. Three years later the Buenos Aires Club travelled to Chile. Needless to say these teams all comprised Englishmen resident in the countries concerned.

The first game reported in Venezuela took place in Caracas in March 1894. In the same season a match of sorts was played at Villa Rica in Paraguay; there was also some cricket in Lima, Peru. The only South American country to engage a professional was Argentina, the Hurlingham Club bringing out William Lacey, the Nottinghamshire cricketer, in the 1890s.

AFRICA

Across the Atlantic, the MCC made a pioneering tour of Egypt in 1909. The eight fixtures included three two-day matches against All Egypt. The tourists won the series two matches to one. All the Egyptian side were British, either in the Armed Forces or in the Egyptian Civil Service. Richard Moore, the Middlesex cricketer, who was a member of the Civil Service, commented:

> Arabs might make good cricketers. They are strong, very active and extremely powerful and accurate throwers, with of course eyes like hawks. But it is rather early to catch them yet: they do not quite appreciate such a ladylike form of contest. It is quite conceivable that in time something can be done with the people, but at present, shining example is all that is feasible.

Travelling down the East Coast of Africa, little cricket was played in Somaliland or Zanzibar, except when British naval vessels were in port. In Mombasa some cricket was played, supported by a few of the 20,000 Indians resident there. The main cricket centre in British East Africa was Nairobi, where in 1912 there were four grounds, the best being the Gymkhana Ground. The major game of the season was Settlers vs. Officials, established in 1910. Cricket on Africa's western coast owed a great deal to Major F.G. Guggisberg of the Royal Engineers. He had played first-class cricket in England and was later Governor of the Gold Coast (now Ghana). In 1904 the first Gold Coast vs. Lagos match was staged; this was to develop into Gold Coast vs. Nigeria. It is clear that, provided there were sufficient players and the climate was at all suitable, cricket of some standard was played in every British colony before the First World War.

Pelham Warner begins his heavyweight tome entitled *Imperial Cricket* with:

> Cricket is something more than a mere game. It is an institution, a part of the people's life, a creed, one might almost say a passion with some. It has got into the blood of the nation, and wherever British men and women are gathered together there will be stumps pitched.

CONTINENTAL EUROPE

On the continent of Europe, Holland was the major cricketing nation and the Gentlemen of Holland toured England in 1892, 1894, 1901 and 1906. The great Dutch cricketer was C.J. Posthuma, who proved that he was a player of ability when he appeared for London County in the first-class matches in 1903. At the turn of the century there were some 15 Dutch clubs, taking part in a league competition. H.S. Isbrucker, the President of the Dutch Cricket Association, explained the problems facing cricket in Holland: 'There are no private or public residential schools, so that boys get no opportunities of learning the game until they are old enough to go into business or professions, and then only a few of them have the time to spare. There is a leisured class as in England, but of course it is comparatively small.'

The progress of cricket in Denmark was much slower than in Holland, although three English sides played matches there prior to 1914. No Danish side came to England until the 1920s, and a Danish Cricket Association did not emerge until 1953.

Cricket made a solitary appearance in the Olympic Games, when a single match was staged in Paris in 1900. England, represented by the Devon County Wanderers, played France, represented by All Paris. Virtually all the French team were Englishmen resident in Paris. The star of the game was M.H. Toller (a Devon Wanderer), who took 7 wickets for 9 runs. He had played six first-class matches for Somerset in 1897.

Most other European countries saw some cricket including Russia, where matches were staged in St Petersburg. As with the lesser colonies, all that was needed was enough Englishmen and/or the arrival of a British naval vessel. In August 1894 the liner *Lusitania* cruised off Norway and a cricket match (of sorts) was played by the light of the midnight sun, when the liner moored off Spitsbergen.[21]

Quite frequently readers come across some document mentioning a cricket match in some 'foreign' land and announce to the world that cricket was played in year 'x' in that country. In reality it would have been an isolated game involving two English sides.

---

21 Curiously, an 18th-century Russian writer called Charitonow earlier described how his countrymen, while stationed on Spitsbergen, had played a game resembling cricket, 'as was evident by the bats and rude wooden balls they had used, still lying on the mossy ground'. Certainly the British had been known to visit the archipelago since before the Civil War; Horatio Nelson later went to Spitsbergen as a 14-year-old midshipman and was nearly killed when he rashly tried to hunt a polar bear on the ice at night. However, even if the Russians on Spitsbergen invented this particular bat-and-ball game themselves, it confirms a fundamental fact about the origins of cricket: namely, that while various cricket-like games may have been played around Europe from the late middle ages onwards, it was only in The Weald that a peculiar set of social circumstances and characteristics combined to transform a rudimentary 'club-ball' game into a highly sophisticated sport.

THE HISTORY OF CRICKET

Charles, 4th Duke of Richmond playing cricket as a child (said to have been painted by his nurse).

Alfred Mynn (1807–1861), the outstanding all-rounder for Kent, represented his county from 1834 to 1859. (Portrait by William Bromley, c.1848.)

Thomas Hope (1769–1831). This portrait was painted by Jacques Sablet, when Hope was in Rome on the Grand Tour. Hope came from a family of Scottish bankers that had settled in Amsterdam. He moved to London in 1796. The cricket being played is clearly of a makeshift nature.

Cricket in Marylebone Fields, by Francis Hayman (1708–1776), painted about 1747. This is the earliest picture showing a conventional cricket match and demonstrates that the mid-18th-century game was not that far removed from present-day contests. (See page 18.)

Lord's Cricket Ground, 1996. For all the changes in the game and the shift of focus – in terms of pure talent and joie de vivre *– from England to Australia, and then on to the West Indies and, currently, the South Asian subcontinent, Lord's is still considered cricket's headquarters and the home of the ICC.*

Part of a 1996 sponsorship advertisement which used inn-signs to highlight the historical link between the Army and cricket. It advertised an Under 15 county competition, sponsored by the Army, which was won by 'the boys' of Sussex, whose predecessors were among the first to play the game in The Weald at least 400 years ago.

Shane Warne. Because of the difficulty in controlling the length and direction, bowling leg-breaks or googlies and capturing wickets at a reasonable cost has required special skills. The Australian Shane Warne is the leading exponent of this rare art at the present time.

Ian Botham, England's best-known post-war cricketer. A great all-rounder who used his cricketing fame to build a career in the media and the theatre, as well as raising large sums of money for charitable causes.

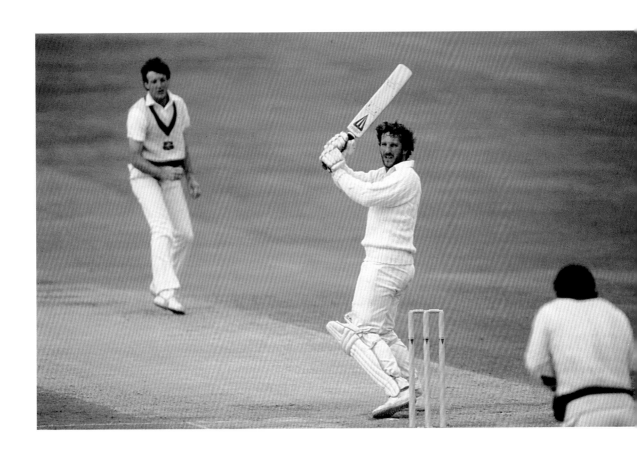

Brian Lara, the first cricketer since Bradman to hold, simultaneously, the records for the highest innings in both Test and first-class cricket. He was also the first batsman to top 500 runs in a single innings in County Championship cricket.

C.L.R. James, a talented cricketer and friend of Learie Constantine, came to England to work as a journalist. In the 1950s he orchestrated a campaign to have Frank Worrell chosen as the West Indies' captain.

Jubilation as India win the first Lombard Under 15
World Challenge, against Pakistan at Lord's in
1996.

Eden Gardens, Calcutta,
the largest Test Match arena.
The South Asian subcontinent's
enthusiasm for cricket has been
on the increase over the past
30 years.

*England's
team celebrate
victory over
New Zealand
at Lord's
in the 1993
Women's
World Cup.*

*Arjuna Ranatunga, captain of the Sri Lankan team which won the 1996 World Cup.
This victory overturned the presumed hierarchy among the Test-playing countries
and gave a tremendous boost to the game in Sri Lanka.*

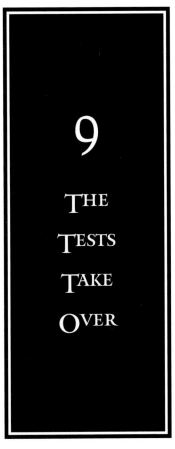

Armageddon may well be at hand. As one writes the talk is all of War–War–War! Cricket is naturally pushed into the background – naturally and rightly – big a part as the greatest of games plays in our national life. Yet when the thrilling call – Who is on our side? – goes forth, the debt the nation owes to cricket ought not to be forgotten. In spite of occasional squabbles – Sydney barracking, Bloemfontein incidents, and the like – cricket has perhaps done more than anything else to weld together in links of sympathy the Mother Country and her wide-spread children.

The principal cricket magazine of 1914 carried this cartoon on page 1, posing the question: was it patriotic to play cricket when the nation was at war?

9

THE
TESTS
TAKE
OVER

The quotation on the previous page was part of the editorial in *World of Cricket*, published on 8 August 1914, four days after war had been declared against Germany.

Some 40 County Championship matches remained to be played on the day war broke out (no first-class overseas touring side had come to England in 1914); Surrey were leading the county table. No immediate decision was taken, so the planned games continued as if nothing had happened. It was not long, however, before counties found themselves without some of their best players – a few were called to the colours in the middle of matches. The Kennington Oval was requisitioned for military purposes and Surrey borrowed Lord's for two home games.

On 27 August, W.G. Grace wrote to the press:

> I think the time has arrived when the county cricket season should be closed, for it is not fitting at a time like the present that able-bodied men should play day after day and pleasure-seekers look on. There are so many who are young and able and yet are hanging back. I should like to see all first-class cricketers of suitable age, etc., set a good example and come to the help of their country without delay in its hour of need.

Three days later, Field Marshal Earl Roberts, the victorious Commander-in-Chief of the Boer War, made some very pointed and public remarks about the same subject. The following day, the Surrey Committee met and decided to abandon their two remaining matches, leaving Surrey as Champions. This effectively ended first-class cricket in England. It would not resume until 1919.

In Australia the 1914–15 season of Sheffield Shield matches was played through. A.G. Moyes, who had been picked for the Australian team for the abandoned 1914–15 tour to South Africa, noted later: 'After the 1914–15 season, we put away our bats, pads and flannels until the sterner work was over. It was the end of an era.'

In South Africa no first-class cricket was played between April 1914 and October 1919. In fact, so little cricket was played during the war that Newlands, South Africa's most famous ground, situated in Cape Town, was only saved from the builders by a public appeal and the mortgagees forgoing their interest for two years.

Cricket, like so many walks of life in Great Britain, suffered a tremendous loss as a result of the slaughter during the war. No less than one first-class cricketer in eleven lost his life during the conflict (of those who had played domestic English cricket between 1900 and 1914). By accident or design the current England Test players were more fortunate. Seventeen county players had been selected for the last home Test series (in 1912). Not one lost his life in the war. Six of the ten professionals spent part or most of the war playing cricket in the Bradford League – Sydney Barnes, Schofield Haigh, John Hearne, Bill Hitch, Jack Hobbs and Frank Woolley – while Wilfred Rhodes appeared in his local Huddersfield League. Other past or future Test players in the Bradford League included Charles Llewellyn (South Africa and Hampshire), George Gunn (Nottinghamshire), Cecil Parkin (Yorkshire and Lancashire),

Wally Hardinge (Kent) and Ernest Tyldesley (Lancashire). With the Lancashire League closing down in 1917 and 1918, the Bradford League established itself, for a time, as the centre of top-class cricket in England.

In the south of England many local clubs closed down, while others operated on a very reduced scale. The MCC had played 163 matches in 1914; during the war this came tumbling down to an average of 30 per season, all of them against public schools.

As the war dragged on, the initial notion that playing cricket was unpatriotic faded, giving way to the view that the game provided healthy exercise and a brief diversion from the stark reality. In 1918 a series of three matches (for suitable charities) was arranged in London between 'England' and a Dominion side picked from Australian and New Zealand forces stationed in England. When, in November of the same year, the Armistice was announced, almost immediately plans were afoot for an official Australian tour to England for 1919. This did not materialise, but the Australian military authorities stepped in to sponsor a forces side (Australian Imperial Forces, A.I.F.), which arranged a series of matches against the first-class counties. They proved very popular and might be described as the hors d'oeuvre to the ten Test Match series which were to become the central feature of inter-war cricket: England vs. Australia for The Ashes.

POST-WAR COUNTY CRICKET

The inter-county matches, which resumed after a break of four seasons in 1919, were strange affairs. The counties had voted to play two-day games, in place of the traditional three-day, and arranged the Championship fixtures accordingly. When they realised what they had done, most counties were aghast. Lord Harris, still the figure of authority at Lord's, was bemused and took the attitude that the counties would soon realise their error. Forty-five per cent of the 1919 Championship matches ended as draws, compared with 30 per cent in 1914. The two-day scheme was abandoned for 1920, when 31 per cent of the games were drawn.

The majority of counties spent the 21 inter-war years lurching from one financial crisis to another. Moreover, the problem of there being too many counties, which had caused concern before the war, was exacerbated by the promotion of Glamorgan to the Championship in 1921.

After wins in 1920 and 1921 by Middlesex, the Championship became a straight fight between Yorkshire and Lancashire. In the 18 summers from 1922 to 1939, Yorkshire were Champions 11 times and Lancashire five. Nottinghamshire and Derbyshire won once each. At the bottom of the table in the same period, Northamptonshire finished with the wooden spoon eight times and Worcestershire four times. The northern counties' domination of the Championship was primarily due to the flight of the southern working class from cricket as a profession and the fact that fewer and fewer amateurs could afford the time for full seasons of Championship cricket. Middlesex were particularly hard hit by this second problem. The county had four England-class amateurs: Gubby Allen, Ian Peebles, Robbie Robins and Greville Stevens. All of them only had time to play intermittently. If the four had been financially independent, Middlesex would certainly have challenged the northern domination more than they did. Another anti-cricket spectre which affected amateur participation was the call of the golf course. For example, Leonard Crawley (Cambridge University and Essex) was considered one of the most brilliant young batsmen of his day, but he turned to golf, playing four times in the Walker Cup.

THE ASHES

However, it was not the County Championship which interested the general public (apart from in Lancashire and Yorkshire), but the England vs. Australia Tests. Nationally cricket captured the headlines in England roughly in four-year cycles, and in between each cycle came the second-hand interest from the series in Australia.

Accurate figures for attendances at Test Matches in England are unobtainable, but relatively speaking they were on a par with those in Australia, taking into account the smaller size of English grounds and the fact that Tests in England were confined to three days in 1921 and 1926 and four days thereafter. However, it was agreed that if the series was tied after four games, the fifth would be played out. In Australia all the inter-war matches were continued until a definite result was achieved, which could be seven days or, in one extreme case, eight. The attendance figures for the five inter-war series in Australia make interesting reading:

Attendance figures for the inter-war Ashes series in Australia

Tour	Total attendance	Days	Average per day
1920–1	491,182	24	20,465
1924–5	687,134	31	22,165
1928–9	863,608	33	26,169
1932–3	761,107	26	29,273
1936–7	943,513	26	36,288

In England the media, at first through increasing sales of popular newspapers and then through wireless broadcasting and cinema newsreels, helped to focus interest on the Tests and divert it away from domestic first-class cricket. The appearance of a megastar boosted the image further. He first appeared in the 1928–9 series. His name: Don Bradman.

There were, however, four Ashes series prior to the rise of Bradman. After the Australian Forces games of 1919, the England team went out to Australia in the winter of 1920–1. England, chosen and financed by the MCC, were led by the Essex captain Johnny Douglas. They were simply overwhelmed. Australia won all five matches, a sequence of victories which neither side had previously recorded. This was not, however, the end of England's humiliation and Australia's success. Both teams boarded the *RMS Osterley*, which left Fremantle on

22 March, bound for Toulon. They then crossed France by train and arrived in England in mid-April to continue the battle for The Ashes. There was no respite for England, as the Australians won the next three Tests by ten wickets, eight wickets and 219 runs. The fourth match was ruined by rain and the fifth was a high-scoring draw.

The fundamental reason for England's lack of success is generally attributed to the terrible losses suffered during the war, but it is probably more likely to be due to the basic difference between cricket in Australia and England. By 1919 most cricket in Australia was competitive and formed around the 'leagues', which were now well established in all the former Australian colonies. This competitive cricket developed young talent much faster than was the case in England, where most cricket was of a social nature. English club cricketers played in top-class cricket until they were in their 50s, which kept the game at a much more sedate pace. Only in Lancashire and Yorkshire did younger players evolve more quickly through competitive league matches. On the whole, talented cricketers of possible Test Match ability were reared much more slowly, although they did appear in the end. Exactly the same pattern was to occur after the Second World War, Australia trouncing England in the first few Test series, then gradually England's equality coming through: a tortoise and hare syndrome.

The Australian side of 1920–1 was fortunate to find a pair of outstanding fast bowlers, Jack Gregory and Ted McDonald, and the ideal man to control them, Warwick Armstrong. R.C. Robertson-Glasgow, who played for Oxford University and Somerset in 1921, wrote of the Australian captain:

> Armstrong was the nearest thing to W.G. Grace that Australia had produced, both in bulk and ability. He somewhat resembled The Old Man in his method of bowling, rolling the ball from leg for as long as you pleased, with a sort of comfortable assiduity and strainless guile. As a batsman, he had become rather slow of foot (he weighed about 20 stone in 1921), but he still drove with great power and could stick at need. As a captain Armstrong was reckoned among the astutest tacticians … he was not a man of many words, but the few that he uttered were apt to be noticed.

Armstrong had toured England in 1902, 1905 and 1909, but missed 1912 because of the quarrel between the Board and the players. On three of his four tours he had achieved the 'Double' of 1,000 runs and 100 wickets.

It was perhaps not a coincidence that, like that of Grace, his reputation suffered from derogatory remarks after he had retired. The story of Armstrong reading a newspaper while fielding in the 1921 Test at The Oval has grown out of proportion with the years, like the Grace yarn of the bails and the wind.[22]

---

22 In Armstrong's case, paper was blowing across the playing area and, in order to help clear the debris, he picked up a newspaper and for a moment or two glanced at the racing results. The 'Grace yarn' refers to WG's supposedly claiming, when bowled once, that the wind had blown the bails off.

Warwick Armstrong,
captain of the formidable
1921 Australian touring side
to England, was a formidable
figure in his own right.

Jack Hobbs, the professional who was
the perfect gentleman. Hobbs played
for Surrey from 1905 to 1934, and his
batting aggregates in first-class cricket
of 61,760 runs and 199 centuries
remain records which are unlikely to
be broken. He was knighted in 1953
for his services to cricket.

Behind the scenes was Australia's greatest cricket administrator, Ernest Bean of Victoria. He put the Victorian Cricket Association on its feet and also the Australian Board of Control. His obituary in the Victorian CA Annual Report of 1938–9 noted:

> Those who remember the stormy period during the settlement of the government of State and Commonwealth cricket must ever pay homage to the untiring efforts of Ernest Bean. Fearless in his defence of the right and courageous in his outlook for the future of the game, his outstanding personality has passed into the cricket history of his State and of Australia.

For England, the man behind the scenes was still Lord Harris. In 1921 he chaired the annual meeting of the Advisory County Cricket Committee, as well as its sub-committee, and was chairman of the Board of Control which selected the Test Selectors. No one at Lord's made any significant decision without consulting Lord Harris.

Following the 1921 Ashes series, the next meeting between the two combatants took place in the Australian season of 1924–5. Australia had lost McDonald to the magnet of Lancashire money, although he had to spend two years qualifying for residence (in 1925 he took 205 wickets at 18 runs each for his county), and lacked a top quality replacement to open the bowling with Gregory. England had found in Herbert Sutcliffe a batsman to partner Jack Hobbs: the pendulum was swinging away from Australia, but they still won the series by four matches to one.

Back in England in 1926, the first four Tests were drawn, two, at Trent Bridge and Old Trafford, being marred by rain. All depended on the Fifth Test at The Oval. Australia gained a first innings lead of 22. Hobbs and Sutcliffe began England's second innings with an opening partnership of 172 and Australia collapsed to 83 for six. Three wickets were taken by a fast bowler in his second Test and three by a 48-year-old Yorkshireman in his last Test against Australia. England won the series. The young fast bowler was Harold Larwood, a miner from Nottinghamshire; the veteran was Wilfred Rhodes, who had last played for England in 1921 and made his Test debut in 1899. Larwood was described as a 22-year-old with a very promising future.

Reporting on the 1927–8 domestic season in Australia, *The Cricketer* magazine notes:

> D. Bradman (N.S.W.) promises to develop into a real dasher. Bradman is very sound in his methods and the way he jumps to meet anything well up is refreshing. He is the latest recruit to the little band who have made a century in their first Shield match. Bradman charmed the Melbourne crowd by the easy and fearless manner in which he jumped out and drove Blackie to the fence.

The Ashes series of 1928–9 was one of two heavy-weights slogging it out. England had all the luck on their side in the first match (the first Test ever played in Brisbane). They not only caught Australia on a sticky wicket in the final innings, but the home side were forced to bat with two men absent. England thus began the rubber with a win by the huge margin of 675 runs. Thereafter the bat ruled. Hobbs and Sutcliffe had been reinforced by the emergence of Walter Hammond, the Gloucestershire all-rounder who was to succeed Hobbs as the most reliable batsman in England. He hit 905 runs in the series – a record. Australia had found two batsman of great potential in Don Bradman and Archie Jackson. Jackson made a century on his Test debut in the fourth match; Bradman scored two hundreds in this his first Test series. England won the rubber four matches to one, thus setting the scene for an exciting series in England in 1930. England won the opening Test at Trent Bridge; Australia won the second at Lord's. The third was a high-scoring draw and the fourth a rain-ruined one. The destiny of The Ashes therefore depended, as it had done in 1926, on the fifth and final Test at The Oval. It was arranged that the match would be a timeless one. England, on winning the toss, made the seemingly high score of 405. Australia capped that and were finally all out for 695. They went on to win by an innings in six days, one being washed out by rain.

The tour was a personal triumph for Bradman. He made a record 974 runs in the Test series (breaking Hammond's record), including a new highest Test score of 334, in the third match at Headingley. This Test record was added to his first-class record of 452 not out made for New South Wales against Queensland at Sydney the previous January.

Geoffrey Tebbutt of the Australian Press Association wrote:

Few cricketers have ever captured the public imagination like Bradman. His record-breaking feats, his astounding consistency, were alone, of course, enough to keep the mass sporting mind concentrated upon him in a season in which the rubber created such tremendous interest; but it was his youth, his romantic and meteoric rise to first-class rank, his utter imperturbability when confronting bowlers of world-wide renown, which caused him to become the most-talked-of man in England between May and August this year.

Pelham Warner, in his book of the 1930 series, simply stated: 'He seems to have brought run-getting to a certainty.' Over the next twenty years Bradman was to eliminate the word 'seems' from Warner's comment.

Bradman's batting was exceptional, but in both England and Australia pitches had become so bland during the 1920s that batting completely overwhelmed bowling. The scoring in the County Championship rose at an incredible rate and in 1928, a summer of slightly above average rainfall, 414 first-class centuries were recorded, 105 more than the previous summer. Five batsmen reached over 3,000 runs – only ten instances of such an aggregate had been logged in the history of first-class English cricket until then.

Drastic measures were required and before the start of the 1929 season it was agreed to increase the size of wickets by one inch in height and one inch in width, and also to adjudge batsmen out lbw even if the ball had hit the bat or hand before hitting the pad (this curious rule lasted for just five seasons). In addition, the rolling of pitches before innings was reduced from ten minutes to seven. These three regulations applied only to County Championship

THE HISTORY OF CRICKET

matches. In 1930 they also applied to Minor County matches, but the 1930 Australian touring team refused to allow the larger wickets for their matches. In March 1931, however, the Australian Board of Control stepped into line and sanctioned the use of the larger wicket.

BODYLINE

In Bradman cricket had thrown up a personality the like of which had not been seen since the heyday of Grace. In the Australian summer of 1931–2, when the South Africans toured Australia, Bradman's batting average in the Test series was 201.50. England were due to tour Australia in 1932–3; the editor of *Wisden* writing in January 1932 stated: 'At the end of the forthcoming season we have to send a team out to Australia and it would be idle to suggest that the undertaking is being approached with great confidence.'

The editor, C. Stewart Caine, felt that there was uncertainty about who should captain England, that apart from Larwood the bowling was thin, and that with Hobbs retiring, would a suitable partner be found to open with Sutcliffe?

As the summer of 1932 unfolded some optimism seeped into the English newspapers, and with hindsight it is worth quoting *The Cricketer* magazine of 17 September 1932: 'It is fashionable to run down our bowling, but, possibly, either Mr Brown, Verity or Mitchell might surprise their batsmen; there is Tate to keep a length and get one or two of their early batsmen out; nor should we forget Larwood and Voce of Nottingham and G.O. Allen.' This quote is also of interest in that Freddie Brown, an amateur, is given as 'Mr Brown' and Gubby Allen, another amateur, as 'G.O. Allen'; whereas the professionals are just surnames – Verity, Mitchell, Larwood and Voce.

So many books have been written – and are still being written – on the 1932–3 Ashes series (the so-called Bodyline tour), that in the public mind it remains the best remembered of all Test rubbers. Douglas

Don Bradman, the greatest batsman of all time and Australia's idol through the 1930s and 1940s. After he retired as a player, Bradman became a leading administrator in Australian cricket.

Jardine, the Oxford and Surrey amateur, was selected as England's captain at the beginning of July 1932 and spent the next two months in discussions with such cricketers as Percy Fender, the Surrey captain until 1931, Arthur Carr, the former England and current Nottinghamshire captain, and Frank Foster, the Warwickshire bowler who had used 'leg-theory' tactics in 1911. The consensus of opinion which Jardine garnered led him to believe that Bradman's Achilles' heel was fast bowling aimed at the leg stump. Nottinghamshire possessed in Harold Larwood the fastest and most accurate bowler in England as well as a very good contrasting partner in Bill Voce, who was left arm. Voce usually bowled round the wicket. The England touring party also included two other young fast bowlers, the Middlesex amateur Gubby Allen and the Yorkshire professional Bill Bowes.

The tour began with the normal warm-up games, three of which featured Bradman. He scored successively 3, 10, 36, 13, 18 and 23. He was omitted from the Australian team for the First Test, being declared unfit. Aside from a brave and quite brilliant innings of 187 by Stan McCabe, the Australian batsmen were completely out of their depth against Larwood. He took ten wickets and England won by ten wickets. The Australian crowds were well known for their barracking in the past, but it was obvious from the outset of the tour that the England captain, Jardine, had a contempt for Australians in general, and the crowds soon realised that in him they had discovered a perfect 'stage villain'. He was scrupulously fair in all his dealings, but he was brought up with the notion that colonials had to be kept in their place.

For the Second Test Bradman was fit; Jardine replaced the slow spin of Verity with Bowes, thus playing all four of his fast men. Australia batted first. The score was a modest 67 for two when Bradman came in. He was bowled first ball by Bowes, or rather, played on as he moved outside his off-stump to pull the ball to leg. In the second innings Bradman redeemed himself with a splendid 103 not out, the highest score in the game and one which won the contest for Australia.

With the series at one match each, there was tremendous interest in the Third Test played at Adelaide. England, batting first, made a poor start but recovered to reach 341. The ill-feeling which had been building up in Australia against the England side and their tactics burst out when Australia batted. The Australian captain, Bill Woodfull, was hit twice by deliveries from Larwood, and then the Australian wicketkeeper was hit on the head by a ball from the same bowler. Australia were dismissed 119 in arrears. Before the match had been terminated in England's favour, the Australian Board of Control sent the following cable to the MCC at Lord's:

BODY-LINE BOWLING HAS ASSUMED SUCH PROPORTIONS AS TO MENACE THE BEST INTERESTS OF THE GAME, MAKING PROTECTION OF THE BODY BY THE BATSMEN THE MAIN CONSIDERATION. THIS IS CAUSING INTENSELY BITTER FEELING BETWEEN THE PLAYERS AS WELL AS INJURY. IN OUR OPINION IT IS UNSPORTSMANLIKE. UNLESS STOPPED AT ONCE IT IS LIKELY TO UPSET THE FRIENDLY RELATIONS EXISTING BETWEEN AUSTRALIA AND ENGLAND.

Stan McCabe. The way he hooked the short-pitched
deliveries of Larwood and Voce during the Bodyline tour –
he hit 187 not out in the First Test – proved he possessed
extraordinary qualities as a batsman.

Harold Larwood, the
outstanding fast bowler
between the two World
Wars. His controversial
bowling during the 1932-3
tour to Australia is still
the subject of debate,
and that particular Test
series has provoked more
books than any other.

The MCC's reply began as follows: 'We, the Marylebone Cricket Club, deplore your cable. We deprecate your opinion that there has been unsportsmanlike play. We have fullest confidence in captain, team and managers and are convinced that they would do nothing to infringe either the Laws of Cricket or the spirit of the game.'

The MCC went on to say that if they felt it desirable the Australian Board should cancel the rest of the tour. This, however, the Australians declined to do. After two more cables it was agreed to set up a committee to discuss 'Bodyline'.

England went on to win the Fourth and Fifth Tests, taking the series four matches to one. The Australians brought in a new fast bowler, Harry Alexander, for the Fifth Test, but he was not very effective, taking one wicket for 54 runs. It was his sole Test appearance.

The tour may have ended, but the ill-feeling generated did not dissipate. Quite apart from cricketing matters there had been serious political problems between England and Australia for several years. Some commentators had hoped that the Test series might be the cause of an improvement in relations between the two countries and not the reverse. The world economic crisis of 1931 affected Britain more than many countries because it was so reliant on exports and its shipping trade. By the end of 1931, 2,900,000 – a fifth of all workers – were unemployed. The new National Government under Ramsay MacDonald decided on a policy of protectionism and placed a 10 per cent duty on all imported goods, but with exemption for Empire products. A special Imperial Conference met in Ottawa in 1932 to agree a system of exchange between Britain and the Dominions and colonies. Australia, however, instead of reducing tariffs on British goods entering the country, increased still further the duty paid on non-British imports. Britain at the same time would not place duties on imported foodstuffs, because of the general policy of keeping food prices in Britain down. Australia's economy was dealt a severe blow as the prices of the raw materials and foodstuffs which it exported went into a steep decline.

The Secretary of State for the Dominions was the Rt Hon. J.H. Thomas, while Lord Hailsham was both a cabinet minister and President of the MCC. Despite the volume of words written about this tour, it remains unclear what role the politicians played in deciding how the MCC should respond to the Australian Board of Control. It is worth noting that Lord Harris, for so long the effective controlling voice at Lord's, had died in March 1932, aged 81. The main conciliatory force during the hubbub was the Governor of South Australia, Sir Alexander Hore-Ruthven.

The sub-committee set up by the Australian Board to look into the ways of framing laws to eradicate Bodyline comprised four Australian Test players, Roger Hartigan, Bill Woodfull, Monty Noble and Vic Richardson. Its deliberations did not take long and on 21 April 1933 (before the England side had arrived home) the Australian Board cabled the MCC with a suitable amendment to the Law, but headed the cable with: 'Australian Board adopted following addition to Laws of Cricket in Australia.' The Laws had always been in the charge of the Marylebone Cricket Club, so this unilateral declaration was fighting talk.

The Australian Board's representative in England, Dr Robert Macdonald, made it clear that if the MCC did not agree with this Australian law amendment, then the proposed 1934 Australian tour to England might well be cancelled.[23]

The MCC did not bow to Australian pressure, however. They wrote back to the Australian Board saying that the Board was incorrect to use the term Bodyline. The English bowlers had not bowled at the batsmen's bodies, but had used 'leg-theory', bowling at the leg stump. It was the Australian batsmen who had converted the bowling to Bodyline by moving in front of the stumps to play the bowling.

The MCC proposed to consult the county captains during the 1933 English season and to view any dangerous 'leg-theory' bowling that occurred. However, they felt that dealing with the matter through cables was unsatisfactory and that a Special Meeting of the Imperial Cricket Conference should be called to discuss the problem.

The MCC then went on to the attack and told the Australian Board that the barracking that the English cricketers had been subjected to during the tour was thoroughly objectionable. Furthermore, the Board had apparently done nothing to prevent it. The MCC were of the view that if the barracking at this level continued they would consider whether they should send any more England sides to Australia.

Because of injury Larwood scarcely bowled in 1933 (though he played in 13 matches for Nottinghamshire as a batsman) and Voce took some time to recover from his winter's work. However, spectators in England did not have long to wait to see how 'leg-theory' worked. The best reported example was at the show-case match at Lord's between the Universities. Cambridge had in their side a very promising 22-year-old fast bowler, Ken Farnes. He bowled to a leg trap and hit several of the Oxford batsman. The *Wisden* report of the match contains the following: 'Grant also bowled round the wicket, but happily, although this style of attack was genuine leg-theory, it had no element of real danger until the second and third days when Farnes, inclined to drop the ball rather short, was on.'

Bill Bowes also employed 'leg-theory', knocking out Frank Watson when Yorkshire played Lancashire and Walter Keeton when Yorkshire opposed Nottinghamshire. Learie Constantine, the West Indian fast bowler, forced W.R. Hammond to retire hurt when the West Indies played England in the Second Test in 1933.

All these incidents occurred prior to the Imperial Cricket Conference meeting at Lord's. The MCC, having seen the consequences first-hand, began to change their mind. No definite decision was reached at the ICC meeting, but cables between the MCC and the Australian Board adopted a more gentle tone. The MCC were thus able to switch to the Australian viewpoint gradually and without loss of face.

The county captains met to discuss the whole issue. The result of their meeting was that it was felt unnecessary to change the Laws, but they agreed that direct attacks on the

---

23   Robert Macdonald (1870-1945) had played for Queensland, but in 1908 emigrated to England, setting up a dental practice in Leicester. He was Honorary Secretary of Leicestershire CCC in 1922-9 and 1937-9, but also represented Australia at ICC meetings.

batsman by bowlers was against the spirit of the game. The Australians accepted that the captains would make sure that Bodyline bowling was not used in 1934 and the Australian side set sail for England on 9 March 1934.

The three main actors on the English side in the Bodyline drama – Jardine, Larwood and Voce – were not part of the 1933–4 winter of cable, counter-cable and meetings. Jardine was in India as captain of an England Second Eleven (only Jardine and Verity of the 1932–3 Australian trip were part of this side); Larwood and Voce remained in their Nottinghamshire homes.

Both Jardine and Larwood had had books published during 1933 firmly defending 'leg-theory' bowling. Was either of them happy that the MCC had performed a U-turn? Jardine saved the Club any embarrassment by giving an interview to an Indian newspaper saying that he would not play for England in the forthcoming Ashes series. He gave no reason for his statement.

Larwood reported fit to bowl for the 1934 campaign. The press were keen that he should play for England, but the MCC implied that the Selectors would not choose him unless he made some sort of apology for the way he had bowled in Australia. This he refused to do. When the England team for the First Test was being picked, Larwood suffered a 'diplomatic' injury. He played for his county on the same date as the Test was staged. Just before the Second Test, the Lancashire team complained that Larwood and Voce had bowled 'leg-theory' against them; the Chairman of Lancashire was T.A. Higson, who was also a Test Selector. The Nottinghamshire captain, A.W. Carr, along with both Larwood and Voce, issued statements to the press attacking the inconsistencies in the MCC's stance. This effectively closed the Test door to both bowlers.

Australia went on to win the Test series two matches to one. Bradman's batting average for the series was 94.75; the best by an Englishman, Maurice Leyland, was 68.28.

The editor of *Wisden* covering the 1934 summer began his review with: 'No matter the angle from which it may be viewed it is next to impossible to regard the cricket season of 1934 as other than unpleasant ... I deplored the attitude of a certain section of the press in what seemed to me an insane desire constantly to stir up strife.'

The 'difficulties' with the press had been increasing ever since the war. Even in the first post-war Ashes series, Rockley Wilson, an amateur touring as part of the England team, had caused controversy by his reports on the matches, in which he criticised English tactics. Before the war it was common for one or two of the amateurs to earn money by reporting the matches in which they took part. The journalists in the 1930s tried to obtain sensational stories from professionals. Australia was not immune from the press either: for some weeks before the 1932–3 series, Don Bradman was involved in a dispute with the Australian Board, as to whether he could play in the Tests and report the games.

There were no examples of 'leg-theory' bowling in County Championship matches in 1935, and in 1936 Bill Voce made his peace with the MCC and resumed his international career. Larwood had made it clear that he did not wish to take part in Test cricket, though he was the outstanding bowler in first-class English cricket in 1936. Jardine did not continue in Championship cricket after 1933, but his final first-class appearance did not take place until 1948, for an England XI against Glamorgan.

BRADMAN'S DOMINATION

Gubby Allen was appointed captain of the 1936–7 MCC side touring Australia. Bradman took over as Australia's captain. England made a splendid start to the Test series, winning the first two games, with Voce picking up 17 wickets and Allen 12. Bradman's innings were 38 & 0, 0 & 82. Thereafter the rubber belonged to Bradman. In the Third Test he hit 270, in the Fourth 212 and in the Fifth 169. Australia won all three, thus taking The Ashes by three wins to two. Public interest in the Tests was enormous and broke the attendance records that had been set during the previous series. In contrast, interest in the MCC matches

Rockley Wilson, a master at Winchester College and occasional county cricketer for Yorkshire. At the age of 41, he was unexpectedly chosen to tour Australia in 1920-1 and made his Test debut that winter. However, he caused problems by sending reports of the tour to the press, and as a result future cricketers were banned from reporting England matches in which they were taking part.

against the State sides dwindled and the MCC were accused of employing these matches purely for practice. The divide between first-class and Test cricket was widening.

It is impossible to say how much of the increase in the crowds was due to the presence of Don Bradman, but William Pollock, reporting the tour for the *Daily Express*, wrote:

And he (Bradman) is probably the greatest gate attraction cricket has ever seen – a far greater money-spinner at the turnstiles than were WG, Ranji, Jack Hobbs. Nearly £30,000 was taken at the gates in the third Test in Melbourne. I should say that Bradman drew at least £2,000 into the ground when there was a prospect of him batting. Yet all 'the King of Australia' (as he is called) gets is, say, £5 a day – which is precisely what Sievers, Ward, Rigg – others who do not draw a penny to the gates are paid. It is all slightly absurd. What would happen if Bradman thought he would go on strike and not play unless he was paid, say, a thousand pounds per Test? The Board of Control would throw a fit and run round in circles – but they would have to pay up. The crowds would not come if Bradman were not playing.

Len Hutton, the Yorkshire and England opening batsman, who created a new Test record of 364 in 1938 and later became the first professional picked to captain England in the 20th century.

Pollock is incorrect about W.G. Grace, who attracted more attention, but Bradman comes second only to WG.

Australia's next tour of England was in 1938. If anything Bradman dominated the proceedings to an even greater extent than on his previous visits. He captained the side. His first-class average for the summer, 115.66, was the highest ever recorded; his Test average was 108.50. He scored a century in each of the three Tests in which he batted; the Old Trafford Test was totally washed out by rain and, at The Oval, he twisted an ankle and could not bat in either innings. The first two Tests were drawn; Australian won the Test at Headingley and England overwhelmed the visitors at The Oval, when Len Hutton, the young Yorkshire opening batsman, created a new Test record, making 364. England went on to reach 903 for 7 declared. Australia had both Bradman and Fingleton injured and unable to bat. The match result was thus a foregone conclusion long before the official end. With the rubber tied one win each, Australia retained The Ashes. The next meeting of the two countries was scheduled for Australia in 1940–1, but the Second World War intervened.

COUNTY FINANCES

If record receipts and attendances were being established for England vs. Australia matches, the public's enthusiasm for cricket at English first-class level was not so keen. In the seasons of 1935 and 1936 every single first-class county made a loss on its normal trading, and these losses were only partly off-set by the handouts from international cricket. For 1934, 1935 and 1936, even with the Test Match handouts, only seven of the 17 counties showed a profit over the three seasons. Matters were particularly serious for Sussex; the report on the 1936 season included the following paragraph:

> Wensley, after promising great things with an innings of 106 not out against Cambridge, could not keep his place in the side. During the winter Sussex decided to dispense with his services and also those of Greenwood, Pearce and George Cox (senior) who had charge of the Hove nursery.[24] The loss of £2,000 last year, increasing their overdraft to £6,000, promoted this action on the part of the County Club, whose Secretary and Assistant-Secretary voluntarily assented to salary cuts to assist in a financial recovery. The players followed suit in agreeing to a reduction of wages.

Similarly the report for Leicestershire for 1934 noted:

> The one distressing feature of the season was in the matter of finance … Indeed, on the occasion of Shipman's benefit the attendances were so poor that the player found himself some £60 out of pocket as a result of the match … During the season a suggestion was made that Leicestershire should amalgamate with Lincolnshire, but naturally nothing came of the proposal and the Leicestershire authorities decided to carry on in the hope of better support in the future. (An appeal later cleared their £5,000 debt).

In March 1937, the Advisory County Cricket Committee asked the MCC to appoint a Commission to investigate the problems facing county cricket. The Commission was led by William Findley, who had recently retired as Secretary to the MCC. The Commission duly reported its findings and recommendations a year later, only to have its most controversial points rejected by the counties, including the reduction of the Championship from 17 to 15 county teams. The counties did, however, recommend increasing the number of balls per over to eight, a point not suggested by the Commission. (The eight-ball over was used in the County Championship in 1939 and in some wartime matches, but in 1946 the counties reverted to six balls.)

LEAGUE AND CLUB CRICKET

The number of 'overseas stars' featuring in county cricket did not increase, despite the success of Ted McDonald, the Australian fast bowler with Lancashire. Instead some overseas players and quite a number of competent first-class county men preferred cricket in the leagues. The outstanding figure in the Lancashire League was the West Indian all-rounder Learie Constantine. He played for Nelson in the 1930s, and the club

---

24   In common with other first-class counties, Sussex had a 'nursery', i.e., a number of young paid players under the tuition of a coach.

regularly attracted larger crowds for their Saturday matches than those attending the average inter-county game. Constantine was paid about £25 per match (for a Saturday afternoon); England Test players in 1934 were paid £40 per Test (i.e., £10 per day). Nelson CC had a membership of about 2,000 in the 1930s, larger than several of the first-class counties, while Rawtenstall CC's membership was nearly 3,000. The Central Lancashire League, particularly the Rochdale Club, proved equally prosperous in the inter-war period. Over in Yorkshire, the Bradford League was shorn of its First World War stars, but its home-grown professionals played very keen cricket which was watched by large crowds. Other leagues that flourished were the Birmingham League and the North Staffordshire.

In the South of England no major leagues existed; the Club Cricket Conference continued to assist clubs with fixture problems and advise on such matters as third-party insurance. It was designed 'to foster amateur cricket on non-competitive lines'. The Conference picked representative sides to oppose such teams as the Royal Navy, the Army and the MCC.

Immediately after the First World War Oxford and Cambridge nurtured a number of cricketers destined for notable England careers. Douglas Jardine and Percy Chapman were famous examples. There was a trough in the mid-1920s, but in 1930 the University Match included Freddie Brown, the Nawab of Pataudi and Alan Melville, all later Test captains. Public interest in the University Match declined. In 1932, 24,000 paid during the three days, in 1939 the number was 15,663, and it was noted that this was a considerable improvement on the three or four preceding games.

The redbrick universities were beginning to build up their cricketing strength. The Universities Athletic Union (UAU) was founded and in 1927 inaugurated a knock-out competition, Manchester being the first Champions. There was also a representative side which played a limited number of games, including one against the Club Cricket Conference.

Despite the demise of country house cricket (except in isolated pockets), most of the wandering clubs founded before 1914 were revived in 1919, and yet another clutch was hatched. The most notable, with year of formation, were the Invalids (1920), Gloucestershire Gypsies (1922), Googlies (1923), Grasshoppers (1924), Stragglers of Asia (1925), Jesters (1928), Romany (1929), Arabs (1935) and Forty (1936).

Amongst the handful of the country house sides, the most famous was Sir Julien Cahn's team, based at Stanford Hall on the Nottinghamshire/Leicestershire border. Cahn was reputed to spend about £30,000 per year in the 1930s on cricket and ran a team, comprising mainly young county amateurs and young overseas players, which was as good as the lesser first-class counties. Indeed, on several occasions the team opposed first-class counties in three-day matches, as well as playing all the first-class touring sides to England in the 1930s, except Australia. Through his generosity both the Nottinghamshire and Leicestershire county clubs were kept financially viable. Other upholders of country house cricket included

Hubert Martineau of Holyport, near Maidenhead; Sir Walter Lawrence at Hyde Hall, Sawbridgeworth; and Fred Hunter at Bystock, near Exmouth.

Public school cricket, with the two-day Eton vs. Harrow match at Lord's its highlight, continued to flourish. In fact the number of schools featured in *Wisden* almost doubled between 1914 and 1939, when the number reached 102 and the *Almanack* devoted 90 pages to reports, scores and averages.

THE WRITTEN WORD

One place in which cricket still ruled the English sporting world was the written word. The press devoted much space to cricket at all levels, with local daily papers giving the detailed scores of club matches in their area as well as the national press covering international and County Championship matches. The number of books published increased throughout the inter-war period. The *Wisden* covering 1939 listed over 100 cricket books in print and available from English bookshops.

The reporting of cricket matches was transformed – from the careful, plodding description of each innings – by the pen of the *Manchester Guardian* correspondent, Neville Cardus, whose stint as cricket reporter began shortly after the First World War. His reports have been described as literary essays and though some readers found his similes high-flown, his style made an impact on most of his contemporaries. R.C. Robertson-Glasgow, the Oxford and Somerset cricketer, was a journalist with, successively, the *Morning Post*, *The Daily Telegraph*, and *The Observer* in the 1930s, and wrote in a manner both lyrical and humorous. Pelham Warner preceded Robertson-Glasgow at the *Morning Post* and founded and edited the only national weekly cricket magazine of the time, *The Cricketer*, which began publication in 1921. These three had their newspaper contributions reprinted in book form.

The period also saw the publication of *A History of Cricket* by H.S. Altham, which had first appeared in serial form in *The Cricketer*. Altham set a new standard for such a work, the detail of which was heavily reliant on the researches of F.S. Ashley-Cooper and H.T. Waghorn. The former of these was the major statistical and historical expert on cricket from about 1902 until his death in 1932. An historian with more imagination and greater erudition was P.F. Thomas, whose series *Old English Cricket* came out in six booklets between 1923 and 1929. In 1935 and 1937, G.B. Buckley published two books containing a mass of fresh data gleaned from pre-1837 newspapers.

DOMESTIC CRICKET IN AUSTRALIA

In Australia between the wars the Sheffield Shield continued as the principal domestic competition. Queensland joined the Shield in the 1926–7 season and thus from 1927–8 there were 24 Shield games per season, six for each state. There were very few full-time professional cricketers. Australian Test players were paid at about the same rate per international as English ones, but the fees they received for playing Sheffield Shield cricket were little more than nominal. Luckily, players with a job did not need a lot of time off work, unless they were in the Test team.

Between 1919–20 and 1939–40, New South Wales and Victoria each won the Shield nine times; South Australia won three times. Victoria created a new record by scoring 1,107 in one innings against New South Wales in 1926–7; and in 1929–30 Bradman (as noted previously) hit 452 not out for New South Wales against Queensland, another record. The Shield games had been timeless; in 1927–8 this was changed to four days, with 5 ½ hours' play per day. The eight-ball over was established throughout the period and was popular, with no move to revert to six-ball overs. Indeed it was not until the 1979–80 season that Sheffield Shield matches changed to six-ball overs.

Australian club cricket usually comprised matches played over two Saturdays, with four hours' play on each day. Schools cricket, which is mainly state-controlled, had its own organisation, which provided a direct route to District and State cricket.

In an article in the 1935 *Wisden*, the Australian Judge, H.V. Evatt, described how Australian cricket was currently run and pointed out how democratic it was in comparison with the English system. Any resident in Melbourne or Sydney was free to join his District club. He could then vote for the club's delegate to the State Association, and the Committee of the State Association elected representatives on to the Australian Board of Control. In England much of the power still rested with the MCC, whose membership elected their own Committee. However, the membership was limited to a given ceiling and, with certain exceptions – mainly public school or university players – there was a long waiting list.

NOTABLE CRICKETERS

The cricket world was dominated by Don Bradman from 1930. His career figures dwarf not only those of his contemporaries, but of all who came before and after him. Critics have complained that he was not the greatest stylist, but that slight criticism meant little to his legion of admirers. Second to Bradman among Australian batsmen were Charles Macartney, whose career spilled over from pre-war days, then Bill Ponsford, who for a brief moment set new batting records, and lastly Stan McCabe.

Of the fast bowlers, the pair of Gregory and McDonald were by far the most outstanding. The trio of slower bowlers who were most successful at Test level were all leg-break specialists: Clarrie Grimmett, Arthur Mailey and Bill O'Reilly. Bradman commented that Grimmett bowled like a miser and Mailey like a millionaire: Grimmett's length was perfect, while Mailey had a vicious spin and a well-concealed 'wrong-un'. Of the three Bradman placed O'Reilly on a pedestal by himself.

England began the post-war era with three great professionals: Jack Hobbs, Frank Woolley and Wilfred Rhodes. Robertson-Glasgow commented: 'Hobbs was the greatest English batsman I've seen and tried to remove. He was the most perfectly equipped by art and temperament for any style of innings on any sort of wicket against any quality of opposition.' Hobbs's career, which had begun for Surrey in 1905, closed in 1934, when he was 51. By that time he had overtaken Grace's records of most runs and most hundreds in a first-class career (his record still stands) and he was the first man to reach 5,000 runs in Test cricket. In England he was generally referred to as 'The Master'

Batsmen scoring over 4,000 Test runs at an average of 50.00 or more (to September 1996)

	Tests	Innings	Not out*	Runs	Highest	Average	100s
D.G. Bradman (Australia)	52	80	10	6,996	334	99.94	29
H. Sutcliffe (England)	54	84	9	4,555	194	60.73	16
K.F. Barrington (England)	82	131	15	6,806	256	58.67	20
E.D. Weekes (West Indies)	48	81	5	4,455	207	58.61	15
W.R. Hammond (England)	85	140	16	7,249	336*	58.45	22
G.St A. Sobers (West Indies)	93	160	21	8,032	365*	57.78	26
J.B. Hobbs (England)	61	102	7	5,410	211	56.94	15
L. Hutton (England)	79	138	15	6,971	364	56.67	19
G.S. Chappell (Australia)	87	151	19	7,110	247*	53.86	24
Javed Miandad (Pakistan)	124	189	21	8,832	280*	52.57	23
S.M. Gavaskar (India)	125	214	16	10,122	236*	51.12	34
A.R. Border (Australia)	156	265	44	11,174	205	50.56	27
S.R. Waugh (Australia)	81	125	26	5,002	200	50.52	11
I.V.A. Richards (West Indies)	121	182	12	8,540	291	50.23	24
D.C.S. Compton (England)	78	131	15	5,807	278	50.06	17

Frank Woolley had started with Kent in 1906 and was also 51 when he retired, in 1938. A left-handed batsman, he was an accomplished left-arm bowler, either medium pace or slow. A brilliant slip field, he still holds the record for the most catches by a non-wicketkeeper in a first-class career.

Wilfred Rhodes was the great slow left-arm bowler, who also developed into a very effective opening batsman. His talents have previously been noted in the pre-war era, since his career began for Yorkshire in 1898. He continued until 1930, by which time he was the only bowler to take 4,000 first-class wickets, a pinnacle still unique to him.

The two outstanding English batsmen whose careers began in the early post-war days were Herbert Sutcliffe, the Yorkshireman who opened for England with Hobbs; and Walter Hammond, born in Dover, but whose cricket was for Gloucestershire. Bradman noted of Hammond: 'He was a batsman of the classical, majestic school. Of lovely athletic build, light as a ballet dancer on his feet, always beautifully balanced, Hammond was the outstanding batsman between 1918 and 1938.' (Bradman overlooks Jack Hobbs, who was England's premier batsman until 1927.)

Herbert Sutcliffe (left), with his Yorkshire opening partner Percy Holmes, put on a record 555 for the first wicket against Essex in 1932. He formed an equally successful partnership for England with Jack Hobbs. A very talented defensive batsman on bad wickets, he was just as much at home as a fast-scoring player on easier pitches.

Wilfred Rhodes (right), who played for Yorkshire from 1898 to 1930, captured a record 4,204 first-class wickets and developed from a modest batsman to perform the 'Double' 16 times.

Robertson-Glasgow wrote an illuminating paragraph on Sutcliffe:

Herbert Sutcliffe is the serenest batsman I have known. Whatever may have passed under that calm brow – anger, joy, disagreements, surprise, relief, triumph – no outward sign was betrayed on the field of play. He was understood, over two thousand years in advance, by the Greek philosophers. They called this character megalo-psychic. It is the sort of man who would rather miss a train than run for it, and so be seen in disorder and heard breathing heavily.

The outstanding English fast bowler was Harold Larwood, and of the slower practitioners, Bradman points to the left-arm spinner Hedley Verity, the man who took over Wilfred Rhodes's post for Yorkshire. Hammond commented: 'Now hostility is not at all the same thing as say Bodyline. It marked Verity's bowling – he talked with his fingers – and he was a man who bowled as if in a mental abstraction, the batsman being just the obstacle. He had that quality which never lets a batsman rest, never allows him an easy stroke.'

'Tich' Freeman, the Kent leg-break bowler, who played from 1914 to 1936, broke many county records and was the only bowler to top 300 wickets in an English first-class season. He had a perfect length, but his guile never really disturbed the great Australian batsman.

The Second World War was to prove a watershed as far as English and Australian Test bowlers were concerned, but several young batsmen – such as Len Hutton, Denis Compton and Bill Edrich of England, and Lindsay Hassett and Sid Barnes of Australia – were to re-establish themselves in post-Second World War cricket.

THE HISTORY OF CRICKET

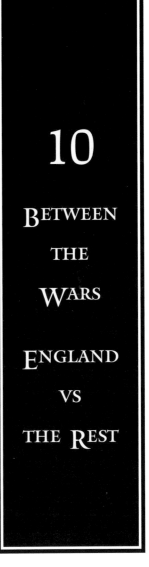

The battle for The Ashes, the great Bodyline controversy and the amazing Don Bradman filled the sports pages and the cricketing public's imagination. The press were either having a post-mortem on a rubber just completed, or attempting to forecast the outcome of the next encounter. In the years between Australian tours to England, the other sides touring England were used to try out potential candidates for the serious matches against Australia.

International cricket between the six countries who, by 1939, comprised the Test-playing nations was very much a case of England versus each of the others. The number of tours between the other five was very limited. England (or the MCC to be technically correct) sent 12 touring sides in total to India, New Zealand, South Africa and the West Indies, and received the same number in return. The table below lists all the other main tours, excluding interchanges between Australia and New Zealand (the former treating New Zealand on about a par with Tasmania).

Major tours undertaken by the Test-playing nations between the wars, other than those involving England

Home Country	Visiting Country	
Australia	South Africa (1)	West Indies (1)
South Africa	Australia (1 full, 1 half)	
India	Australia (privately organised)	
West Indies	Nil	
New Zealand	South Africa (1 half)	No full tours

The five countries were involved in only six Test series among themselves, of which three were Australia vs. South Africa. The table reveals starkly how The Ashes series dominated cricket and why even South Africa who, with England and Australia, were joint founders of the Imperial Cricket Conference, did not loom large in the minds of the general public, in England at least.

The Imperial Cricket Conference was not then the annual meeting of minds that it has now become. After 1912, it did not reconvene again until 1921, when the main item of business was the use in Australia of the eight-ball over. The next meeting took place at Lord's on 31 May 1926; apart from the three founders, India, New Zealand and the West Indies were represented. It is evident that the man who got the six

10

BETWEEN

THE

WARS

ENGLAND

VS

THE REST

countries round the table was Lord Harris. New Zealand had possessed a central governing body for cricket prior to the war, but the West Indies' Board of Control had only been created a few months before while the MCC were touring the Caribbean and – was it a coincidence? – Lord Harris was on holiday in Trinidad. The Board was formed by the Hon. Laurie Yearwood and H.B.G. Austin of Barbados and A.C. O'Dowd of British Guiana. India had no Board of Control, but prior to the ICC meeting, Lord Harris, who represented England, informed the other delegates that he wanted India represented (and that was that). So the ICC expanded from three to six countries, and the meeting agreed that a set of draft rules for the body should be prepared and another meeting held in about eight weeks to ratify those rules. At this latter meeting, Lord Harris took the chair and among other rules defined a Test Match as 'a match played between sides duly selected by recognised governing bodies of cricket representing countries within the Empire'.

The definition was, to put it mildly, a loose one and led to the very strange situation in which, in the winter of 1929–30, two MCC sides, neither representing the full England strength, simultaneously toured the West Indies and New Zealand and both played official Test Matches. Be that as it may, cricket has to thank Lord Harris for the way he bulldozed the game into rapid expansion at its highest level, no doubt believing that it would bind three more countries to the Empire and one day those three countries would reach the same cricketing standard as England and Australia. It took a long time, but Lord Harris was right, in his way, on both counts. The winning of the 1996 World Cup by Sri Lanka, the holding of that event on the South Asian subcontinent and the participation of so many members of the former Empire is Lord Harris's legacy.

SOUTH AFRICA

Although it had been one of the founder members of the Imperial Cricket Conference, South Africa cannot be ranked at the same level as either England or Australia during the inter-war period. As the leading administrator in South Africa pointed out in 1927, there was a major problem. H.L. Crockett, Chairman of Natal Cricket Association, noted:

> The question of turf wickets in South Africa is, in the writer's opinion, one of paramount importance to South African cricket viewed from an international standpoint. If South Africa intends to keep her place as one of the 'Big Three' in world cricket, it behoves her to leave no stone unturned to prepare and train her players up to the high standard required of this ambition. If she does not, she may find herself displaced by other countries whose cricket is in the ascending scale ... South Africa has laboured under a severe handicap in the Tests she has played against England and Australia in those countries because South African players have learnt all their cricket on matting wickets.

Crockett himself believed in actions as well as words, for, in the same year, Natal had created a turf wicket at their headquarters in Durban. He gradually persuaded the other Provinces that his comments made sense. In Cape Town a grass pitch was used for Test cricket for the first time in 1930–1, Johannesburg pitches were of grass for the Currie Cup in 1934–5. When the MCC toured South Africa in 1938–9 the only major games they played on matting were in neighbouring Rhodesia.

Initially there was a snag attached to the turf pitches: they were much too bland. They were bland in Australia, too, but there the occasional 'sticky dog'[25] gave them some variety. In South Africa the batsmen seemed in total control. In the Test series against England in 1938–9, the scores grew until, in the final Test, the match dragged on for ten days and was still a draw, because the England team had to leave to catch the boat home (see pages 174–5). No less than 14 batsmen in that series averaged more than 40 per innings. The leading South African bowler, Eric Dalton, managed a wicket for every 38 runs he conceded and even the best English bowler, Hedley Verity, averaged 29 runs per victim.

The overall results achieved by South Africa in Tests between 1919 and 1939 bear out H.L. Crockett's concern. South Africa played 15 inter-war Tests in England and won just two. Of the 13 Tests they played against Australia, Australia won ten, and the rest were drawn.

As in the pre-1914 period the major domestic competition in South Africa remained the Currie Cup. During the 1920s, the competition was dominated by Transvaal, so much so that the Transvaal Test cricketer Fred Susskind wrote:

> One cannot help being impressed by the imposing part which the Transvaal has played in South African cricket, as well as by the almost immeasurable superiority she has shown over all her opponents. At any time during these years she could have placed a second eleven in the field capable of doing almost as well as her first eleven – capable, at any rate, of beating any one of the other Provinces.

In order to level down Transvaal, in 1937 a portion of the Province was turned into a separate cricketing entity, North Eastern Transvaal Cricket Union, which fielded its own Currie Cup side. Apart from the two Transvaals, the other inter-war Currie Cup sides were Western Province, Natal, Griqualand West, Orange Free State, Eastern Province and Border, plus Rhodesia, who took part only in 1930–1 and 1931–2. The Rhodesian correspondent to the official *History of South African Cricket*, vol. 3, commented: 'From then (1931–2) the Colony had little encouragement and less co-operation from Union centres to continue in this (Currie Cup) sphere.'

While England had lost great hordes of the population to soccer, in South Africa the game of rugby was increasingly more popular than cricket, not least because it was cheaper to play.

---

25 A sticky dog is a pitch which has become soft and very difficult after rain.

The longest Test: ten days and still drawn, South Africa vs. England 1938–9 (5th Test)

Played at Kingsmead, Durban, on 3, 4, 5, 6, 7, 8, 9, 10, 11 (no play), 13, 14 March.
Toss: South Africa. Result: MATCH DRAWN

South Africa	1st innings			2nd innings	
A. Melville (capt)	hit wkt b Wright	78	(6)	b Farnes	103
P.G.V. van der Bijl	b Perks	125		c Paynter b Wright	97
E.A.B. Rowan	lbw b Perks	33		c Edrich b Verity	0
B. Mitchell	b Wright	11	(1)	hit wkt b Verity	89
A.D. Nourse	b Perks	103	(4)	c Hutton b Farnes	25
K.G. Viljoen	c Ames b Perks	0	(5)	b Perks	74
E.L. Dalton	c Ames b Farnes	57		c and b Wright	21
R.E. Grieveson (wkt)	b Perks	75		b Farnes	39
A.C.B. Langton	c Paynter b Verity	27		c Hammond b Farnes	6
E.S. Newson	c and b Verit	1		b Wright	3
N. Gordon	not out	0		not out	7
Extras	(B2, LB12, NB6)	20		(B5, LB8, NB4)	17
Total		**530**			**481**

England	1st innings			2nd innings	
L. Hutton	run out	38		b Mitchell	55
P.A. Gibb	c Grieveson b Newson	4		b Dalton	120
E. Paynter	lbw b Langton	62	(5)	c Grieveson b Gordon	75
W.R. Hammond (capt)	st Grieveson b Dalton	24		st Grieveson b Dalton	140
L.E.G. Ames (wkt)	c Dalton b Langton	84	(6)	not out	17
W.J. Edrich	c Rowan b Langton	1	(3)	c Gordon b Langton	219
B.H. Valentine	st Grieveson b Dalton	26		not out	4
H. Verity	b Dalton	3			
D.V.P. Wright	c Langton b Dalton	26			
K. Farnes	b Newson	20			
R.T.D. Perks	not out	2			
Extras	(B7, LB17, W1, NB1)	26		(B8, LB12, W1, NB3)	24
				(5 wickets)	
Total		**316**			**654**

THE HISTORY OF CRICKET

The longest Test *continued*

England	1st innings				2nd innings			
	O	M	R	W	O	M	R	W
Farnes	46	9	108	1	22.1	2	74	4
Perks	41	5	100	5	32	6	99	1
Wright	37	6	142	2	32	7	146	3
Verity	55.6	14	97	2	40	9	87	2
Hammond	14	4	34	0	9	1	30	0
Edrich	9	2	29	0	6	1	18	0
Hutton					1	0	10	0

South Africa	1st innings				2nd innings			
Newson	25.6	5	58	2	43	4	91	0
Langton	35	12	71	3	56	12	132	1
Gordon	37	7	82	0	55.2	10	174	1
Mitchell	7	0	20	0	37	4	133	1
Dalton	13	1	59	4	27	3	100	2

Fall of wickets	SA	E	SA	E
Wkt	1st	1st	2nd	2nd
1st	131	9	191	78
2nd	219	64	191	358
3rd	236	125	191	447
4th	274	169	242	611
5th	278	171	346	650
6th	368	229	382	–
7th	475	245	434	–
8th	522	276	450	–
9th	523	305	462	–
10th	530	316	481	–

Of the three South African tours to England – 1924, 1929 and 1935 – only the last one made a financial profit. The first tour party comprised has-beens; the second, which contained only three of the first party, was made up of promising youngsters; while the third saw many of those youngsters flourish, having gained experience, notably Ken Viljoen and Bruce Mitchell as batsmen and Bob Crisp as a fast bowler. Mention must also be made of the two Nourses, father and son. 'Dave' Nourse (1878–1948) had a first-class career spanning 1896 to 1936, and he played in 45 Tests as a very sound batsman. His son, Dudley (born 1910), played from 1931 to 1952, including 34 Tests, and was another outstanding batsman.

THE WEST INDIES

The West Indies possessed one man who, above all others, could see beyond the individual colony in which he resided. He was H.B.G. Austin, a member of the Barbados aristocracy, whose family had grown wealthy through their sugar plantations. He was one of five brothers who played first-class cricket in the West Indies and it is probable that he would have captained the 1900 West Indian side to England had he not been fighting in the Boer War. As it was, he led the 1906 and the 1923 teams to England. Learie Constantine noted in his autobiography: 'He managed West Indies cricket alone and it has never been so well managed since. To me personally he has been immensely kind (though I believe he is a little cold, not so much because of my turning professional as for my deserting, as it seems

Learie Constantine typified the exuberance of West Indian cricket with his fast bowling, attacking batsmanship and electric fielding. Coming to England, Constantine made himself a household name in the Lancashire leagues.

to him, West Indies cricket.)' Austin was knighted in 1935, when he was Speaker of the Barbados House of Assembly. As was noted in Chapter 9, Constantine moved to England to join the Lancashire League. As a result, he was not available for the West Indian tour to England in 1933, except when released by Rochdale.

The principal inter-colonial tournament in the West Indies remained the same as before 1914, involving Barbados, Trinidad and British Guiana (Jamaica being too far away to compete). Picking a team to go to England for 1923 was thus none too easy. There was no way of comparing Jamaican players with those in the three other colonies and, even worse, the two major bowlers – George Francis (Barbados) and George John (Trinidad) – were classed as professionals and excluded from the tournament. Francis was picked for the tour, which was just as well, since he was easily the side's best bowler. No Tests were played and the team, which attracted little notice from the public, returned a modest record.

The first post-war MCC tour to the West Indies took place in 1925–6, the English side being of strong county standard. Three matches were played against representative West Indian sides. The MCC won one; the other two were drawn.

F.S. Gough-Calthorpe, the touring captain, reported back to the MCC that in his opinion the West Indies were equal in strength to South Africa and were deserving of Test Match status: effectively this was confirmed at the May 1926 ICC meeting (previously noted).

In 1928, therefore, when the West Indies returned to tour England, a series of three Test Matches was on the fixture list. All three were lost. The team were handicapped because the one top-class wicketkeeper, George Dewhurst, had to cry off and his absence, added to poor slip fielding, meant that the fast bowlers lost heart. Learie Constantine, who performed the 'Double', was the one player to go home with an enhanced reputation.

The second post-war MCC visit, which came in 1929–30, was a very high-scoring tour. Four Tests were played. The series was tied one all, with the other match drawn, when the final Test (to be played to a definite result) began. The match lasted nine days, and, like the later one in South Africa, had to be abandoned as a draw, because the English side's boat home was scheduled. The improvement from the West Indies viewpoint was largely due to the emergence of a young Jamaican batsman, George Headley. He hit 703 runs in the Tests at an average of 87.87. The English side, however, lacked the current top-class players, such as Harold Larwood, Maurice Tate, Walter Hammond and Herbert Sutcliffe.

Charles Macartney, the former Australian Test batsman, was impressed by the growing strength of the West Indies and persuaded the Australian Board of Control to arrange for a West Indian tour to Australia the following season. Much would depend on the ability of Constantine and Headley. Bradman noted later:

> Constantine became a great favourite with the crowds in Australia as he did in other countries and without hesitation I rank him the greatest all-round fieldsman ever seen... One could understand why his name became first on the list of all Lancashire League cricketers. In this class of cricket, where matches are decided in one afternoon, I cannot envisage a player with better qualifications. In a quarter of an hour of terrific speed bowling or unorthodox hitting he could swing the fortunes of a match.

From that description Constantine was a man born before his time, since he would have made an ideal One-Day International cricketer. On this trip to Australia he did little in the Tests: his career Test record shows a batting average of 19 and a bowling average of 30.

Headley duly topped the 1,000 run mark for the tour, but he could not carry the side and Australia won the series by four matches to one. The tour lost money. It was 21 years before the West Indies returned.

Headley enjoyed two very successful tours to England, in 1933 and 1939, being by a long way the outstanding batsman on each visit. Constantine, who had missed the 1933 tour, returned in 1939 and took over 100 first-class wickets. England won both series. The MCC tour to the West Indies between these two dates provided the West Indies with their first rubber. They beat England by two matches to one. Headley scored 270 not out in the final crucial Test, which the West Indies went on to win by an innings. The MCC touring party lacked one or two key players; nevertheless, it was a great milestone in West Indian cricket.

Before leaving West Indian cricket, mention should be made of the inter-war English tours financed privately. These were of particular help to isolated Jamaica. Five of these trips were confined purely to that island, three being organised by Lionel Tennyson, the Hampshire captain and grandson of the poet. The sides brought out by Tennyson were as powerful as the MCC teams and gave Jamaican cricketers, including young Headley, as good a testing as if the island had been competing in the West Indian annual tournament.

NEW ZEALAND

New Zealand cricket suffered from being a satellite of Australia, to the extent that a touring team from New Zealand to its large neighbour attracted no attention. The public ignored it and the State sides put out second elevens. On the other hand, plenty of Australian teams were keen to come to New Zealand. New South Wales, Victoria and Melbourne CC all visited in the 1920s and played major matches. The Australian Board sent a strong team in 1920–1, which was watched by large crowds and overwhelmed the local teams. Vernon Ransford, who led the Australian tourists, advised the New Zealand Cricket Council that more money was needed to provide better grounds and coaching; schools also needed to be encouraged to improve their game.

The MCC sent their first post-war side out in 1922–3, under the veteran Test captain Archie MacLaren. Like the Australians it returned home undefeated, but the enormous cost of travelling meant a financial loss of £1,929.

The costs clearly concerned the New Zealand Council, especially as their principal objective was to send a New Zealand side to England. They decided to finance the venture by setting up a limited company. The main arrangements for the tour, which took place in 1927, were handled by H.D. Swan and Arthur Sims. Swan, who was connected with Essex and London club cricket, had managed the 1922–3 MCC side; Sims was a very wealthy philanthropist, who represented New Zealand at ICC meetings for 40 years. Much of his wealth came from the shipping of frozen lamb to England, where he had been born. He moved to New Zealand with his parents as an infant and later played cricket for Canterbury. It was just as well that the New Zealand Cricket Council had the support of Arthur Sims: the tour made a heavy loss and shareholders only received 10 shillings in the pound.

The 1927 side was led by Tom Lowry. No Tests were played and only seven of 26 first-class matches won. The batting of Stewie Dempster and Roger Blunt, the wicketkeeping of Ken James and the bowling of Bill Merritt were singled out for praise, although the last named received too little help, from both fellow bowlers and fielders.

Not discouraged, the New Zealand Council arranged a second England tour in 1931, again under Tom Lowry. Three Tests were played of which England won one and the other two were drawn. Originally only one Test had been scheduled; however, the relative success of the tourists meant that two more were added.

A third England tour took place in 1937 with the identical result. In between times, the MCC had sent a non-Test-playing side to New Zealand, which in today's terms would be labelled 'Young England'. The team played no less than 18 fixtures there, including four against representative New Zealand sides, all of which were drawn. As in 1922–3, the tour was a social success, but a financial flop – the New Zealand Council lost £3,400.

There can be no doubt that all this effort was worthwhile from the point of view of raising the standard of New Zealand cricket, though there was a major drawback: many of the new generation of top players were no sooner trained than they accepted contracts to play in England. All four of the heroes of the 1927 tour – Dempster, Blunt, James and Merritt – moved to England, as indeed did Chris Dacre, another 1927 tourist. If H.B.G. Austin was cool with Constantine for deserting the West Indies, the New Zealand Council must have been below freezing at the rate their talent disappeared. South Africa lost Bob Crisp and Denys Morkel, Australia had lost Ted McDonald, but in percentage terms of quality, New Zealand suffered more than any other country.

On the domestic front, New Zealand only lost two seasons of first-class cricket (1915–16 and 1916–17) because of the First World War. In 1921 the Council reorganised the Plunket Shield. It had been run on a challenge basis, similar to boxing, but this proved impractical and was switched to a league system. At the same time two Cricket Associations, Hawke's Bay and Southland, which had challenged for the Shield, were demoted to minor status. The country was divided into four Districts, each District having a number of Minor Cricket Associations who could all compete for the Hawke Cup. Meanwhile Auckland, Canterbury, Otago and Wellington were the first-class teams involved in the Plunket Shield.

INDIA

It was evident from the pre-1914 sketch of Indian cricket that the game on the subcontinent was developing in a haphazard manner, more so than in any other prospective Test-playing country. The Bombay tournament between Europeans, Parsees, Hindus and Muslims was not interrupted by the First World War and was without doubt the major competition. There were similar tournaments begun in Nagpur and Karachi in 1919–20, and in Lahore in 1922–3. In the last case, Sikhs played rather than Parsees. The Madras Presidency match between Europeans and Indians was established on a regular basis in 1915–16. Among the rulers of the native states, the Maharaja of Patiala continued his support for the game and the Maharaja of Cooch Behar followed his example. The latter employed two Sussex professionals, George Cox and Joe Vine. His son, Prince Narayan, was educated at Eton and Cambridge, and became a more than useful player who turned out for Somerset in 1909 and 1910.

In 1913 Lord Willingdon, who as Freeman-Thomas had been awarded a blue at Cambridge and then played for Sussex, was appointed Governor of Bombay. He was keen to promote cricket and played in several first-class matches in India. The Armistice was celebrated in November 1918 with a match in Bombay between England, captained by Lord Willingdon, and India, captained by the Maharaja of Patiala. India won by an innings.

Cricket in India seemed destined to continue in a fragmented manner. The Calcutta Club, though believing itself the MCC of India, remained aloof and let a variety of parties arrange matches throughout the country in isolation. Murray Robertson of the Calcutta Club, however, decided that the MCC ought to tour India and began to canvas support. Robertson was one of the Indian delegates who were invited by Lord Harris to attend the 1926 ICC meeting. Harris heard Robertson's plea for a tour of India and, wearing his MCC hat,

persuaded the Club to make suitable arrangements. The various cricket clubs in India put up the money for the tour and in July 1926 the provisional fixture list was drawn up. The list proved far too ambitious; the total of 34 matches had only once been equalled in previous English overseas tours, and they were all crammed into just over four months. R.E.S. Wyatt, the Warwickshire cricketer, was a member of the MCC side and noted:

> The tour, quite apart from the cricket, was a tiring and strenuous one. I'd never seen anything like it before. There were great dinners, lunches and entertainments everywhere we went. Indian hospitality is amazingly lavish. It would never do for only one community to entertain us in any particular town; we would have to go to one dinner given by Europeans, another given by Hindus, another by Mohammedans and sometimes yet a fourth by the Sikhs or the Parsees. Every night was a late night, with cocktail parties and dances, followed of course, next day by cricket.

In order to accommodate the players and travel arrangements quite a number of games were reduced from three days to two. The two principal fixtures were against All India in Bombay and Calcutta. In the first, All India had no European players, but the Maharaja of Patiala played for 'England', as the touring side were beset by injury. The match was a high-scoring draw. The Calcutta match had seven Europeans and four Indians in the home side. The four Indians were C.K. Nayudu, S. Wazir Ali, S. Nazir Ali and R.J. Jamshedji. 'England' won by four wickets. These two games are not considered to be proper Test Matches.

From the historical viewpoint one of the most important events of the tour was a meeting at the Roshanara Club in Delhi between the Maharaja of Patiala, R.E. Grant Govan, A.S. de Mello and the MCC touring captain, A.E.R. Gilligan. The four men agreed that a Board of Control for Cricket in India should be formed: easy enough for the four to discuss the matter, to implement, more difficult. One hurdle concerned the location of the headquarters of the Board. The Secretary of the Bombay Gymkhana, J.S. Spenser, had a letter published 'anonymously' in the press, explaining that the new Board needed to be cosmopolitan, and that cricket in Bombay was cosmopolitan, while in Calcutta it was exclusively European. Rather surprisingly the wealthy Parsee, Sir Dorabji J. Tata, sprang to the defence of Calcutta:

> The remarks dubbing the Calcutta Club as an insolent body of Europeans are very ill-conceived. I certainly do not attach any importance to any remarks made by an irresponsible person. It is absurd to start with the suggestion that Bombay alone should take the lead in the matter. Unless every Province is represented the Committee can never be called and recognised as Central.

After more debates and several preliminary meetings, a provisional Board was set up on 10 December 1927. It was not until December of the following year that the official Board was founded with Grant Govan as President and de Mello as Secretary; the headquarters – Delhi.

THE HISTORY OF CRICKET

Grant Govan and de Mello had already instituted an All-India Cricket Tournament in Delhi in 1926–7, which was to run until the Ranji Trophy commenced in 1934–5. In May 1929, Grant Govan and Colonel Mistry attended the ICC meeting as the official Indian delegates. There was talk of a South African tour to India as well as the MCC making a second visit in 1930–1. Politics then intervened. The Civil Disobedience Movement was launched by Mahatma Gandhi.

History is not made up of what-might-have-beens, but there has been much speculation as to the direction of international cricket if Gandhi's campaign had not virtually wiped out major domestic Indian cricket for a year and, in the case of Bombay, made the authorities suspend the famous Quadrangular Tournament for four seasons. The best-known Indian actively playing cricket at this time was Ranjitsinhji's nephew, Duleepsinhji. He had made his Sussex debut in 1924 and his England Test debut in 1929. The suggestion was that he should leave England and captain India, but Ranjitsinhji was opposed to this, presumably on political grounds? And anyway, with the Civil Disobedience campaign going, when would India be able to play Test cricket?

After preliminary discussions, the MCC abandoned their projected 1930–1 tour to India purely for political reasons, but one Indian refused to be diverted from his cricket by Gandhi. The Maharajkumar of Vizianagram came to England in 1930 and on learning that the MCC had aborted their tour, invited the two best-known English Test batsmen, Jack Hobbs and Herbert Sutcliffe, to join his own select Indian XI, which would tour India (except Bombay) in place of the MCC. Vizianagram arranged a programme of 16 matches plus entry into the Moin-ud-Dowlah Gold Cup tournament. His fixtures went ahead according to schedule. The Moin-ud-Dowlah Gold Cup (which was won by Vizianagram in 1930–1) had been set up at Secunderabad by the Nawab Behram-ud-Dowlah of Hyderabad in 1927–8, and was to continue with some considerable gaps and alterations until 1978–9. Entry was by invitation.

Through his initiative, the relatively unknown Vizianagram moved above the Maharaja of Patiala in the hierarchy of Indian cricket, more especially so when he caught the ear of

The Maharajkumar of Vizianagram (far right) was a major figure in Indian cricket both on and off the field during the 1930s, and captain of the 1936 Indian side to England.

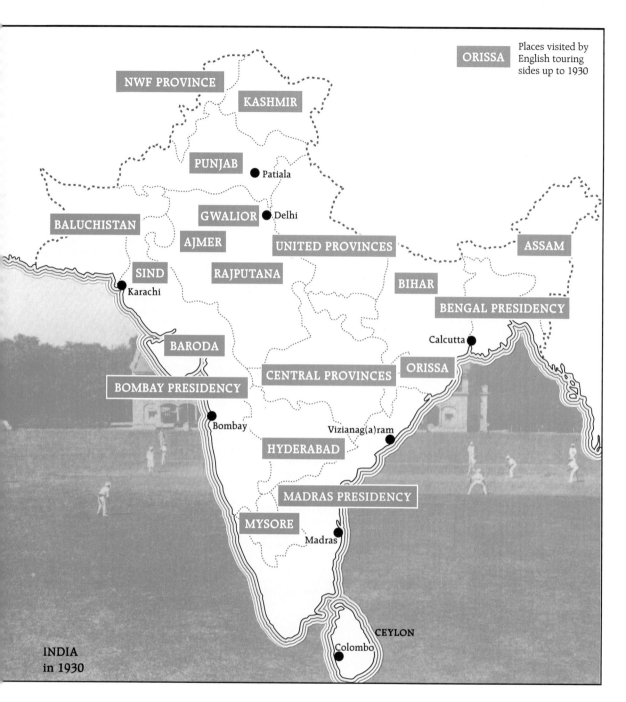

ORISSA

Places visited by
English touring
sides up to 1930

NWF PROVINCE

KASHMIR

PUNJAB
● Patiala

BALUCHISTAN

GWALIOR
● Delhi

AJMER

UNITED PROVINCES

ASSAM

SIND
● Karachi

RAJPUTANA

BIHAR

BENGAL PRESIDENCY

Calcutta ●

BARODA

CENTRAL PROVINCES

ORISSA

BOMBAY PRESIDENCY

● Bombay

Vizianag(a)ram ●

HYDERABAD

MADRAS PRESIDENCY

MYSORE

Madras ●

CEYLON

Colombo ●

INDIA
in 1930

India in the 1930s.

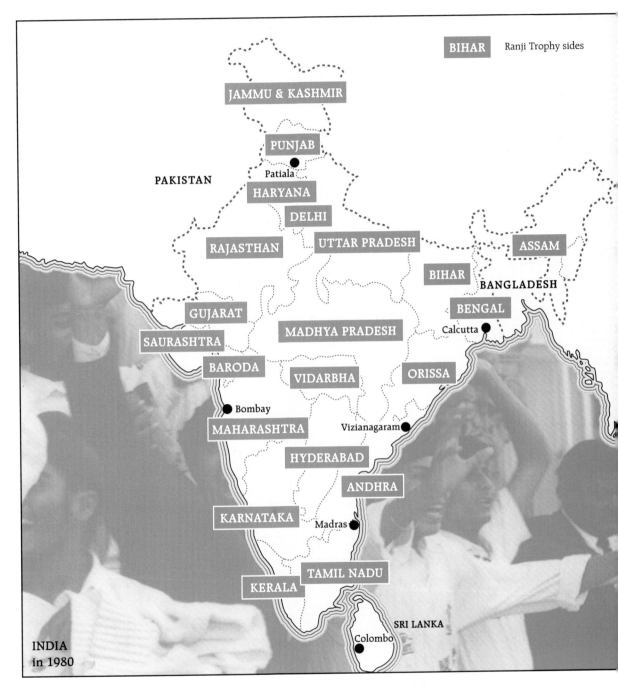

BIHAR Ranji Trophy sides

JAMMU & KASHMIR

PUNJAB

PAKISTAN

Patiala

HARYANA

DELHI

RAJASTHAN UTTAR PRADESH

ASSAM

BIHAR

BANGLADESH

GUJARAT

BENGAL

MADHYA PRADESH

Calcutta

SAURASHTRA

BARODA

VIDARBHA

ORISSA

Bombay

MAHARASHTRA

Vizianagaram

HYDERABAD

ANDHRA

KARNATAKA

Madras

TAMIL NADU

KERALA

SRI LANKA

Colombo

INDIA
in 1980

India in 1980, showing the new divisions and names of the Ranji Trophy sides of that era.

the new Viceroy: none other than Lord Willingdon, who returned in 1931, having been Governor-General of Canada for seven years.

Somewhere along the line Patiala regained the ascendancy and trials for a proposed 1932 Indian tour of England were arranged at his private ground. Patiala rode roughshod over the so-called selection committee, not only picking the team, but making himself captain. Kumar Shri Limbdi was made vice-captain and Vizianagram 'deputy vice-captain'. Vizianagram declined owing to 'reasons of state'. However, this was not the end of the labyrinthine intrigue. Patiala then withdrew and appointed the Maharaja of Porbandar, brother-in-law of Limbdi, in his stead.

Duleepsinhji, meanwhile, was nowhere to be seen, since he was playing cricket in England. However, there was another Indian prince, now aged 22, who was a most promising batsman and had gained a blue at Oxford: the Nawab of Pataudi. He had taken part in Patiala's trials, but then oddly had quit. Within twelve months he was playing Test cricket for England.

The tour went ahead. Not many matches had gone by before everyone realised that the captain (Porbandar) and the vice-captain (Limbdi) had no idea: in all but name C.K. Nayudu, the outstanding all-rounder of the side, assumed the leadership. Although the single Test and seven other first-class matches were lost, the tour proved much more successful than anticipated.

The postponed MCC visit to India eventually took place in 1933–4. The side was led by Jardine, but the captain apart, contained only one member of the 1932–3 squad that had gone to Australia, Hedley Verity.

The lobbying for power between Patiala, Vizianagram, Lord Willingdon and the Board of Control continued. After the fixtures for the MCC had been settled, the next major debating point was the choice of India's Test Selectors. The Board, under the influence of Lord Willingdon, chose to divide the country into three zones, each electing one Selector. The three turned out to be A.L. Hosie, E.L. West and the retired Parsee all-rounder, Dr H.D. Kanga. A.L. Hosie, who was Calcutta's choice, was an experienced cricketer who played for Hampshire when on home leave. C.K. Nayudu was chosen to lead India. Patiala had hopes that his son might be captain, but had made too many enemies for that to be acceptable. The series was won by England two matches to none, with the Calcutta Test drawn. The son of the Maharaja of Patiala did play in the final Test in Madras and was the only Indian to reach 50, so Patiala had some small consolation. Vizianagram, however, took the palm. His team inflicted the only defeat suffered by the MCC during the 34-match tour. Mohammad Nissar and Ladha Ramji bowled out the MCC for 111 and 139. Vizianagram, who captained his side, won by 14 runs.

In order to improve the overall standard of Indian cricket, the Board Secretary, A.S. de Mello, decided that a competition along the lines of the County Championship should be set up. It is hardly necessary to state that such a proposal would invite renewed politicking. Patiala paid for a trophy to be named after Ranjitsinhji, who had died in April 1933;

THE HISTORY OF CRICKET

The Maharajah of Patiala greets Douglas Jardine during the 1933-4 MCC tour of India.
Both are controversial figures in cricket's history. It was during this tour that Jardine
announced his retirement from Test cricket.

Vizianagram paid for a separate trophy named after the Viceroy, Lord Willingdon. De Mello invited all the Cricket Associations affiliated to the Board to compete in the competition. The Associations were divided into four regional zones, with the winners of each zone then going through to the semi-finals. Bombay beat Northern India in the final and, ironically, Lord Willingdon presented Bombay with the Ranji (not the Willingdon) Trophy.

In this first Ranji Trophy season, however, the new competition was overshadowed (at least in the public's attention) by the Bombay Quadrangular Tournament, which resumed when Gandhi was released from jail.

Patiala and Vizianagram, meanwhile, took a more direct interest in the battle for the Moin-ud-Dowlah Gold Cup at Secunderabad. The two princes found their teams facing each other in the final. Vizianagram brought Learie Constantine over to reinforce his side, but Patiala won by three wickets, Lala Amarnath hitting an unbeaten century in the final innings.

The point-scoring between Patiala and Vizianagram did not cease with the Gold Cup. The former, as President of the recently formed Cricket Club of India (designed as India's equivalent of the MCC), was instrumental in the creation of the CCI's new headquarters, the Brabourne Stadium in Bombay. It was named after Lord Brabourne, currently Governor of Bombay. Patiala then, through his Australian cricket professional, Frank Tarrant, organised an Australian touring team to India for the 1935–6 season. Unfortunately, however, opposition by the Australian Board to the proposed tour meant that many of the best players declined the trip. Before these tourists arrived, Vizianagram made a counter move, arranging a George V Silver Jubilee Cricket Festival in Delhi. The briefly forgotten Willingdon Trophy re-emerged as the Jubilee Festival prize: won by Vizianagram's team and presented to him by Lord Willingdon.

The next major decision for the Indian Board was the captaincy of the 1936 Indian team to England. The obvious candidate was the England Test cricketer, now back in India, the Nawab of Pataudi. Pataudi was chosen, but later resigned, being 'unfit'. There were three other possible candidates: C.K. Nayudu, Vizianagram and Patiala's son. The last withdrew and when the votes were counted, Vizianagram won by ten votes to five.

The England tour was not a happy one, with the team split between two camps – Vizianagram or Nayudu. Amarnath, potentially a brilliant all-rounder, was sent home early for disciplinary reasons. The press had a field day as one squabble after another emerged. Vizianagram was nicknamed 'Vizzy' and knighted. The Test series went to England two matches to nil. One man returned to India with an enhanced reputation: Vijay Merchant, who hit 1,745 runs and easily topped the batting averages. An inquiry was set up by the Indian Board to find out what went wrong. Both 'Vizzy' and Nayudu received a measure of blame.

The last major international event before the outbreak of war was the tour of English cricketers under Lord Tennyson in 1937–8. Although Tennyson himself was over the hill as a Test cricketer, the team contained some very talented players, including Bill Edrich, Joe Hardstaff, Norman Yardley and Alf Gover. The 'Test' series of five matches was won by England 3–2. Merchant led India in all the matches and proved a shrewd captain, managing to keep clear of the cliques as far as he could. Patiala had his great day, when Tennyson's team opposed the Cricket Club of India at the official opening of his brand new Brabourne Stadium. The CCI collapsed to 189 all out in response to Tennyson's 367 but, following on, managed to save the game, with Vijay Merchant scoring 63 and Lala Amarnath 64. Patiala died three months later.

CEYLON

In comparison with the highly charged machinations in India, cricket on the island of Ceylon was a sedate affair. The Ceylon Cricket Association was formed in July 1922, and the country was most fortunate to have at this time an outstanding sports administrator, Dr John Rockwood. S.S. Perera comments:

> No individual since 1920 has spent so much money for so many young cricketers. Time and money seemed to have been of no concern. As with Vanderspar,[26] he selected the talented young cricketers of the period in his teams against visiting teams and for local matches. Dr Rockwood provided blazers for the whole Ceylonese team to Bombay in 1920. A regular headline in the sports pages of the local newspapers was: 'Dr Rockwood's Latest Enterprise'. His hospitality was unbounded. Ceylonese cricket owes him much. How the Doctor found time to preside over the destinies of so many sports organisations will never be known. Dr Rockwood was solely responsible for the Nondescripts Ground at Maitland Place in 1915 and the building of the pavilion. He was Ceylon's Sir Julien Cahn.

On the international stage Ceylon's cricket came to public notice when the MCC or Australian teams stopped off in Colombo for a one-day game *en route* for an Ashes series. The Ceylon authorities made much of these frequent brief visits, but from the visiting teams' viewpoint they were hardly more than a chance to stretch their legs before resuming the sea voyage.

The first 'proper' post-war English tour to Ceylon came as part of the MCC 1926–7 visit to the subcontinent. Four matches were played – against the Europeans, Ceylonese, Up Country XI and All Ceylon. The second similar MCC visit, again with four matches, followed in 1933–4. In 1936–7 came the third inter-war English tour, by Sir Julien Cahn's Team. They played five matches, and Bob Crisp, the South African Test cricketer who was a member of Cahn's side, commented:

> As far as cricket goes we received our first shock in the first match played in Colombo. The Singhalese are very fine cricketers, quick of feet and eye, and supple of wrist. Their best side – which would always take for granted F.C. de Saram – is about the strength of one of the weaker first-class county sides. Sir Julien was impressed enough to suggest a tour of England by a Ceylon side.

In fact in 1929 preliminary preparations had been made for such a tour, but the plans fell through. Ceylon (or Sri Lanka, as it became) did not finally tour England until 1979. F.C. de Saram, mentioned by Crisp, had in 1934 become the first Ceylonese to gain a cricket 'blue', playing for Oxford in the University Matches of 1934 and 1935.

---

26   George Vanderspar (1858–1940) played for Somerset in 1880, but from 1884 to 1908 was the principal organiser of Ceylon cricket. He took teams from Ceylon to Calcutta in 1884–5, and Madras in 1885–6 and 1891–2.

There were many matches between teams from Ceylon visiting India and vice versa, but most were of a minor character. The major Indian tour to the island was in 1930–1, when Vizianagram brought over his side, including Hobbs and Sutcliffe. Eight matches were played. Dr Rockwood picked the teams to oppose Vizzy in the three major fixtures. In the one game against All Ceylon, the local side scored 312 against the tourists' 358, before the game drifted to a draw.

The major domestic match immediately after the First World War was, as it had been before, Europeans vs. Ceylonese. As the seasons went by the Ceylonese strength waxed while the Europeans' waned and the fixture was abandoned after 1933. There was a Club Championship which the Ceylon CA inaugurated in 1924. Most games were of one-day duration.

The great nursery of Ceylonese cricketers was the island's equivalent of Eton vs. Harrow: Royal College vs. St Thomas' College. The fixture was established in 1879 and a hundred years later celebrated its centenary with a fine *History*. The Royal College sent a school team on a tour of Australia in 1936.

EAST ASIA AND THE PACIFIC

Cricket flourished in Ceylon between 1919 and 1939, but the same cannot be said of India's other British neighbour, Burma. When the 1926–7 MCC side went to Ceylon, they also travelled to Rangoon, where they opposed Rangoon Gymkhana and All Burma. The home sides were entirely European. Ceylon Europeans had toured Burma in 1894, playing four matches, and the repeat tour took place in 1912. Records of Burmese playing cricket are sparse.

Moving east and south from Burma, cricket made better progress in the Federated Malay States and Straits Settlements. The most famous international match of the inter-war period was played on 3, 4 and 6 June 1927, when Malaya beat the Australians by 39 runs. An Australian side led by Charles Macartney and containing several Test cricketers played nine matches: three in Singapore, two in Kuala Lumpur and in Ipoh, and one each in Seremban and Penang. The Malayan victory came in Kuala Lumpur, but the home side suffered a severe reverse in the return fixture. The majority of home players were Europeans, but Lall Singh, who appeared in two games, went on to gain a Test cap for India. Sir Julien Cahn's side, which had been in Ceylon in 1936–7, travelled on to Malaya and played four matches. The main domestic cricket was the inter-state games, with Selangor possibly the strongest side.

Straits Settlements played five matches against Shanghai between 1919 and 1939; Singapore opposed Hong Kong six times; and Hong Kong and Shanghai met annually between 1920 and 1936. The summary scores of all these encounters were published in *The Cricket Quarterly*, 1966, pages 149–153.

Domestic cricket continued in the Fijian Islands between the wars. There were also several visits from overseas teams, although unfortunately the visits by Bradman's

Kuala Lumpur Cricket Ground.
Throughout the Empire
cricket grounds were laid out,
some more opulent than others.

Australians and Allen's England side were both rain-ruined. On each occasion the single match scheduled was washed out. The two major tours to Fiji were by New Zealand sides in 1924 and 1935–6. Cricket was still largely segregated, with the Europeans in Suva having the best facilities, and the standard of play by both Europeans and Fijians had stagnated. The arrival of Philip Snow, as Administrator of Fiji and Western Pacific in 1938, was destined to transform the lethargic scene.

NORTH AMERICA

The leading light in Canadian cricket during the 1920s was Norman Seagram of Toronto, a wealthy philanthropist. He organised a tour to England in 1922 in which the Canadians, playing leading amateur clubs, failed to win any of their 11 matches. They were

however socially successful; several Cabinet Ministers attended a dinner in the Canadians' honour at Westminster. Seagram arranged for the Free Foresters to tour Canada the following summer. The Foresters returned home unbeaten. Various cricket leagues were established during the early post-war years, not only in Toronto and eastern Canada, but also in the west, where British Columbia, Alberta, Saskatchewan and Manitoba competed in an annual tournament.

Arthur Mailey organised an Australian tour of North America in 1932. The single defeat inflicted on this near Test standard side was at Brockton Point in Vancouver. A year later, Sir Julien Cahn toured North America and played ten matches in Canada. The Hon. R.C. Matthews, a former Minister in the Canadian government, organised a short tour to England in 1936. The team greatly improved on the record of the 1922 side and beat a fair MCC team at Lord's by 76 runs. Matthews paid the expenses of the side. The Canadians set up a national Cricket Association in 1928 with the aim of improving standards.

Across the border in the States, Philadelphian cricket continued to decline. The famous pre-war clubs closed, notably Frankford in 1926 and Germantown in 1927. The few remaining clubs competed with those of New York for the Dewar Cup, but it was small-scale stuff. The one great enthusiast who kept cricket alive was Karl Auty of Chicago (1878–1959), who was English by birth. He founded a local league in 1924, organised matches between Chicago and St Louis and published a well-produced cricket annual. It is odd to think of cricket being played in Chicago in the Prohibition era, at the same time as Al Capone was dominating organised crime in the city.

Over on the west coast, the actor and former cricketer C. Aubrey Smith ran a regular side in California, for whom such players-cum-film stars as David Niven, Errol Flynn and Boris Karloff appeared, but the games were as much social occasions as matches.

SOUTH AMERICA

Cricket in South America reached its zenith during the 1930s. In 1932 a South American side toured England, won two of their six first-class matches and played 18 games in all. The tour was organised by E.W.S. Thomson, Honorary Secretary of the Argentine CA; the captain was C.H. Gibson. Although the main party came from Argentina, there were members from Brazil and Chile as well. This tour had been preceded by two in the opposite direction. The MCC went out in 1926–7 under the now veteran Pelham Warner. The principal games were against Argentina. The MCC won by two matches to one. Games were also arranged in Uruguay, Chile and Peru. The home sides were entirely British expatriates. One point of future historical interest was the presence in the MCC team of Lord Dunglass, the future Sir Alec Douglas Home, Prime Minister. The ubiquitous Julien Cahn took a side to Argentina in March 1930; the three 'Tests' resulted in two draws and a victory for Cahn. In 1937–8 Sir Theodore Brinckman took a side of good county standard out, playing 11 matches. The tourists shared the rubber with Argentina, each team claiming a single victory. Meanwhile, the domestic club matches and games between the South American countries continued much as they had done in Edwardian times. However, the break caused by the Second World War resulted in a serious drop in playing standards.

AFRICA

The cricket scene in Africa away from the Union of South Africa and the colony of Rhodesia changed little in the 1920s and 1930s. Kenya maintained the best standard, with its Officials vs. Settlers and Europeans vs. Asians fixtures. M.D. Lyon, the Somerset batsman, went out to Gambia as Resident Magistrate and from 1930 Gambia played an annual match against Sierra Leone, which in 1938 Lyon regarded as up to Minor Counties' standard. The annual Gold Coast vs. Nigeria match was normally of a somewhat higher standard. In 1938 it lasted five days and contained several players who had appeared in English first-class cricket. Both teams were entirely of European origin.

Moving north, there was a well-run club in Khartoum and a good ground at Gordon College in that city; the standard varied depending on the availability of Sudan government officials and other British residents. In Egypt, the All Egypt side was as strong as one of the weaker first-class counties. The centre of Egyptian cricket was the Gezira Sporting Club, where an excellent grass pitch had been laid out. Three other well-maintained grass pitches were Willcocks Sports Ground, Maadi Sporting Club and the Ministry of Education Ground. All these were in Cairo or its environs. In Alexandria, the local club and Victoria College both had grass pitches. Most of the cricket was played by British expatriates, but at Victoria College some Egyptians played and there was a native Egyptian side, mainly comprising Egyptians who had been educated in England.

H.M. Martineau, who has been mentioned before as having a private ground near Maidenhead, brought a team to Egypt for eleven successive seasons up to 1939. In the final year the team broke new ground by flying from Croydon Aerodrome to Marseilles and then transferring to a flying boat, via Rome and Athens, to Alexandria – the first major English team to travel by air. On each tour Martineau's team played a 'Test' series against All Egypt and these three-day games were keenly fought by sides of first-class quality.

THE MIDDLE EAST AND THE MEDITERRANEAN

In 1935, Lord Melchett took a side to Palestine, playing five matches. The opposition were the Army, Royal Air Force, Palestine Police, Haifa CC and Jerusalem Sports Club. The following year, there is a news item which notes that despite the troubles between Arabs and Jews, the Palestine Police managed to complete their normal eleven-match fixture list and were undefeated. Service cricket was also a regular feature of the sporting scene in Transjordan, Iraq and Aden.

Of the British possessions in and adjacent to the Mediterranean, Malta saw a great deal of Services cricket. The Combined Services side on the island was generally very strong and in 1929, for example, beat a touring Incogniti team, which contained several county cricketers, by seven wickets. Gibraltar sent a team to Portugal in 1937 and 1939, as well as entertaining several visiting sides, such as the Cryptics and Yorkshire Gentlemen. Little cricket, however, seems to have been played (or at least reported) in Cyprus or Corfu. Presumably the native Greeks in Corfu were keeping the game alive, since it is still being played there today.

CONTINENTAL EUROPE

The one continental country which apparently took a fresh interest in cricket between the wars was Germany. A cricket league operated in Berlin in the 1930s, and when the Gentlemen of Worcestershire went on tour there in 1937, it seems a great fuss was made of them. The report in *The Cricketer* stated: 'At the early hour of 8.00 a.m. the XI arrived in Berlin to find on the station a large gathering of German sportsmen. Numerous cinema and press cameras were also in evidence ... The Reichsports Führer honoured the Gentlemen of Worcestershire by his presence at two of the matches, entertaining us to tea and attending the final banquet.' The unusual aspect of German cricket was that the players were actually German and not English people resident in Germany, as was the case in France and Italy, for example.

One of the venues for this tour was the 1936 Olympic Stadium. The standard of play was not, however, high and the English side won all three of their matches comfortably.

Holland remained the most active centre of continental cricket. The Free Foresters regularly visited the Netherlands, as did other clubs of that ilk, and in most seasons a Dutch side came to England. Several English professionals went over in the 1930s and were engaged by clubs in The Hague, Haarlem and Amsterdam. The Flamingos were established in 1921 and soon developed into one of the leading Dutch clubs, particularly in relation to matches against English sides.

Denmark's cricket grew steadily. The former Sussex captain H.P. Chaplin (1883–1970), sponsored by the Anglo-Danish Society, spent five months in 1929 as a coach in Jutland. R.P. Keigwin (1883–1972) of Cambridge, Essex and Gloucestershire lived in Denmark for some years and was responsible for arranging tours to and from England. The best batsman in Denmark in the early post-war years was Charles Buchwald. He retired in 1927 and his place was taken by Oskar Jorgensen, who captained Denmark against Sir Julien Cahn's touring side in 1932. One of the major problems for Danish players was the poor quality of their grounds, most of which were also used for football.

The first cricket centre in Switzerland was Zuoz College. The initial match was reported in 1924, when a team of golfers in St Moritz came to the college to inaugurate cricket there. The college continued to play through the 1930s, but the game did not overflow into the rest of the Alps.

THE HISTORY OF CRICKET

THE BRITISH ISLES

Returning to the British Isles before closing this chapter, the islands of Jersey and Guernsey had two excellent centres of cricket in Victoria College and Elizabeth College. From 1924 the MCC sent an annual touring side to the islands and other well-known sides to visit included the Incogniti, Free Foresters, Cryptics and Hampshire Hogs. Sir Theodore Brinckman brought his side there on several occasions. British understatement is at its best in the following note by V.G. Collenette, describing Guernsey cricket: 'Until the beginning of the Second World War, when the garrison was withdrawn, there were many fixtures with the regiment stationed on the island.'

Ireland was in turmoil for the five years following the 1918 Armistice. The wrecking of country estates and the movement of the landed gentry to England had an enormous effect on cricket in Southern Ireland. Only in Dublin itself and in Cork did the game continue as the Free State was established. The Irish Cricket Union was resuscitated in 1923, the year in which the West Indies played Dublin University in Dublin and the Northern Cricket Union in Belfast. League cricket was instituted in Dublin in the 1920s. Despite the division of Ireland into two parts, cricketers on both sides of the border were still united and the traditional game against Scotland was played in almost every inter-war summer.

English authorities have rated three-day matches by Ireland as of 'first-class' standard, but Edgar Shearer, who played for Ireland from 1933, commented: 'Because we love it we tend to claim too much for our Irish cricket. It has never been "first-class" in my time and I think we only try to get our three-day matches classified as such in the belief that it will help us get visits from Dominion sides.'

Ireland did produce two outstanding players in the late 1920s, Edward Ingram and James Boucher, both of whom were up to first-class county standard, as indeed was Shearer himself.

The principal feature of Scottish cricket was the Scottish County Championship. In the 1920s it was mainly a battle between Aberdeen and Perth, but the 1930s belonged to Fife. First-class touring sides to England regularly came to Scotland and played the national side. There was also the annual match with Ireland and occasional games against English counties. John Kerr was for many years Scotland's principal batsman, his career extending from 1908 to 1933. Ian Peebles, born in Aberdeen and educated at Glasgow Academy, was lost to Scottish cricket when he went to qualify for Middlesex and played for England as a leg-break bowler. After the war, Mike Denness, born in Lanarkshire, captained England in 19 Test Matches.

In contrast to Scotland, several Welsh counties participated in the English Minor Counties Championship in the pre-1914 years, notably Glamorgan, Monmouth and Carmarthenshire. Glamorgan were promoted to the English first-class county competition in 1921, and can thus be considered as part of 'English' cricket. In North Wales a County Championship was established in the 1920s, playing mainly weekend matches.

WOMEN'S CRICKET

The playing of cricket by women and girls has yet to be mentioned, the reason being that until the 1930s organised ladies' matches were few and far between. Netta Rheinberg, who played for England and acted as editor of the monthly *Women's Cricket* magazine for 18 years, rightly described women's matches before the 1880s as 'rural romps'. The first ladies' club, The White Heather Club, was founded in 1887 and was allied to country house cricket. In 1890 there was an attempt to run a series of exhibition matches on a professional basis under the title 'Original English Lady Cricketers'. It survived little more than a year, the manager absconding with the funds.

Before the First World War, however, the major girls' public schools began to run cricket teams. At Wimbledon House, which became Roedean in 1898, cricket was played from the 1880s, and Roedean's first inter-school fixture was against Wycombe Abbey in 1899. The early games between the two schools were played at Reigate in Surrey, as a half-way point between High Wycombe and Brighton. In 1899 Roedean also played the White Heather Club. In addition to internal matches, the school had five or so outside fixtures each season.

Cricket seems to have been introduced to Cheltenham Ladies' College by the girls themselves, but the headmistress of the time, Miss Beale, was opposed to competitive sport, regarding competition by girls in any form as 'productive of too great a desire for success and incompatible with their unique emotional and intellectual needs and future family responsibilities'. However, her successor, Lilian M. Faithfull, was a keen sportswoman, and from 1908 onwards outside matches were introduced in hockey, tennis and cricket.

Cricket was certainly well established at Harrogate Ladies' College by 1908, when the school had four teams, including a Baby XI. Two years earlier, they had found it necessary to erect a high wooden fence around their grounds on Duchy Road, 'which protects us from the intrusion of workmen and boys who stood on the bank to watch our games and did great damage to our trees and hedges and caused us much annoyance in other ways'. However, local interest in the girls' cricket could be much more positive. In 1911 the school magazine reports:

> One particularly enjoyable afternoon was spent at Spofforth, when Mr. Pearson most hospitably entertained the team and some of the School. It was during this match that our first century was scored by Miss Henson, the surrounding village crowd shouting admiring comments; one in particular was heard above the others, 'Three cheers for Miss 'Enson, and let the women 'ave their vote!'

From this growing nucleus of public school players Miss V.M.M. Cox organised some matches in the 1920s which led to the formation in 1926 of the English Women's Cricket Association. Australia (1931) and New Zealand (1934) followed suit, and in 1934–5 an

School vs. Staff match at Roedean in 1905. This fixture commenced in 1896 and is still being played. Apart from house matches, Roedean played an average of five cricket matches a season during the Edwardian era.

Cheltenham Ladies' College cricket team in 1908. Until the founding of the Women's Cricket Association in 1926, women's cricket was largely confined to the public schools.

English Women's side under Betty Archdale toured Australia and New Zealand and beat both their national teams. It was very much an upper-middle-class tour, with the players having to pay all their own travel expenses.

In 1937 Australia toured England; the only other major pre-1939 tour was by New Zealand to New South Wales. Holland formed a women's cricket association in 1934, but in South Africa, the West Indies and India women's cricket was almost unknown, save for the odd country-house-style game, prior to the Second World War.

In 1939 the Overseas Educational League sponsored a 'demonstration' tour of Canada by cricketers from Harrogate Ladies' College, Roedean and Newcastle school. War was declared during their visit, throwing their plans for the return journey into disarray. Most of the Harrogate girls, for example, did not finally manage to get back to England until November.

WARTIME CRICKET

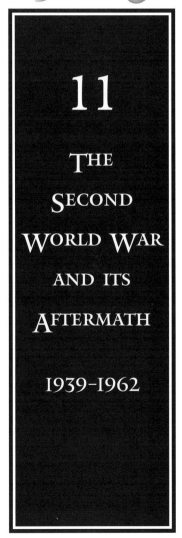

Because of the Blitz and the very real danger of invasion, life in Great Britain during the first years of the Second World War was much more disrupted than it had been in 1914–18. In contrast to the First World War, however, cricket was positively encouraged. Although travel restrictions, if nothing else, meant it was impractical to contemplate the continuation of the County Championship, two new cricketing organisations were founded and these provided the southern half of England with good-quality weekend matches. The British Empire XI was the brainchild of Desmond Donnelly, who was only 19 when he founded the side.[27] Donnelly's XI was captained by the Sussex batsman Hugh Bartlett, and the side played no less than 37, mainly one-day, matches in 1940.

The second organisation, London Counties, was established by C.J.E. Jones and was a most unusual concept. Charles Jones was a useful club cricketer and later became Secretary of Forest Hill CC. (He was also a civil servant with the Inland Revenue and died in 1966 aged 73.) Jones was concerned that many professional county cricketers, having lost their principal source of income with the abandonment of the County Championship, would find their finances stretched. He therefore created this side and its fixtures in order to provide some income for the players he employed. His plan was that the gate receipts, after expenses, should go to the players. In the end, a percentage of the gate went to charity and the players shared the rest. Both these teams attracted fair crowds and when they met at Lord's in August 1940, the attendance was about 13,000.

The MCC reverted to their 1915–18 format, only playing away matches against public schools. Surrey's ground at The Oval was requisitioned by the military and converted into a prisoner-of-war cage, but Lord's was in continuous use for cricket, mainly for matches involving Service teams. A week of inter-schools cricket was played there each summer, though without the traditional Eton vs. Harrow match.

---

27 Desmond Donnelly later became the Labour MP for Pembroke (1950-68), before resigning the Labour whip and sitting as an Independent. He was also a political journalist and died in 1974 aged 53.

11

THE SECOND WORLD WAR AND ITS AFTERMATH

1939-1962

Bruce Mitchell in the Western Desert. In the period 1940–3, many first-class cricketers gravitated to North Africa and in particular the Gezira Club in Egypt. The strong South African contingent included the Test opening batsman, Bruce Mitchell.

Australian troops in the Alamein area taking time off to play cricket during the desert campaigns of the Second World War.

Flight Lieutenant Walter Hammond, England's captain and leading batsman of 1939, joined the RAF and later led England in the 1945 Victory Tests against Lindsay Hassett's Australians.

For two or three years, Lord's had a rival in North Africa. The Gezira Sporting Club in Egypt, which possessed the best cricket ground in that country, drew quantities of servicemen in their rest periods from the fight against Rommel. Dudley Nourse, the South African Test batsman, makes the following note in his autobiography:

> I doubt whether any nations are quite as sportsminded as the British people. As soon as we (the South African Troops) were settled in Egypt the various regiments began to lay concrete wickets. If there was not an awful amount of time for cricket, at least we were going to enjoy ourselves as, and when, we were able to. Stationed about 40 miles outside Cairo as we were, we would always think in terms of the possibility of arranging a match in our time off.

The South African forces in Egypt could pick a side which contained four Test players plus seven Currie Cup representatives; New Zealand had a number of first-class players in the country, including their Test batsman Martin Donnelly and the fast bowler Tom Pritchard. England cricketers stationed in Egypt were Hedley Verity and Norman Yardley, together with a pair of youngsters who would rise to fame after the war: Jim Laker (later of Surrey) and Ron Aspinall (later of Yorkshire). From 1941 to 1943 no less a personage than the current England captain, Walter Hammond, serving as an officer in the RAF, was stationed in North Africa. Part of his responsibilities was the promotion of sporting facilities in Egypt.

The games played in Egypt, while involving top-quality players, were friendly one-day affairs. Only in India did competitive first-class matches survive. With residential qualifications for Ranji Trophy teams being a matter of weeks rather than years, several well-known English cricketers were drafted into the Championship, the most notable being the young England Test batsman Denis Compton. Two outside events interrupted the cricket: Gandhi renewed his campaign for independence, which caused the cancellation of the 1942 Bombay tournament; and the Japanese carried out an air raid on Madras, which resulted in panic for a few months and the abandonment of much cricket in the area.

The Japanese also caused problems in Australia. The 1939–40 season of Sheffield Shield games was played out, but after that the major matches during the war were staged in aid of charity. The possibility of a Japanese invasion looked very real in 1942; Darwin suffered air raids and travel was restricted. Club cricket continued on a reduced level with some of the country cricket clubs having to close for the duration.

In New Zealand the two main competitions, the Plunket Shield and the Hawke Cup, took place in 1939–40. Thereafter both competitions went into abeyance. It had been intended that an Australian side would tour the country in 1939–40 but, like the proposed MCC visit to India, the trip was cancelled.

Retrospectively the most important development of the game during the Second World War occurred in South Africa. It had nothing to do with the Currie Cup – no matches were played – but was the inspiration of S.J. Pitts, Chairman of the Transvaal Cricket Union and Vice-President of the South African Cricket Association. In 1939, Lord Nuffield, the millionaire who founded Morris Motors, gave the sum of £10,000 to be used for the expansion of cricket in Southern Africa. Pitts thought up a scheme involving schoolboy matches played during the Christmas holidays. From this series of matches a representative schoolboy team would be chosen. The job of putting the scheme into practice was given to C.J. Offord. The first programme took place in January 1940 and Offord continued to mastermind the arrangements for the first decade. It was largely due to this Nuffield scheme that South Africa at Test level could, from a small base, compete on equal terms with England and Australia during the 1950s and 1960s. Test cricketers were drawn almost exclusively from the white English section of society.

Because of travel difficulties during the war, Jamaica once again found itself isolated from the other major cricketing entities of the Caribbean. So far as first-class games were concerned, for much of the war it simply was a matter of Trinidad against Barbados, though in the later stages British Guiana joined the other two.

1945–8

The war in Europe ended on 8 May 1945. In England teams drawn from both the Australian Infantry Forces and the Royal Australian Air Force had already begun a programme of matches for the 1945 season. These programmes were extended and to an

The inner sanctum of the MCC: the Long Room of the Lord's pavilion as it was during the Victory Tests in 1945.

extent merged. The result, at the top level, was a series of five 'Victory' Tests between the Australians stationed in England and the best available England side. The first took place at Lord's on 19, 21 and 22 May, when crowds each day averaged some 20,000. England were led by their pre–war captain, Walter Hammond; Lindsay Hassett, a member of Bradman's 1938 team to England, captained Australia. The venue for three of the 'Tests' was Lord's, the other games being played at Bramall Lane, Sheffield, and Old Trafford, Manchester. The series was tied two all, with one draw. A note on the Old Trafford game reported that German prisoners of war were paid three farthings an hour to renovate the ground in readiness for the 'Test'.

Throughout 1945 the 17 first-class counties took stock, arranged a few friendly one- or two-day games and began engaging professionals for 1946. The two wartime substitutes, British Empire and London Counties, continued their fixtures for 1945, then announced that any activity in 1946 would be minimal.

When the 1945 season ended, the popular Australian Services side was directed to India for a ten-match tour. There were three 'Tests'; two were drawn, and India won the other game. India were led once more by their currently outstanding batsman, Vijay Merchant. This time he proved to be an ultra-defensive leader, a point epitomised in the Bombay 'Test', when his declaration set Australia 20 minutes to make 113 runs. This negative approach was of immediate concern to the Indian cricket authorities, since it had been agreed to send a side to England for the 1946 season.

The political situation in the country was becoming chaotic. Rioting had already affected one of the Australian Services matches, when the mob invaded the pitch and demanded that play cease in order to show sympathy for the rioters who had been killed the previous day. The British government were drawing up plans for their withdrawal from India. The rulers of the princely states were not happy, since they were hoping for some sort of semi-independent status. One possible avenue for influencing decisions in London was the captaincy of the 1946 touring side. Who should reappear on the cricketing scene but the Nawab of Pataudi, the former England Test cricketer? He had not taken part in serious cricket for ten years. Was it a coincidence that his father-in-law was the Nawab of Bhopal, the man who was leading the princes in their political manoeuvres? Mihir Bose, in his Indian history, states that it was unlikely that the move to appoint Pataudi as captain had any consequences for independence. Be that as it may, the Indian Board did appoint Pataudi rather than Merchant as India's captain. In view of the turmoil on the Indian subcontinent, the point must be made that this touring side, unlike its predecessors of the 1930s, did not split into factions and Merchant, who could have felt slighted at the loss of the captaincy, batted quite brilliantly throughout the summer.

The 1946 season in England was out of the ordinary for obvious reasons. About 100 English first-class cricketers had lost their lives in the Second World War (half the 1914–18 total), the most famous being Hedley Verity, the Yorkshire and England spin bowler, who died fighting in Italy. Nevertheless, after six years of war and little serious cricket, the public welcomed whatever was on offer.

Despite appalling weather, which meant that two of the three Tests with India were rain-affected draws (England won at Lord's), both the tourists and the first-class counties made profits. The 1946 season was the first time since the Championship was expanded that all the counties balanced their books from gate receipts, subscriptions and Test Match profits (without the need for some patron digging into his pocket).

So far as England were concerned the selectorial eye was on the projected tour the following winter to Australia. The interest of the cricketing public thus moves away from India and all its difficulties to the Antipodes and to the uncrowned king of Australia, Don Bradman.

The Australian Board had arranged a short tour of New Zealand for March 1946. Bradman, who was a member of the Board, representing South Australia, declined the trip. Outside cricket he had had business problems during 1945. The stockbroking firm for which he worked went bankrupt and he was setting up on his own. He did, however, play in two first-class friendlies in Australia in 1945–6 (the Sheffield Shield would not resume until 1946–7). Bradman stated that he would not decide whether to play against England in 1946–7 until the time for selection came. In the event, he chose to play, led Australia and was highly successful. By contrast Walter Hammond, who led England again, failed with the bat. Hammond, like Bradman, had personal problems unconnected with cricket.

With Bradman scoring runs, and with two new fast bowlers, Ray Lindwall and Keith Miller, Australia were too good for their English visitors, winning the series by three matches to nil with two draws. As in England in 1946, the first-class Australian States reported large profits and high memberships.

The next country to be involved in a Test match series (if one ignores the single Australia vs. New Zealand game of 1945–6) was South Africa, who visited England in 1947. The sun shone that year and attendances at first-class matches in England were estimated at nearly three million, a record. Again the counties prospered. England beat South Africa by three matches to nil, with two draws. Denis Compton and Bill Edrich, the Middlesex batsmen, broke many records and enabled their county to wrest the Championship from the north of England for the first time since 1921.

In preparation for the fight for The Ashes, scheduled for the English summer of 1948, Australia were to entertain India, while the MCC were sending a team to the West Indies.

India was now a divided subcontinent. The Indian Independence Act of July 1947 effectively created the Dominion of Pakistan and there was terrible carnage as the Muslims left in India tried to reach the new country, while Hindus in Pakistan fled to India. Some estimates put the death toll at one million. In the midst of this traumatic upheaval, the Indian Cricket Board was determined to select a United Indian side to visit Australia. A.S. de Mello, now President of the Board, had a pre-tour booklet issued with the inscription: 'Dedicated to Sports About the Only Thing In Which India's Unity is still left.'

Keith Miller, Australia's great all-rounder in the early post-war years. He formed a lethal fast bowling partnership with Ray Lindwall and was a hurricane middle order batsman.

The biographies of the 17 players selected were given. For one reason or another Vijay Merchant (the appointed captain), S. Mushtaq Ali, R.S. Modi and Fazal Mahmood withdrew. India therefore faced their first ever five-match Test series of five days each with a weakened side. They were opposed by Bradman and the team that had demolished England the year before. Australia won four matches to nil, with one draw.

THE RISE OF THE WEST INDIES

If India were embarrassed by the absence of their principal players and the resultant defeats, then England, or the MCC, were doubly so in the West Indies during the same season. Of the basic England eleven which had beaten South Africa in 1947, only four agreed to tour the Caribbean. Gubby Allen, who had last represented England in 1936–7, was resurrected as captain (just as India had brought back Pataudi in 1946). The four top England batsmen – Len Hutton, Cyril Washbrook, Bill Edrich and Denis Compton – were nowhere to be seen; likewise the two best England bowlers, Alec Bedser and Doug Wright. Not a single match was won on the tour. England had totally under-estimated the continuing improvement in West Indies cricket and the emergence of three quite outstanding batsmen: Frank Worrell, Everton Weekes and Clyde Walcott. The West Indies, moreover, were still largely free from controversy, although the question of the captaincy and whether it should remain the prerogative of the white cricketers was uppermost in the Selectors' minds. For 1947–8 they hedged their bets, appointing their greatest pre-war batsman, George Headley, for two Tests and white cricketers, Jeff Stollmeyer and John Goddard, for one Test each. The campaign to remove the notion that black men were 'incapable' of leading a West Indies team overseas had not yet gathered momentum.

This compromise was workable in the West Indies, but the Selectors had to make a firm decision the following season, since, for the first time, it had been agreed to send a Test team to India. The Selectors chose John Goddard, not Headley, but the latter was picked as part of the touring side. Of equal interest in terms of the future was the fact that the most talented of the three 'Ws', Frank Worrell, refused the terms offered by the Board. He had had a taste of the sort of income top-quality cricketers could earn since, for the 1948 summer, he had joined Radcliffe in the Central Lancashire League at a reported salary of £500 (a sum considerably more than was earned by first-class county players at the time). Like Constantine before him, Worrell's independence set him aside from his contemporary black colleagues.

A year later, the West Indian Selectors remained faithful to the white captaincy policy, when they continued with Goddard for the 1950 West Indian side to England. The West Indies had won the series in India. Worrell rejoined his friends Weekes and Walcott for the England tour and the Selectors took a gamble on two totally unknown spin bowlers, Alf Valentine and Sonny Ramadhin.

THE HISTORY OF CRICKET

A FAREWELL TO BRADMAN

Before relating the deeds of that tour, it is necessary to return to 1948 and the first post-war Australian visit to England. Bradman hesitated, but eventually accepted the captaincy. England achieved little more than they had 18 months before in Australia and the tour was one long triumphant march as Lindwall and Miller brushed aside the England batsmen and the crowds turned out to say farewell to the greatest batsman the world had ever seen. The Test series was a 4–0 win for Australia, culminating in the total destruction of England in the final Test at The Oval – all out for 52. Australia in reply reached 117 when their first wicket fell. Bradman entered the field and was cheered all the way to the wicket. He required four runs in this last Test to achieve the incredible Test career batting average of 100. He was bowled second ball for nought, the most emotional moment in 20th-century cricket history. The pattern of England-Australia Test results was repeating the sequence that had occurred after the First World War. The Australians made a record profit. There was a little niggle that spectator numbers at Championship games had dropped, but then 1947 had been a record summer and the weather was not so kind in 1948.

THE WEST INDIANS ARRIVE

The next four Test series, prior to the West Indies in England, were popular and predictable. The West Indies beat India at home; England beat South Africa away, as did Australia. The 1949 England vs. New Zealand series in England proved a joke because the authorities decided that the Tests should be of three days' duration. All four were drawn, even though there were virtually no weather interruptions. We can now go back therefore to Goddard's West Indians in England.

By now England had pensioned off half the pre-war stalwarts who had continued their Test careers after 1945, and a new generation of players was developing. The debacle in the Caribbean of 1947–8 did not provide a real measure of the strengths of the two sides and though the West Indies had some formidable batsmen, they had not really been tested on English wickets. The West Indian bowling was an unknown quantity. England won the First Test, at Old Trafford, by the substantial margin of 202 runs, even without the two major Test players of post-war years, Denis Compton and Alec Bedser. The Second Test was at Lord's. The two unknown slow bowlers, Ramadhin and Valentine, spun the West Indies to an historic and unexpected victory, prompting the composition of a famous calypso about 'those two little pals of mine, Ramadhin and Valentine'. From then on England fell apart and the tourists won the Third and Fourth Tests by margins of 10 wickets and an innings and 56 runs respectively. Valentine took 33 wickets in the four games, Ramadhin 26; Worrell hit 261 and 158 in his single innings in the last two matches.

The first influx of West Indian immigrants to England had begun a year or two prior to this success, so the visitors had a fair sprinkling of supporters at their matches. The initial win at Lord's produced an improvised West Indian band which chanted and sang its way round the outfield. A decade later such exuberance would be stamped on, but the novelty of it all caught the traditionalists by surprise.

Michael Manley in his *A History of West Indies Cricket* commented on his side's success: 'To the Caribbean, the victory was more than a sporting success. It was the proof that a people was coming of age. They had bested the masters at their own game on their home turf. They had done so with good nature, with style, often with humour, but with conclusive effectiveness.'

With such obvious talent, it is astonishing that the West Indies were to play six Test series against either England or Australia between their great 1950 series and 1961, yet fail to win a single one. To many minds in the West Indies the lack of success at the highest level during those years was due to the continued belief that a white man had to captain the side overseas. It was all the more odd given that, in Frank Worrell, the team possessed a natural leader who was also an automatic choice on the grounds of his cricketing ability. The man who led the campaign to install Worrell as captain was the black journalist C.L.R. James (see plate section). He had come to England in 1932 and been a close colleague of Constantine. He returned to his native Trinidad in 1958, taking up the appointment as Editor of the paper *The Nation*. James notes in *Beyond a Boundary*: 'Immediately I was immersed up to the eyes in The Case for West Indian Self-Government; and a little later, in the most furious cricket campaign I have ever known, to break the discrimination of sixty years and have a black man, in this case Frank Worrell, appointed captain of a West Indies team.'

The catalyst for his campaign had been the strange appointment of John Goddard to lead the West Indies on their second post-war trip in 1957. Goddard had had to come out of virtual retirement. Michael Manley describes the move as the same as the English people reinstating Charles I after Oliver Cromwell.

England won the 1957 series comfortably. The wiles of Valentine and Ramadhin had been mastered by Tom Graveney, Peter May and Colin Cowdrey. Goddard carried the can, but England had a near perfect attack in Fred Trueman and Brian Statham as their fast bowlers and Jim Laker and Tony Lock as spinners. This combination had beaten Australia in the preceding English summer, with Jim Laker's off spin creating a world record at Old Trafford when he took 19 of the 20 Australian wickets. In something of a gamble, Trueman had been omitted from the match to allow an extra batsman, Sheppard, to play.

With the retirement of Bradman and the gradual fading of Lindwall and Miller, Australia's star declined from 1951. England had won the 1953 series in England, the 1954–5 series in Australia and then the 1956 series just mentioned.

COUNTY CRICKET IN CRISIS

Curiously the rise of England's Test team through the 1950s was in inverse proportion to the general popularity of English cricket, judged by the number of spectators. The small downturn back in 1948 was not a simple blip, but the beginning of a general decline in

England vs. Australia (Laker's Match): Fourth Test Match, Manchester, 26-28, 30-31 July 1956

England	1st innings		
P.E. Richardson	c Maddocks b Benaud	104	
M.C. Cowdrey	c Maddocks b Lindwall	80	
Rev. D.S. Sheppard	b Archer	113	
P.B.H. May (Capt.)	c Archer b Benaud	43	
T.E. Bailey	b Johnson	20	
C. Washbrook	lbw b Johnson	6	
A.S.M. Oakman	c Archer b Johnson	10	
T.G. Evans (wkt)	st Maddocks b Johnson	47	
J.C. Laker	run out	3	
G.A.R. Lock	not out	25	
J.B. Statham	c Maddocks b Lindwall	0	
	B 2, l-b 5 w 1	8	
		459	

Australia	1st innings			2nd innings	
C.C. McDonald	c Lock b Laker	32	c Oakman b Laker	89
J.W. Burke	c Cowdrey b Lock	22	c Lock b Laker	33
R.N. Harvey	b Laker	0	c Cowdrey b Laker	0
I.D. Craig	lbw b Laker	8	lbw b Laker	38
K.R. Miller	c Oakman b Laker	6	b Laker	0
K. Mackay	c Oakman b Laker	0	c Oakman b Laker	0
R.G. Archer	st Evans b Laker	6	c Oakman b Laker	0
R. Benaud	c Statham b Laker	0	b Laker	18
R.R. Lindwall	not out	6	c Lock b Laker	8
L. Maddocks (wkt)	b Laker	4	lbw b Laker	2
I.W. Johnson (Capt.)	b Laker	0	not out	1
			B 12, l-b 4	16
		84		**205**

Australia Bowling	1st innings							
	O	M	R	W	O	M	R	W
Lindwall	21.3	6	63	2				
Miller	21	6	41	0				
Archer	22	6	73	1				
Johnson	47	10	151	4				
Benaud	47	17	123	2				

England Bowling	1st innings				2nd innings			
Statham	6	3	6	0	16	9	15	0
Bailey	4	3	4	0	20	8	31	0
Laker	16.4	4	37	9	51.2	23	53	10
Lock	14	3	37	1	55	30	69	0
Oakman					8	3	21	0

England win by an innings and 170 runs

numbers through the turnstiles. In 1955 Ronald Aird, the MCC Secretary, speaking at the annual meeting of County Secretaries, noted that most counties were no longer self-supporting through gate receipts and membership subscriptions. Even the additional income from Test Match profits was hardly bridging the gap between income and expenditure. Various ideas were tried out to entice spectators back. Drawn matches were blamed and a scheme limiting first innings to 85 overs was tried. The standard 75-yard boundary was introduced so that the crowds could enjoy more sixes. The idea of a knock-out competition, which had been mooted in 1945, was dusted off and then shelved. By 1958 fewer people watched the 700+ days of Championship cricket than saw the 42 league matches played by Arsenal.

Leslie Deakins, the practical Secretary of Warwickshire, realised that gate receipts from Championship matches were not to be relied upon. Through his county's Supporters Club he organised a very successful Football Pool. This enabled Warwickshire to transform their run-down Edgbaston Ground into a venue fit for Test Matches and made Warwickshire prosperous both on the field and in the balance book. Other counties copied his ideas, Supporters' Groups being set up on similar lines by most. So the County Championship survived through Football Pools!

The shortage of money had one very serious long-term effect on English cricketing standards. The counties could not afford to raise players' wages in line with those enjoyed by sportsmen in other fields. Many talented youngsters were therefore discouraged from making cricket a career. The working class boy was already more in tune with soccer than cricket and the money to be earned as a footballer was simply an added incentive which cricket did not possess. The other side of the coin was the public schoolboy. His parents could no longer afford to pay his expenses so that he could play as an amateur; the taxman had seen to that during the austerity of the Labour government between 1945 and 1951. The boy could earn vastly more in the professions, than by electing to be either a shamateur or a professional cricketer.

The cricket press was continually printing ideas for revamping first-class county cricket. One suggestion was to run the Championship along the lines of the Sheffield Shield or Currie Cup, by drastically reducing the number of matches and thus giving genuine amateurs a chance to play again. In fact, as will be detailed in the next chapter, the 1960s were to see the beginning of a fundamental change, but Rowland Bowen, one of the leading students of the game in the 1960s, remained unaware of what was in the offing. He began the final chapter of his book of cricket history (written in 1969–70) with:

> The theme of this book is of rise, life and decline. It is my view that by the end of this century cricket will still be found fairly world-wide, but played as a game for pleasure (even at the club cricket level) as all games and sports should be played or indulged in. Its rise was an accident of geography and social history, and, maybe, of one or two other local factors: its esteem during the best part of

THE HISTORY OF CRICKET

its healthy life was something quite definitely accidental as it became a kind of hand-maiden of the British Empire; and its decline was as inevitable as was the decline of that Empire.

What Bowen missed in his sweeping statement linking the decline of cricket with the decline of Empire was that in three major countries, as well as the islands of the Caribbean, cricket positively boomed after they became independent. The three countries were Pakistan, India and Ceylon (Sri Lanka).

PAKISTAN, INDIA AND CEYLON

After the Gandhi-led campaign for freedom, it might be suspected that India's new government would be anxious to remove the outward traces of British rule as soon as practical. Under Prime Minister Pandit Nehru, however, cricket was not only tolerated, it was positively encouraged. Nehru, having been educated at Harrow and Cambridge, was no newcomer to cricket; it was a basic part of his upbringing. The West Indies tour of independent India in 1948–9 was greeted by huge crowds and tremendous enthusiasm. During their visit to the subcontinent, the West Indies also pioneered the first major tour to Pakistan. The authorities in Pakistan had an unenviable task. They were faced with building a national cricket team from a few broken fragments, and were not helped by the political geography which split the country in two halves. Furthermore, East Pakistan, which was formerly the eastern section of Bengal, had no tradition of first-class cricket. Bengal's cricket had always been centred on Calcutta.

West Pakistan incorporated three former Ranji Trophy Cricket Associations: North West Frontier Province (NWFP), Sind and Northern India. There were just four decent cricket grounds (i.e., up to first-class standard): Lawrence Gardens in Lahore, the Sind CA ground in Karachi, the NWFP ground in Peshawar, and the former Indian Army Ground in Rawalpindi. Of the old princely native states, Bahawalpur was the only one of substance in the new country. Through the efforts of Mr Justice A.R. Cornelius, a Board of Cricket Control was formed in April 1948 and the new Pakistan government was quick to support this venture. The following year came the first Pakistan *Cricket Annual*, which proudly published the details of the first first-class overseas tour by Pakistan – to Ceylon, a few weeks prior to the *Annual's* appearance. The *Cricket Annual* makes no bones about the importance of cricket in the new state:

Cricket is not a game meant only for amusement or physical exercise as many people seem to think. It is also a great education and training for both the young and the old. Physically it develops every muscle of the body. Mentally it teaches cheerfulness in defeat and modesty in victory. It checks the growth of selfishness and creates a spirit of comradeship. Cricket is a democratic game in which wealth or poverty, high or low position, make no difference. It is perhaps the only game

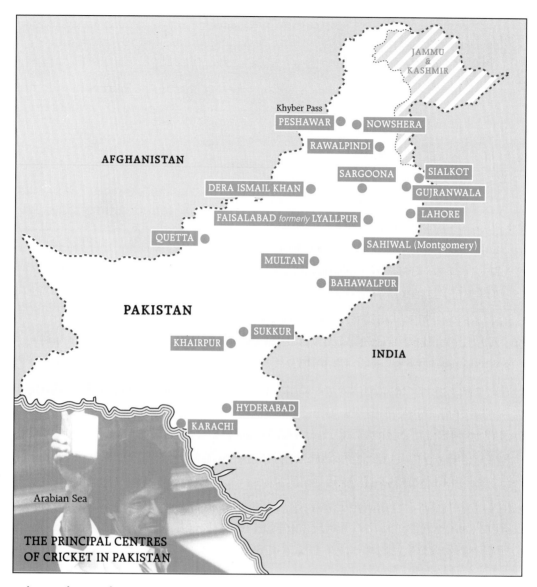

Pakistan, showing the centres of cricket. On the formation of Pakistan, most of the established subcontinent Cricket Associations were in independent India.

that builds up a sound character and an adaptable temperament that are helpful to a man, not only on the cricket field, but also in the wider field where the struggle for existence goes on.

This comment hardly agrees with the remarks made by Rowland Bowen, but echoes similar sentiments published in England a hundred years ago. Cricket in England might well be on

THE HISTORY OF CRICKET

a downward path in the 1950s, but the reverse was most surely the situation on the subcontinent.

An MCC team toured India in 1951–2 and visited Pakistan, playing unofficial Tests there. As soon as the tour was over, Pakistan applied to join the Imperial Cricket Conference and was admitted at the July meeting in England that summer. A few months later came the first official Pakistan Test series, against India. Pakistan were led by A.H. Kardar, who had been a member of the 1946 Indian side to England under Pataudi. In this first Test series, India won two games, Pakistan one and two were drawn. Later tours between the two countries were often marred by political tensions, but this initial visit was harmonious. S.K. Gurunathan ends his report on the tour with: 'That they were a popular side the record attendances at each centre amply proved. They played the game in the right spirit and did much more. They will be welcome in this country again.'

Pakistan were granted a full tour of England in 1954. The Chairman of the Pakistan Selection Committee, Hassan Mahmood, Chief Minister of Bahawalpur, bore the entire cost of training the selected team for one month at the Bahawalpur Stadium. Despite a very wet summer, the Pakistan side flourished and the Test series was tied with one victory to each country.

The subsequent book on the tour contained a Foreword by Mohammad Ali, the Pakistan Prime Minister, who commented:

> It was for the first time that a visiting team defeated a formidable English team on British soil on their first venture. In spite of the handicap of the vagaries of the English weather the members of our team gave an excellent account of themselves and raised Pakistan's prestige high in the international cricket world. By winning so many County matches and emerging with honours even in the Test rubber – they have carved for Pakistan an honourable place in the cricket world. I hope our team's triumph will prove a source of inspiration to our young cricketers.

The Prime Minister was now also the President of the Board of Control for Cricket in Pakistan. This hands-on support from the government was useful in many ways, but it meant that Pakistan Test cricket was entwined in the politics of the country to an even greater extent than in the days of the Raj.

What Pakistan lacked when they joined the ICC in 1952 was a first-class competition on the lines of the Ranji Trophy. Mr Justice Cornelius, who had founded the Board, was the architect behind the Qaid-i-Azam Trophy (Qaid-i-Azam means 'The Great Leader' and refers to Jinnah, the founder of Pakistan). Cornelius invited various provincial clubs to enter a competition for this trophy in 1953–4. Seven provinces – East Pakistan, Baluchistan, Punjab, Karachi, Sind, NWFP and Bahawalpur – together with teams from the Railways and the Services agreed to compete, but East Pakistan and Baluchistan withdrew. No qualification rules were laid down, which enabled the Amir of Bahawalpur to collect a very strong side, and he duly won the trophy. The detailed history of the trophy and its ever-shifting rules and competing teams is beyond this history, but can be found in the *ACS&H Guide to Pakistan First Class Cricket*.

There was a certain reluctance on the part of both England and Australia to tour the subcontinent. Australia had a three-week visit in 1956, but their first full tour was not until 1959–60. The MCC went in 1951–2, but there was a ten-year gap before the second post-war trip. A.S. de Mello of the Indian Board of Control had the idea of filling the voids by bringing Commonwealth teams to India. He asked George Duckworth (1901–1966), the former England and Lancashire wicketkeeper, to act as manager. It was arranged that a series of unofficial 'Tests' would be included in the itinerary. Some critics doubted that such a mixed team would work or attract many spectators. Duckworth engaged players from England, Australia and the West Indies; those from the last two countries were mainly engaged in league cricket in England. The tours confounded the critics by being both harmonious and popular. There were three major tours, each with over 20 fixtures. Then, in the 1960s and 1970s, four more Commonwealth teams made briefer visits. The initial venture took place in 1949–50, and the *Wisden* report noted:

> Particularly well provided with batting talent, the Commonwealth team soon adapted themselves to Indian conditions of hard ground, glaring light and frequent changes from turf to matting pitches. They maintained an unusually high rate of scoring and, although the general level of bowling did not reach quite such a high standard as the batting, it was usually effective because of grand support in the field. Indeed, the fielding ability left perhaps the biggest impression on the Indian public.

Another initiative of de Mello was to arrange an Asian Cricket Conference. In 1948–9 representatives of India, Pakistan, Ceylon, Burma and Malaya met in Calcutta for what proved to be the first and only time. Of the group the unexpected member is Burma. A cricket federation had been formed there – Pakistan sent a side to Burma in 1952–3 – but changes in the Burmese government since then have meant that the vast majority of foreign nationals, at least from cricket-playing countries, have left. Rowland Bowen in 1970 makes the simple statement: 'The game is dead in Burma.'

This was certainly not the case in that other appendage of the old Indian Empire, Ceylon. Like Burma, Ceylon achieved independence in 1948. Cricket was well established at the major public schools on the island. The Ceylon Cricket Board were working hard to extend this interest into the 'National' schools, and were also keen to arrange a tour to England. (The Board had been formed in June 1959, soon after the Ceylon Cricket Association had celebrated its 25th anniversary.)

Several Ceylonese players came to England in order to take part in county cricket: Laddie Outschoorn (Worcestershire, born Colombo 1918) and Gamini Goonesena (Nottinghamshire, born Colombo 1931) were two examples. Ceylon toured Malaya in 1958, soon after that country gained independence. Nine matches were played, including Ceylon vs. All Malaya, staged in conjunction with the independence celebrations. Clive Inman (born Colombo 1936) was Ceylon's star batsman on the trip and went on to a successful career in county cricket with Leicestershire.

MALAYA

A Malayan Cricket Association had been formed in 1948, but the internal war against the communist insurgents restricted cricketing activity. In 1959 Malaya took part in a three-sided tournament in Hong Kong, with Bangkok as the third competitor. The contest had an amazing finish. When the ninth Malayan wicket fell against Hong Kong, 91 runs were still required. Malaya won!

NEW ZEALAND AND FIJI

In New Zealand, the Plunket Shield resumed after the war. It was expanded twice in the 1950s: Central Districts joined in 1950–1 and Northern Districts in 1956–7. The New Zealand national side won its first Test in 1955–6. The West Indies came for a four-match series and New Zealand, under John Reid, won the final Test at Auckland. Reid, who was the Kiwis' outstanding batsman at this time, appropriately hit the highest score in this historic match. The series itself was won 3–1 by the West Indies. The nearest New Zealand got to winning a rubber was in South Africa in 1961–2, when the series was tied 2–2.

Across the Pacific, the enthusiasm of Philip Snow led to a great revival in Fijian cricket. The islanders toured New Zealand in 1948 and 1954 and opposed the Plunket Shield sides with some success.

THE AMERICAS

In 1949, the efforts of Lewis Gunn resulted in the formation of the Canadian Cricket Association. He also acted as player-manager when the first properly representative Canadian team toured England in 1954. Gunn, together with Donald King (1918–1977), the Cricket Association's Secretary, gradually increased the numbers of people involved in Canadian cricket. King reported in 1965 that there were 84 cricket grounds in the country, most of them in public parks.

A fairly strong side represented the MCC on its first post-war tour of North America in 1959. The side were undefeated in 25, mainly one-day, matches. Only two of these games were in the United States, where cricket was at a very low ebb. The few teams in the New York area were principally made up of West Indians resident there; in southern California, the Hollywood influence kept the game alive. Other than that, cricket was played in sundry scattered outposts. In 1961, however, John Marder almost single-handedly created a national United States Cricket Association, and two years later he revived the long defunct

United States vs. Canada match. Born in Nottingham in 1911, Marder emigrated to the States as a young man, where he was educated at Boston University. He later lived in California, although he died in London in 1976.

Argentina continued to be the main South American cricketing country (excluding British Guiana), but as the British influence waned the standard of cricket fell. The MCC sent a team out in 1958–9. The tourists won both 'Tests' against Argentina by a large margin. The side also visited Brazil, playing four games there, but the standard was very low.

SOUTH AFRICA

In South Africa, the development of cricket through the Nuffield Scheme and other youth policies paid dividends when a very young side under Jack Cheetham (1920–1980) toured Australia in 1952–3. The Australians thought so little of the team, that they demanded a £10,000 guarantee before agreeing to the visit. Cheetham's youngsters by dint of brilliant fielding and teamwork tied the Test series two matches each and caught the public's imagination to the tune of a £3,000 profit. When the MCC toured South Africa in 1956–7 the home side again tied the Test series; but the following season, Australia had regrouped and Richie Benaud's leg-break talent had matured. He took over 100 first-class wickets on the tour, and Australia won the Test rubber.

South Africa's first-class cricketers were almost all amateurs, and most retired from top-level cricket around the age of 30. This worked in one way against the standard of the game – the most talented disappearing when at their peak – but it also gave great encouragement to youngsters, since the Currie Cup sides were always looking for new talent to fill their vacancies. It was still the practice for the Currie Cup to be put in abeyance when a Test side toured South Africa; thus almost every other season was blank so far as competitive first-class cricket was concerned. Even when the competition was operating, the provincial teams only played six such matches per season. In 1951–2 the competition was split into two sections. They joined back together ten years later, but the differing standards of the teams made many matches one-sided and spectator numbers dropped.

Like most aspects of life in South Africa, cricket was divided along racial lines and this division hardened with the elevation to power of the Nationalist Party in 1948. The various sections of the black community had their own cricket governing bodies. These merged to form the South African Board of Control in 1947, and the first competition under this body began in 1951. Outside South Africa this cricket received almost no publicity and the first that most English people knew of its existence was the arrival of Basil d'Oliveira in England in 1960, on his appointment as professional with Middleton, the Central Lancashire League club. He had been brought there under the auspices of John Kay, a Manchester-based journalist, and the broadcaster, John Arlott. D'Oliveira's ability had been noticed by the cricket press in the autumn of 1958, when he captained the first non-white South African touring side to East Africa.

THE HISTORY OF CRICKET

In the same year that d'Oliveira joined Middleton, a referendum of white voters in South Africa opted to leave the Commonwealth and declare South Africa a republic. In theory this caused the world governing body of cricket, the Imperial Cricket Conference, a major problem. The ICC was only open to Commonwealth countries, and only Commonwealth countries who were members of the ICC could play Test cricket. South Africa duly left the ICC, but England, Australia and New Zealand simply ignored the second rule. An ICC statement declared that 'there was nothing to prevent matches played by South Africa being called Tests, though these were not recognised as official by the ICC'. Even so, the representative matches between South Africa and these three countries continued to be included in all the official Test Match records. The campaign to prevent South Africa from playing Test Matches was, in 1960, still some years distant. (India, Pakistan and the West Indies had never played Tests against South Africa.)

ELSEWHERE IN AFRICA

The Kenya Kongonis of Nairobi remained the best-run club in British East Africa, and A. Davies of the Kongonis was the architect behind the first MCC tour of that section of the continent in 1957–8. Matches were played not only in Kenya, but also in Uganda and Tanganyika. In 1961–2 a side raised by Freddie Brown, the former England captain, made a similar tour. Apart from the Englishmen resident, the main cricketers came from the Indian communities in the three colonies, all of which achieved independence in the early 1960s. It was as a result of these tours that Basharat Hassan from Nairobi came to England and had 20 successful years in county cricket with Nottinghamshire.

The colonies of West Africa were a real backwater in cricketing terms. There were several tours to England by the Nigerian Cricket Association in the early 1950s, but the sides were in fact composed of Englishmen stationed in Nigeria and home on leave. Matches between Nigeria and the Gold Coast continued – one for Europeans and one for Africans – and in 1956 the two separate Nigerian Cricket Associations merged. Matches were also played between Sierra Leone and Gambia.

Despite the intensive cricket in Egypt during the war, the game took a downward path as the number of British residents dwindled. An Egyptian club did come to England in 1951, playing the MCC at Lord's; however, the club formed in 1935 for native Egyptians does not seem to have survived the abolition of the monarchy in 1953.

CONTINENTAL EUROPE

In Holland in 1958 the Nederlandsche Cricket Bond celebrated its 75th anniversary by being given the title 'Koninklijke' (Royal). Some cricket had continued during the German occupation, though the game remained a pastime for a select few. The Free Foresters toured most years and the 1951 South African touring team to England visited Holland, setting a precedent for the Australians and West Indians to follow. The major Dutch club, Flamingo, made frequent tours to England. The Dutch cricketers, like the Danes, suffered from having no cricket grounds as such in their country, soccer and hockey grounds being converted by the use of matting wickets.

In Denmark, a Danish Cricket Association was not formed until 1953. Two years later the regular series of matches against Holland commenced, which is still being played.

In summary, the years 1945–60 saw the popularity of cricket in the British Isles, Australia and New Zealand go into decline after the initial post-war boom. Contrasting with the downward trend was the surge of enthusiasm in the West Indies and South Asian subcontinent.

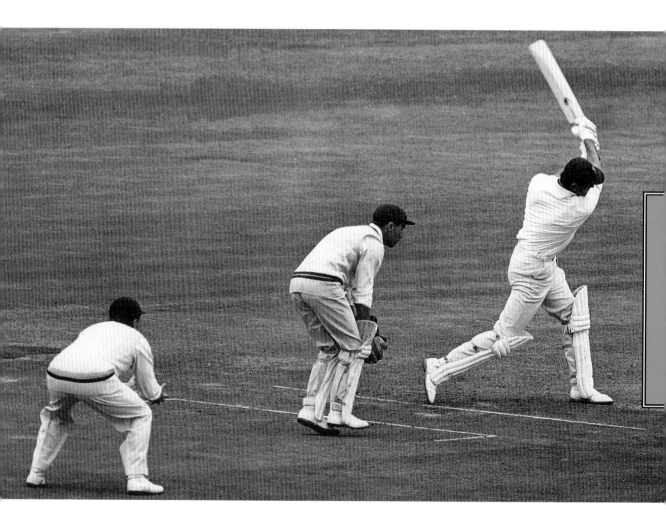

THE HISTORY OF CRICKET

The dominant feature of 1960s English cricket was the need for someone, somehow, to replenish the bank account. While the public enjoyed the talents of Colin Cowdrey, Ted Dexter and Raymond Illingworth, the administrators scratched their heads. There was an acute lack of funds at both professional and amateur level.

Although the initiative in England seemed to be in the hands of the professionals, it was an amateur problem which was to cause the ramshackle structure of English cricket to be revamped. In 1966 a body called the MCC National Cricket Association applied to the Advisory Sports Council (later simply the 'Sports Council') for a grant, to assist the MCC Schools' tour to South Africa. The application was turned down on the grounds that the MCC National Cricket Association was not a body which represented the whole of English cricket. Indeed, no such body apparently existed.

THE SEARCH FOR A CENTRAL ENGLISH BODY

To understand how this situation had come about, it is necessary to go back to 1935, when the Central Council of Physical Recreation (CCPR) was founded to encourage people to take up sport, and to provide the governing bodies of individual sports with a central organisation. Whatever cricket input there was, it was certainly of little moment. In 1957 the CCPR asked Sir John Wolfenden, a former headmaster of Shrewsbury School, to chair an inquiry into sport. The result of this inquiry was a report called *Sport in the Community*, published in 1963. Among the report's findings was the recommendation that cricket required a national body to negotiate with government in such fields as taxation, grant assistance, local council rates and the extension of playing facilities.

Ted Dexter –'Lord Ted' – was just in time to be a 'Gentlemen'. The photograph shows him batting for the Gentleman against the Players at Lord's in 1962, the year that the fixture ceased.

As a direct result of Wolfenden's report, the government created the Sports Council, which was made up of 31 members appointed by the Secretary of State for the Environment. The government handed a considerable annual sum to the Council, to be distributed to worthy sporting causes.

12

TIME

FOR

CHANGE

In response to Sir John Wolfenden's comment on cricket's lack of a national body, Billy Griffith, the MCC Secretary, announced in October 1964 the setting up of the MCC National Cricket Association, to be made up of the following organisations:

- MCC
- National Club Cricket Association
- First-Class Counties
- Minor Counties Cricket Association
- English Schools Cricket Association (ESCA)
- Combined Services
- MCC Youth Cricket Association.[28]

It seemed to meet the criteria of a national body, but the Sports Council decided otherwise. The 1966 rebuff caused the MCC to form a sub-committee to decide what steps should be taken to create a national organisation which would satisfy the Sports Council.

The Minister of Sport, Denis Howell (Labour MP for Small Heath, Birmingham), was consulted and his opinion was that the MCC itself ought to be the national body. In order to become so, it would have to expand its existing committee to include all the bodies listed above.

The MCC Committee rejected this idea and decided on the setting up of a new body called the MCC Cricket Council, under which there would be two main organisations: one dealing with first-class county and Test cricket, the other with amateur cricket. The first body was styled 'the Test and County Cricket Board' (TCCB) and the second was in fact the National Cricket Association (NCA).

The creation of the TCCB meant the disappearance of two long-standing bodies: the Advisory County Cricket Committee (formed in 1904) and the Board of Control for Test Matches at home (formed 1898). These two bodies in reality had been little more than sub-committees of the MCC.

The new set-up satisfied the demands of the Sports Council for the purposes of giving grants to cricket. By this tortuous manoeuvre, therefore, amateur cricket from 1968 could gain government funding.

THE COUNTY CASH CRISIS

The finances of county cricket were not so easily solved. The initial attempt to analyse the ills of county cricket and produce a cure was the 1937 Findlay Report. At an average of six-year intervals fresh reports were issued by new sub-committees, ending in the Clark Report of 1966. As has been noted, the finances of county cricket were in dire straits in the 1930s. They then improved beyond all recognition in the first few years after the war, before going into steep decline – the numbers going through the turnstiles halving from two million

---

28 NB. No mention of the Women's Cricket Association.

THE HISTORY OF CRICKET

to one million and then halving again to 500,000 and to 300,000 in the later 1960s. The carefully considered reports, set up by the authorities at Lord's, proposed nothing substantial to put the invalid back on his feet, or if they did, the counties threw the scheme out.

In 1945 a knock-out cup had been recommended. This finally came to fruition in 1963, about ten years too late – and 90 years after the first, abortive, knock-out cup! Even then it only appeared after a dry run in 1962, when Mike Turner, the Leicestershire Secretary, organised a pilot scheme in the Midlands. Gillette Industries sponsored the 1963 Cup, which involved only the first-class counties and was a 65 overs-per-side, one-day competition. It certainly caught the public's imagination. For the first time ever, Lord's was sold out for a county game before a ball was bowled. As half the counties were knocked out in the first round, the receipts, despite the good crowds, did not have a great effect on county finances once they had been divided up.

The next idea to improve attendances came in 1966. It was agreed that if both sides approved, a Championship match scheduled for Saturday, Monday and Tuesday could be played instead on Saturday, Sunday and Monday. A number of counties arranged such games and again there were reasonable crowds. It was illegal to charge gate money on a Sunday, so spectators were offered programmes or scorecards to buy instead. Because of pressure from religious groups, matches could not begin until 1.00 p.m. The idea for such weekend cricket had been around for some time but, like the Gillette Cup, it became a reality too late to make much difference to the bank balances. Out of the cricket on Sunday, though, developed the limited overs Sunday League, sponsored by John Player and Son. It was introduced in 1969, and charging gate money on a Sunday became legal. The numbers attending county matches doubled, moving back up to the 600,000 mark.

The new league did not, however, solve the riddle of how to persuade spectators to watch three-day county cricket. There is not the space here to delve into all the myriad minor adjustments which the counties made in order to produce 'Brighter Cricket'. The points system for the County Championship altered bewilderingly; instructions to groundsmen on the preparation of pitches spewed forth; counties were fined if the team's over-rate dropped fractionally, as if hundreds more spectators would flock to see a side bowling 19 overs an hour, as against 18. In real life only two factors saw crowds increase: one was fine weather, the other a successful team.

A way was found to give the weaker counties a chance of being successful. The rule allowing counties to employ only cricketers born or resident in that county was still fairly strictly enforced and clearly favoured the most populous shires (after Surrey's run of titles in the 1950s, Yorkshire came back in the 1960s, winning the title six times). In 1968 the counties agreed to the instant registration of one overseas player per team. Yorkshire declined the offer, but most of the other counties engaged a notable Test player, the plum being Gary Sobers, the West Indian all-rounder, who joined Nottinghamshire. It was a moot point, overall, whether the additional expense of the star was covered by the increase in membership or the gate.

Anti-apartheid demonstrators picket Lord's during the campaign to stop South Africa touring England in 1970. The campaign proved successful and South Africa were out of Test cricket for over 20 years.

Basil d'Oliveira. Because of apartheid in South Africa, the talented all-rounder d'Oliveira moved to England to pursue a career in first-class cricket. So successful was he for Worcestershire, that he played in 44 Tests for England.

THE BASIL D'OLIVEIRA AFFAIR

An external factor in 1970 was to negate most of the benefit of the Sunday League receipts and the 'star' factor. This was the cancellation of the visit of the South African touring team. The voices of those in England who wanted a ban placed on sporting links with South Africa because of apartheid had grown more strident during the 1960s. In the case of cricket, protests took the form of disrupting matches played by South African touring sides. Matters came to a head in the autumn of 1968. England were scheduled to tour South Africa and duly selected their team. Tom Cartwright, the Warwickshire all-rounder, was forced through fitness problems to withdraw from the party and the Selectors picked the Cape Coloured cricketer, Basil d'Oliveira, as his replacement. D'Oliveira had been playing on and off for England since 1966. The Prime Minister of South Africa, B.J. Vorster, then told the MCC that d'Oliveira was not acceptable as a member of the touring party. His government believed that d'Oliveira had been chosen as a result of political pressure and the proof of this was that d'Oliveira, a batsman, was taking the place of Cartwright, a bowler (though both could be termed all-rounders). The tour was cancelled.

South Africa were due to tour England in 1970, but through 1969 a Stop the Tour campaign gathered momentum. The newly formed MCC Cricket Council met for the first time to decide whether to bow to the pressure of the campaign and made the decision to allow the tour to proceed, but with a restricted fixture list. Barbed wire was erected to protect the cricket squares on grounds where matches were to be staged. The British government leaned heavily on the Cricket Council and almost at the last moment it was agreed to cancel the visit. The South Africans were told that tours to and from South Africa by officially appointed teams would not resume until the South African side was selected on merit and not simply confined to the white section of the nation.

The abandonment of the tour meant that professional cricket would lose a considerable sum of money. The previous 1965 tour had resulted in a large profit, part of which had been distributed to the counties. South Africa had a particularly attractive side, containing a number of brilliant cricketers, including the brothers Peter and Graeme Pollock, Mike Procter and Barry Richards.

Graeme Pollock, one of several brilliant South African players whose careers at the highest level were ruined by political events outside their control.

To replace the South Africans, the TCCB arranged a series of matches between England and the Rest of the World, captained by Gary Sobers. These games did not particularly interest the public, despite the presence of some world-famous names. The Cricket Council applied to the Sports Council for £200,000 to compensate the counties for the lost revenue. Cricket received £75,054. Every county except Leicestershire made a loss in 1970 and the professional game searched for finance outside cricket. Trent Bridge, for example, was saved by the building of a multi-storey office block in one corner of the ground.

THE GROWTH OF SPONSORSHIP

A third one-day limited overs competition, this one sponsored by Benson & Hedges, was introduced for the 1972 season and the loss-making County Championship reduced to 20 matches per side. There had been a suggestion that six Test Matches be played when Australia toured in 1972, but when the success of the first One-Day International was understood (played in Melbourne between Australia and England in 1970–1), three One-Day Internationals were arranged as well as the standard five Tests. Prudential were brought in as sponsors of these one-day matches and paid £30,000 for the privilege.

Despite the money coming from the now four main sponsors, the counties still remained in a parlous state. The numbers paying at the gate for County Championship games were hardly worth counting – the spectators were almost entirely county members. In 1974 it was reported that Gloucestershire, Hampshire, Middlesex, Nottinghamshire and Yorkshire were 'in serious financial difficulties'.

The source of revenue for the counties over 100 years is clearly shown by the percentage figures from the annual accounts of Nottinghamshire CCC:

One hundred years of Nottinghamshire CCC's accounts

	1887	1907	1927	1947	1967	1987
			(%)			
Match Receipts	50	45	44	38	14	3
Members' Subscriptions	50	55	56	48	30	14
Supporters' Association	–	–	–	–	35	–
Tests, Broadcasting, Adverts and Sponsorship	–	–	–	14	21	83

Minor receipts have been ignored in the above table.

Monies received from the TCCB by the six counties with Test Match venues

	1970	1975	1980	1985	1990	1995
£	4,469	33,934	140,000	243,293	323,351	717,195

In terms of basic cash, as opposed to additional income through catering and sales of souvenirs, the amounts of money received from the TCCB by the six counties with Test Match venues can also be seen to have grown over the years (see opposite page). Inflation has to be taken into account, but even so the income from international matches combined with broadcasting fees and sponsorship rose substantially, reaching the point where counties once more made a surplus, in most cases in the early 1990s.

Sponsorship entered the amateur game as well. The whisky firm, Haig, sponsored a National Village Knock-Out Competition, which began in 1971; while the oil company, Esso, sponsored the ESCA Schools Competition. In 1973 the Wrigley Cricket Foundation assisted the National Cricket Association in introducing cricket to schoolchildren.[29]

CLUB, LEAGUE AND SCHOOL

Meanwhile, the face of club cricket in the south of England altered dramatically. The Club Cricket Conference, to which most major clubs in the Home Counties belonged, had a rule that member clubs could not compete in organised leagues. The Malden Wanderers' representative, Jimmy Walker, was the first to express the view that the south needed competitive cricket. After much heart-searching the Club Cricket Conference altered its constitution and the Surrey Clubs Championship started in 1968. Hertfordshire began a league in the same year, followed by Kent and Sussex in 1971; Middlesex's league began in 1972. It was not long before the leagues acquired sponsors.

The leagues in the north and midlands continued much as before, but those areas which had not traditionally had leagues also joined the new fad. Cricket was following the pattern set down by soccer in the 19th century.

Schools cricket also changed. The English Schools' Cricket Association (ESCA) had been founded in July 1948, when twelve individual counties which had Schools Cricket Associations joined together to form a national body. The new body, however, had little to do with public schools, and it was not until 1965 that an ESCA team opposed a public schools side at Lord's in a two-day game which, unfortunately, was a rain-ruined draw.[30] The best eleven out of the two teams were then selected to play the Combined Services. The Public Schools vs. Combined Services had been the culminating public schools match for many years. The days when Eton vs. Harrow was part of the social calendar had now gone for some time.

---

29   The Foundation was formed in June 1969 for an initial period of five years to support the NCA in developing and fostering the game at grass roots. In 1973 it specifically gave grants for coaching courses for boys and girls and for the training of coaches.

30   The one player who appeared and later made a name for himself in county cricket was David Acfield of Brentwood School, who played for Essex from 1966 to 1986.

MR CRICKET

Gubby Allen. An all-rounder of Test class who led England in Australia in 1936-7, Allen made an even greater mark as an administrator at Lord's after the Second World War. He was the Lord Harris of his day.

Through all these changes, the chief 'engineer' at Lord's was G.O.B. 'Gubby' Allen. For twelve years, up to his retirement in September 1976, Allen held the key role of Treasurer of the MCC. It was no coincidence that Lord Harris had been Treasurer from 1916 to his death. Allen had known Harris and, after a gap inadequately filled by Pelham Warner, had effectively assumed Harris's role.

Ian Peebles, the Middlesex and England cricketer, described Allen as 'Mr Cricket'. Like Harris before him, Allen was a member of the MCC Committee early in life (on election in 1935, he was ten years younger than any other member). Geoffrey Moorhouse in his book on Lord's comments: 'Allen's own rise to eminence in the club began immediately the war was over, when he noted with despair that the Committee was still packed with "Lord Hawke's yesmen" (Hawke, a dear old man but not very clever, had died in 1938) and decided that they must be replaced by people who thought for themselves.'

THE ICC AND THE WORLD CUP

While English cricket struggled with its finances, there were changes at the highest level – the Imperial Cricket Conference. After South Africa's exclusion in 1961, the most important suggestion put to the ICC came in 1962 from Pakistan. Their delegate proposed that a 'junior section' be set up. Like almost every new proposal the decision was deferred, but in 1965 the constitution was changed, the title of the ICC became the *International* Cricket Conference, and Ceylon, Fiji and the USA were admitted as 'associate members'. Curiously the report of the meeting to agree all this ends with: 'A very long meeting produced nothing fruitful.'

The Netherlands, Denmark, Bermuda and East Africa became associate members in 1966, and in 1971 the possibility of a World Cup was mooted. This took four years to mature and was staged in England in 1975. Sponsored by Prudential, who paid £100,000 for the privilege, and played in fine weather, the World Cup was a great success: 158,000 spectators attended the 15 matches, including 26,000 who watched the West Indies beat Australia in the final at Lord's. The game began at 11.00 a.m. on 21 June and did not end until 8.43 p.m.

The ICC meeting four days after the final immediately decided that a second World Cup would be a worthwhile venture; cricket's major tournament was set on its way. Sri Lanka, which had changed its name from Ceylon on becoming a republic in 1972, had participated in the World Cup as one of two ICC associate members (East Africa being the other), in order to make the numbers up to eight. It applied for Test Match status at the 1975 ICC meeting, but was turned down.

The second World Cup took place in 1979, the West Indies retaining their title. Simultaneously the associate members of the ICC took part in a junior competition, the ICC Trophy. This was masterminded by J.R. Gardiner, Chairman and Secretary of the ICC Associate Members' World Cup Committee. Mr Gardiner himself donated the Trophy and all the medals for the competitors. Somehow he managed to get 15 squads of cricketers to come to England for a competition which lasted a month. It is worth recording the countries which took part in this pioneering adventure: Argentina, Bangladesh, Bermuda, Canada, Denmark, East Africa, Fiji, Israel, Malaysia, the Netherlands, Papua New Guinea, Singapore, Sri Lanka, the United States and Wales. Wales replaced Gibraltar, which had to withdraw at the last moment. Sri Lanka beat Canada in the final.

This new competition should be regarded as a major step towards developing cricket worldwide. For the first time the non-Test-playing countries had an organised tournament as a focal point, and though some of the cricket played in the competition was of a low standard, there is no doubt it greatly encouraged the playing of cricket in the associate countries. Through it first Sri Lanka and later Zimbabwe graduated to Test Match status.

During the 1960s the ICC had debated and eventually reached decisions on two bowling matters of importance: the definition of bowling as opposed to 'throwing'; and the 'front foot' law for bowlers. Both decisions were incorporated in the Laws in 1969. The 1970s saw long discussions on 'dangerous' fast bowling, with proposals for limiting bouncers, and the related problem of slow over-rates. During the 1980s the behaviour of some players towards both umpires and opponents became unacceptable, and the need arose for third umpires and referees. The ICC expanded further in 1984, when Italy was elected as a non-voting 'affiliated member', and by 1996 there were no less than 46 members.

SOUTH AFRICA AND THE REBEL TOURS

For more than 30 years, the political problems of South Africa occupied more of the ICC's time than any other topic. In 1983 the annual conference was described as 'more of a political convention than a cricket debate'.

When the organisation's title was altered to 'International', South Africa did not reapply for admittance. Tests and tours between South Africa, Australia, New Zealand and

England continued on schedule until 1970, with the exception of the 1968–9 England visit, previously mentioned. At the 1971 Conference South Africa's racial policy was condemned, but it was left to individual countries to decide whether or not to continue playing against South Africa. In 1974 there was a proposal that the body representing non-white cricket in South Africa should be admitted to the ICC, but this was rejected because it represented only non-white players. Four years later a delegation from the ICC agreed to visit the country to see if cricket there was now being run on multiracial grounds. They found that the South African cricket authorities were making strenuous efforts to develop multiracial cricket, and in 1980 the South African Cricket Union was invited to reapply for ICC membership. This initiative turned out to be wishful thinking on the part of England and Australia; it was clear that the other members would not entertain South African membership. South African delegates came to London to attend ICC meetings in 1981, 1982 and 1983, but failed to gain admittance to those meetings. The England tour to the West Indies in 1980–1 nearly came to an abrupt end when Guyana expelled Robin Jackman, the Surrey and England bowler, on the grounds that he had played in South Africa. The Second Test, due to be played in Georgetown, Guyana, was then cancelled. The England team left Georgetown and flew to Barbados, while the various West Indian governments conferred. The tour continued without the Guyana leg. The West Indies then threatened to cancel New Zealand's tour to the Caribbean on the grounds that New Zealand and South Africa still played rugby against each other.

The first English 'rebel' tour to South Africa (breaking the ICC ban) took place in 1981–2, England being led by Graham Gooch, the Essex batsman. Of the top English cricketers only Ian Botham and Bob Willis declined a tour offer. At the ICC meeting in 1982 it was announced that England had banned all the players taking part in the tour from Test cricket for three years. The following South African season a rebel party from the West Indies toured. The players were banned for life from playing in matches under the auspices of the West Indian Board (although the ban was rescinded for the 1989–90 season). There were continuous repercussions. At one point the Australian government banned from entry into the country all cricketers who had toured South Africa with unofficial sides, but the boycott proved unworkable. The West Indian Board instructed its touring party to England of 1984 not to play counties which used players who had South African connections. The counties refused to be told what players they could choose and the West Indian Board eventually retracted the demand. The most devastating action in the South African affair came in 1982–3, when a team from Sri Lanka went to South Africa. The Sri Lankans faced a life ban from cricket at home, but would earn in a few months more than they would in a lifetime of Sri Lankan cricket. At a stroke Sri Lanka lost half their pool of 24 top-quality players.

Australia suffered a severe blow in 1985–6, when 15 leading players under Kim Hughes, who had captained Australia in the 1983 World Cup, formed another rebel tour to South Africa. From the South African viewpoint, this was the most successful rebel tour, with the 'Test' Matches well attended and the One-Day Internationals played to full houses.

The man at the forefront of the development of cricket in South Africa – not only the rebel tours, but the coaching of cricket outside the white community – was Ali Bacher. He had captained South Africa against Australia in 1969–70, and in 1987 was Managing Director of the South African Cricket Union. The *Protea Cricket Annual* of that year noted:

Dr Bacher is a realist. He knows that the future of this country lies not in continued white domination of the sport – a natural phenomenon because the game is coached to a very high degree in all the best white schools in South Africa, and has nothing to do with apartheid – but in the development of the other races in this country. That is why this man has started in motion a movement among the black aspiring cricketers that is certain to produce an abundance of cricket talent that will make the world sit up and take notice.

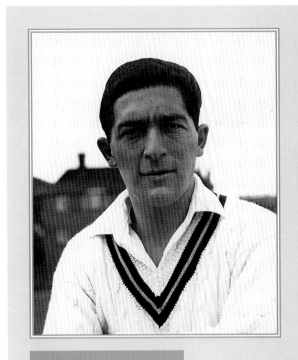

Ali Bacher, who was the South African captain when the anti-apartheid campaign ended his country's participation in Test cricket. He worked tirelessly to have South Africa reinstated.

In 1989–90 another England rebel side, under the England Test captain Mike Gatting, set off for South Africa. The tourists were banned from Test cricket for five years. They had agreed to go on a second tour to South Africa in 1990-1, but in 1990 came news of Nelson Mandela's release and the move to end apartheid. In June 1991 the two controlling bodies of cricket in South Africa joined together as the United Cricket Board of South Africa. The same month all remaining apartheid laws were removed from the statute book, and Ali Bacher came to the July meeting of the ICC at Lord's, when South Africa was readmitted to the Conference. From the selfish viewpoint of a cricket follower the main effect of the isolation of South Africa through the 1980s had been that most Test teams were unrepresentative of their countries' full strength because rebel-tour players were serving bans. This situation naturally produced some unrealistic Test Match and One-Day International results.

The other controversy of the time – Kerry Packer and the Australian broadcasting franchises – also meant that for the best part of three years certain cricketers were omitted from the official national squads. For example, English Test cricketers such as Tony Greig, Dennis Amiss, Derek Underwood and Alan Knott played in the 1977 series in England against Australia, but were not eligible again until the England tour of Australia in 1979–80. Of the Packer players, in fact, only Underwood was chosen for this tour. Knott's international career resumed the following summer in England. Amiss and Greig did not play for their country after 1977, and Greig retired from Sussex county cricket in 1978.

In essence, Packer simply exploited the fact that Test cricketers other than those playing in English county cricket were still poorly paid in the 1970s.

Kerry Packer, reputedly Australia's wealthiest man, ran among other enterprises the Australian independent TV company, Channel Nine. He put in a bid for the exclusive rights to top cricket in Australia, and although his bid was much higher than that offered by the Australian Broadcasting Commission (ABC), the Australian Cricket Board accepted ABC without listening to Packer's proposals. In the winter of 1976–7, Packer and his agents decided to try to contract major Test cricketers, both in Australia and outside, with a view to staging international matches independent of both the Australian Cricket Board and the ABC network. At the time of the Melbourne Test between Australia and England, celebrating the Centenary of Test cricket (which, by an extraordinary coincidence, resulted in exactly the same margin of victory for Australia – by 45 runs – as in the first ever Test, played on the same ground: see pages 230–1) no less than 28 top players in Australia had signed contracts with the Packer organisation. Forty other cricketers, 18 of whom were from the West Indies, were also in the process of being contracted.

All negotiations were carried out without the knowledge of the Australian Board and the news was not made public until the 1977 Australian touring team arrived in England. Only four of that squad had not signed for Packer.

From England's viewpoint Packer's major signing was the current England Test captain, Tony Greig of Sussex. The ruling body for cricket in England, the Cricket Council, met and instructed the England Test Selectors not to pick Greig as captain for the forthcoming Ashes series, although the England players signed by Packer could be chosen for the Tests. If the English authorities had decided to omit from selection players who had signed for Packer, then the whole Test series and Australian tour would have collapsed, since clearly the Australian Board would have had to act likewise.

Kerry Packer came to England and opened discussions with the official cricket authorities in the hope that his programme of 'Super-Tests' could be run without clashing with the Australian Board's 1977–8 fixture list. The talks fell down when the Australian Board refused to agree to Packer's demand for exclusive TV rights as soon as the existing contract with ABC ended. When the ICC met at Lord's on 26 July 1977, the mood of

Kerry Packer, the media tycoon who shook Australia's cricketing establishment in the 1970s and created his own 'Super-Tests'. Many of today's innovations, such as coloured clothing and cameras in the stumps, are due to him, and One-Day Internationals assumed a much higher profile as a result of his intervention.

reconciliation had switched to a formal 'declaration of war' between the two parties. The clause which the ICC agreed unanimously, and which really divided the cricket world into two camps, read: 'No player who after October 1 1977 has played or has made himself available to play in a match previously disapproved by the Conference shall thereafter be eligible to play in any Test Match.'

Kerry Packer applied for an injunction and damages in the High Court against the ICC and TCCB. The hearing began on 26 September 1977, the plaintiffs being World Series Cricket Pty Ltd and three players – Tony Greig, John Snow and Mike Procter. They sought to quash the clause noted above since it was a restraint of trade.

The hearing lasted 31 working days and ended with Mr Justice Slade announcing that the ICC and TCCB ban of Packer players from Tests was *ultra vires* and void as being in unreasonable restraint of trade. The plaintiffs were awarded costs estimated at £250,000, which were shared between the TCCB and ICC. The 1977 England vs. Australia series, won by England by three matches to nil, was an unhappy one because of the brittle atmosphere between Packer and non-Packer players. The Australian side returned home to begin cricket under the auspices of Kerry Packer.

The World Series Cricket (WSC) involved three teams: Australia, the West Indies, and the Rest of the World, which was captained by Tony Greig. The teams played in three

Australia vs. England: Centenary Test, Melbourne Cricket Ground,
12, 13, 14, 16, and 17 March 1977

Australia	1st innings				2nd innings	
I.C. Davis	lbw b Lever	5			c Knott b Greig	68
R.B. McCosker	b Willis	4	(10)		c Greig b Old	25
G.J. Cosier	c Fletcher b Lever	10	(4)		c Knott b Lever	4
G.S. Chappell (capt)	b Underwood	40	(3)		b Old	2
D.W. Hookes	c Greig b Old	17	(6)		c Fletcher b Underwood	56
K.D. Walters	c Greig b Willis	4	(5)		c Knott b Greig	66
R.W. Marsh (wkt)	c Knott b Old	28			not out	110
G.J. Gilmour	c Greig b Old	4			b Lever	16
K.J. O'Keeffe	c Brearley b Underwood	0	(2)		c Willis b Old	14
D.K. Lillee	not out	10	(9)		c Amiss b Old	25
M.H.N. Walker	b Underwood	2			not out	8
Extras	(B4, LB2, NB8)	14			(LB10, NB15)	25
	Total 138 (9 wickets declared)				Total 419	

England	1st innings				2nd innings	
R.A. Woolmer	c Chappell b Lillee	9			lbw b Walker	12
J.M. Brearley	c Hookes b Lillee	12			lbw b Lillee	43
D.L. Underwood	c Chapell b Walker	7	(10)		b Lillee	7
D.W. Randall	c Marsh b Lillee	4	(3)		c Cosier b O'Keeffe	174
D.L. Amiss	c O'Keeffe b Walker	4	(4)		b Chappell	64
K.W.R. Fletcher	c Marsh b Walker	4	(5)		c Marsh b Lillee	1
A.W. Greig (capt)	b Walker	18	(6)		c Cosier b O'Keeffe	41
A.P.E. Knott (wkt)	lbw b Lillee	15	(7)		lbw b Lillee	42
C.M. Old	c Marsh b Lillee	3	(8)		c Chappell b Lillee	2
J.K. Lever	c Marsh b Lillee	11	(9)		lbw b O'Keeffe	4
R.G.D. Willis	not out	1			not out	5
Extras	(B2, LB2, W1, NB2)	7			(B8, LB4, W3, NB7)	22
	Total 95				Total 417	

contests: first, the five-day 'Super-Tests'; second, one-day limited overs games for The International Cup; and, third, The Country Cup Championship, which took top-class matches to venues outside the big cities.

The major Australian grounds refused to entertain WSC matches, so the Super-Tests had to be played on football grounds and at any other suitable venues. The most important of the many innovations for the matches was the introduction of floodlit games, which attracted good crowds. Crowds at other matches were generally poor, but the 315 hours of

THE HISTORY OF CRICKET

England	1st innings				2nd innings				Fall of wickets				
	O	M	R	W	O	M	R	W		A	E	A	E
Lever	12	1	36	2	21	1	95	2	*Wkt*	*1st*	*1st*	*2nd*	*2nd*
Willis	8	0	33	2	22	0	91	0	1st	11	19	33	28
Old	12	4	39	3	27.6	2	104	4	2nd	13	30	40	113
Underwood	11.6	2	16	3	12	2	38	1	3rd	23	34	53	279
Greig					14	3	66	2	4th	45	40	132	290
									5th	51	40	187	346
Australia	1st innings				2nd innings				6th	102	61	244	369
Lillee	13.3	2	26	6	34.4	7	139	5	7th	114	65	277	380
Walker	15	3	54	4	22	4	83	1	8th	117	78	353	385
O'Keeffe	1	0	4	0	33	6	108	3	9th	136	86	407	410
Gilmour	5	3	4	0	4	0	29	0	10th	138	95	–	417
Chappell					16	7	29	1					
Walters					3	2	7	0					

Umpires: T.F. Brooks and M.G. O'Connell

TV viewing had reasonable audiences. One area in which Packer excelled was in the way the matches were televised, the techniques he used being a vast improvement on the staid methods of the BBC and ABC.

During this first season of Super-Tests, both England and Australia had two series of official Tests. England, now under the leadership of Mike Brearley, the Middlesex batsman, toured Pakistan and New Zealand; Australia hosted Tests against India, then went to the West Indies.

For their home series Australia persuaded the retired Test batsman, Bobby Simpson, to captain their side, which for the First Test contained six Test debutants. Australia won the first two games; India recorded their first ever Test victory in Australia in the third, and won the fourth by an innings; but Australia took the series by winning the fifth match. Despite the rival Super-Tests the crowds were higher than on the previous Indian tour. There were no Indian Test players among Packer's signings.

Australia, represented by the players who had opposed the Indians, flew to the West Indies in February 1978. Unlike Australia, the West Indies included their Packer players in the First Test of the five-match series and won by an innings. The Second Test brought a nine-wicket win for the West Indies, but in Georgetown for the Third Test, the West Indies Selectors omitted some of the Packer players. The rest of them then withdrew and the West Indian Board was faced with finding new faces. When the match began only two of the victorious Second Test team, Alvin Kallicharran (the new captain) and Derik Parry, played. Six West Indians made their Test debut and Australia won by three wickets.

The West Indies fielded a similar side for the Fourth Test and won by 198 runs, but the public boycotted the match, taking the part of the Packer players. Whereas the ground usually held about 25,000, each day fewer than 5,000 turned up. The final Test, in Kingston, Jamaica, ended in chaos (and a draw). Disagreeing with an umpiring decision on the last afternoon, the crowd rioted and sacked the pavilion. The West Indies Board agreed to continue the match into a sixth day, but failed to inform the umpires, one of whom refused to officiate, and no play therefore took place. Australia would probably have won inside an hour.

The England team's tour of Pakistan resulted in three drawn Tests. Pakistan did not have their Packer players for the first two games, but Packer released Mushtaq Mohammad, Zaheer Abbas and Imran Khan for the Third Test. The England players announced that they would not allow the match to go ahead if the Packer players took part. The three withdrew; the game was a very dull draw.

The second leg of England's tour, to New Zealand, was a milestone for the home country, New Zealand beating England for the first time ever in a Test Match – by 72 runs at Wellington. Richard Hadlee took 10 wickets for 100 runs in the match. The series was drawn 1–1.

So ended the first season of Packer cricket.

For the 1978 season in England, the counties decided to continue to contract their Packer players, both the four English ones (a fifth, John Snow, had retired) and those from overseas, although there were some problems. Pakistan were touring England. The Chief Martial Law Administrator, General Zia-ul-Haq, attended a meeting of the Pakistan Board of Control and told the Selectors not to pick Packer players in the squad to tour England. The TCCB meanwhile had reacted swiftly to prevent more English players signing for Packer. The basic tour fee for 1977–8 (to Pakistan and New Zealand) had suddenly jumped from £3,000 to £5,000 and, for the 1978 series of Tests, Cornhill Insurance had been signed as a sponsor at a cost of £1 million spread over five years. England players would receive £1,000 per Test appearance.

England did not select their Packer men for the Test series, but their absence was a minor problem in comparison with Pakistan's weakness for the same cause. England won the three-match series 2–0 and then went on to beat New Zealand 3–0.

For the second Australian season of Super-Tests, the Packer organisation had sorted out many teething troubles and now emerged with a slick marketing campaign: Packer was up against cricket's most prestigious contest, The Ashes. Giveaways, competitions, advertisements, sweat-shirts, a theme song and sponsorship agreements for products were all brought into play by the Packer organisation. They lost one preliminary round to the Australian Board. Jeff Thomson, the Australian fast bowler, had originally signed for Packer in the first year, but withdrew and played in the official 1977–8 Tests. He then switched over to Packer for 1978–9, but 'forgot' that he had signed a contract binding him to the Board. A court case followed and the Board got Thomson back.

THE HISTORY OF CRICKET

Thomson then said he would not play any cricket in 1978–9 – and went fishing! He later resumed first-class and Test cricket, finishing in 1985–6.

By and large Packer won the 1978–9 season. Alex Bannister, cricket correspondent for the *Daily Mail*, began his report on England's tour Down Under with: 'A lone trumpeter on the sparsely filled Hill at Sydney grimly symbolised Australia's embarrassing defeats, domestic confusions and divided loyalties, by sounding the Last Post as England won the sixth Test inside four days and the series by five to one.'

In February the Packer team of Australians went on a tour of the West Indies. The West Indies Board was facing bankruptcy and agreed to co-exist with Packer. Five Super-Tests were staged and apart from a riot in Georgetown, the matches went well. A profit was made and the Board received an *ex gratia* payment. The ICC had agreed to remain united against Packer; the West Indies, however, were in a very weak financial position and Pakistan and India were only toeing the ICC line with difficulty. On the face of it, Australia were the country most opposed to any agreement with Packer.

Almost out of the blue, however, came an announcement in May 1979 that the Australian Board had come to an agreement with Kerry Packer, an agreement which conceded all Packer's demands and seemingly more. The television deal was for ten years and included the cancelling of the proposed Australia vs. India series for 1979–80. This was replaced by the Benson & Hedges World Series Cup of 15 matches between Australia, the West Indies and England. The Board agreed to the use of coloured clothing in this series. Packer agreed to pay the Board A$1,150,000 annually for ten years: it looked a good deal, but the Board neglected to have the sum index-linked. With inflation high, Packer soon had a very cheap package.

So in 1979 the current pattern of international cricket – with annual One-Day International competition matches in Australia, in addition to the usual Test series – emerged out of the Packer conflict. 'Traditional' cricket had had its day at the top level.

POLITICS AND ADMINISTRATION

The two Australian officials who were the principal members of the Board through this difficult period were Bob Parish and Ray Steele. Parish acted as Chairman and Steele as Treasurer. Both came from Victoria. Steele, a lawyer by profession, had won a double blue (cricket and football) at Melbourne University. He was elected to Hawthorn CC in 1954 and moved up to the Australian Board in 1967. In 1961 he had been assistant manager of the Australian team to England. Bob Parish joined the Board in 1958 and was chairman from 1966 to 1969 and from 1975 to 1980. He managed the Australian sides to the West Indies in 1965 and to England in 1968. When Parish retired in 1992, he commented: 'You'll forgive me if I give a lot of credit for the healthy financial position of Australian cricket to one man, who is criticised frequently, and that is Kerry Packer ... I thank him for what he did because I think that was the catalyst that brought cricket to where it is today.'

Bob Parish. After serving as a Victorian representative on the Australian Board of Control, Parish was elected Board chairman in 1966. He was to be Chairman for eight years in all and had served the Board for 33 years when he retired in 1990.

Walter Hadlee, who was captain of the 1949 New Zealand side to England and, after retiring from first-class cricket, became the major figure in New Zealand cricket administration. Three of his sons played first-class cricket.

The President of the West Indian Board during the Packer crisis was Jeffrey Stollmeyer. A Test cricketer from 1939 to 1955, he had captained the West Indies and came from Trinidad. He served on the Board and as a Test Selector for many years before being elected President in 1974. Stollmeyer had supported the appointment of Worrell as West Indies captain and had worked to rid the West Indian Board of its parochial attitudes, but he was not in favour of one-day cricket and the razzmatazz attached to it. He did not, however, resign from the Board until the Packer affair was settled, retiring in 1981. He died as the result of being shot by an intruder who entered his Port of Spain home in September 1989.

THE HISTORY OF CRICKET

New Zealand cricket was very much under the control of Walter Hadlee. He had captained the 1949 New Zealand side to England and after retirement as a player was the dominant figure in the New Zealand Cricket Council. His sons, Richard and Dayle, both played Test cricket, the former being his country's outstanding cricketer.

The great administrator of Indian cricket, A.S. de Mello, had left in sad circumstances in 1951, having antagonised the Bombay CA over matters relating to the Ranji Trophy and what amounted to a vote of confidence at a Board of Control meeting. He walked out vowing that he would leave cricket for ever. Although such former cricketers as 'Ram' Ramchand and Vijay Merchant were appointed to administrative posts, the two personalities who stood above the rest during the 1960–80 period were the Nawab of Pataudi jun., and Sunil Gavaskar. Educated at Winchester and Oxford, Pataudi went on to captain India in 40 Tests, his international career ending in 1975. Gavaskar, he record-breaking batsman, made 106 consecutive Test appearances for India, in itself another record, and captained his country in 46 matches. He retired after the 1987–8 World Cup.

As has been noted, Pakistan cricket was entwined in politics. General Zia has been mentioned as intervening in the Packer problem. By the time of the 1986–7 India vs. Pakistan Test series, the General was President. He turned up for the Third Test in Jaipur as part of his 'Cricket for Peace' campaign. He was trying to put pressure on the Indian government over the disputes between the two countries.

In England, the creation of the Test and County Cricket Board in 1968 signalled the

Sunil Gavaskar, the first batsman to reach 10,000 Test Match runs. He made 106 consecutive Test appearances for India and 125 in all. He retired after the 1987–8 World Cup, having captained India in 47 Tests.

start of a 20-year conflict between that body and the MCC for the control of English cricket. Jack Bailey, who was Secretary of the MCC from 1974 to 1987, resigned on the point of principle that the MCC should not hand over their control of Lord's Ground to the TCCB, and wrote a book on the conflict. As a number of members of the TCCB were also Committee members of the MCC, the trick was to discover which way these 'dual' members were facing at any one time. In the 1970s, the shadow of Gubby Allen still loomed over the Lord's pavilion, but two other administrators rose in importance, George Mann and Doug Insole. Mann, the son of an England Test captain, also led England and Middlesex. At various times he was Hon. Secretary, Chairman and President of Middlesex, and from 1978 to 1983 he was Chairman of the TCCB. Doug Insole, who played briefly for England, captained Essex from 1950 to 1960. In 1959 he was appointed as a Test Selector and was twice Chairman of the TCCB, the first time in 1975–8, at the time of the infamous court case against Packer. Both men were also members of influential sub-committees at Lord's.

FAST BOWLING AND INTERNATIONAL STARS

So much for the politics of cricket and its financial problems. For the public, results on the field of play at international level were far more important. The results of competitions at domestic first-class level assumed less and less significance as the 1960s gave way to the 1970s and 1980s.

The one feature that runs continuously through the 30-year period is the success and fear of fast bowling. The first decades after the Second World War had initially seen the Australian pair of Keith Miller and Ray Lindwall dominate Test cricket, followed by the English trio of Fred Trueman, Brian Statham and Frank Tyson. The middle 1960s produced the West Indian opening pair of Wes Hall and Charlie Griffith. They enabled the West Indies to beat Australia in 1964–5 and England in 1966. Backing up Hall and Griffith were the immensely talented Gary Sobers and the spin bowler Lance Gibbs. Australia's fortunes rose with the advent of Dennis Lillee, whose Test debut came in 1970–1. The arrival of a partner for him in Jeff Thomson enabled Australia to beat England 4–1 in 1974–5, and 1–0 in 1975, before beating the West Indies 5–1 in 1975–6. The West Indies, however, soon found some new fast bowling talents in Andy Roberts, then Michael Holding, Joel Garner and by 1980 Malcolm Marshall, plus other back-ups almost as lethal. Controlling this fast battery was Gary Sobers, followed by Clive Lloyd, both of whom reigned as captain for about a decade, Sobers from the mid-1960s and Lloyd from the mid-1970s. To beat the West Indies was regarded as the Everest of cricket.

England had no fire-power to match the Caribs. In Mike Brearley they produced the country's greatest post-war captain, although, because of the Test programme, Brearley never led England against the West Indies. Ian Botham was England's answer to Gary Sobers, an all-rounder who could command a place in the Test team as either a batsman or a bowler. There was in addition the reincarnation of Arthur Shrewsbury: Yorkshire's Geoff

Andy Roberts.
Between
1973 and 1984
he was one
of the great
West Indian
fast bowlers,
enabling the
Caribbean side
to dominate
the Test scene.

Dennis Lillee, who took 355 wickets
in Test cricket for Australia, was his
country's most effective fast bowler
through the 1970s and 1980s.

Gary Sobers
and David Holford
leave the field during
the 1966 West Indies
vs. England Test
at Lord's. The pair
added an unbeaten
274 for the sixth
wicket. Sobers broke
numerous records
during his Test career
and was unequalled
as an all-rounder
in post-war cricket.

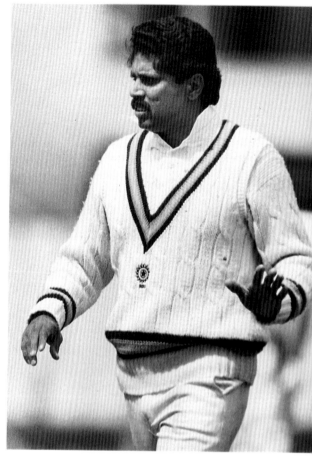

Kapil Dev, India's finest all-rounder. He was the youngest player to reach 100 Test wickets and currently holds the record for most wickets in Test cricket.

Imran Khan (left). His ability as a batsman, fast bowler and especially as his country's captain, ensured that Pakistan in the 1980s were a match for the other Test-playing countries. His final triumph was to lead Pakistan to the World Cup crown in 1992.

Boycott. Australia produced two more dynamic batsmen in the brothers Ian and Greg Chappell. Both captained Australia and played crucial roles in the World Series Cricket. They were to be followed by an outstanding batsman-captain, Allan Border.

Of the other Test countries, Pakistan, on paper, had the most talent, but internal dissension too often meant that the best eleven either were not picked or, if they were, failed to pull together. The brothers Hanif and Mushtaq Mohammad, whose Test careers began in the 1950s, continued respectively until 1970 and 1980. Imran Khan, the notable all-rounder, was the first Pakistani to score 3,000 runs and take 300 wickets, and captained his country in 48 Tests. Two other Pakistani batsmen with long and distinguished careers were Zaheer Abbas and the controversial Javed Miandad.

India relied on a succession of spin bowlers to support the immense batting power of Sunil Gavaskar. Chandrasekhar and Venkataraghavan started playing Test cricket in the mid-1960s and were quickly followed by Bishen Bedi. Kapil Dev, who made his Indian Test debut in 1978–9, was destined to take 400 wickets with his fast bowling and score more than 4,000 runs: in terms of figures India's outstanding all-rounder.

New Zealand's main talents were John Reid and then Glenn Turner as batsmen, but the Kiwis did not rise to the top until the maturing of their fast bowler, Richard Hadlee. His bowling, allied to his batting talent, enabled New Zealand to win rubbers against both Australia and England.

The preponderance of fast bowlers changed cricket as a spectacle in the 1970s and 1980s. The danger of being hit on the

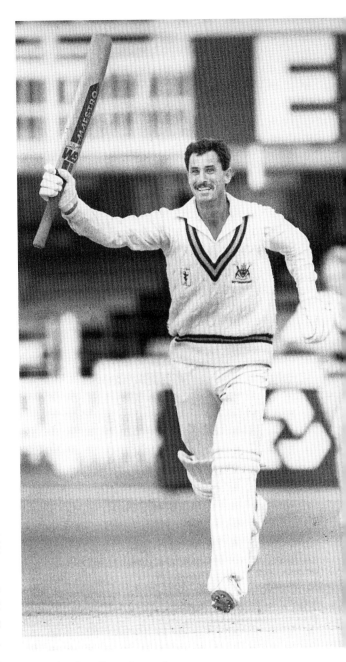

Sir Richard Hadlee, whose talents transformed the New Zealand Test side. He was the first bowler to take 400 Test wickets and from modest beginnings he developed into a formidable batsman.

head by a ball travelling near to 100 mph was first fully appreciated by Mike Brearley in 1978 (maybe he possessed more brains than most cricketers). He wore a strange protective headpiece under his cap. Within a year, the motorbike type helmet had arrived and within a few summers almost everyone was hidden from view by a helmet and grille. Viv Richards, the greatest batsman of the 1980s, was one of the small band who ignored the protection. Extra padding arrived in the form of arm-guards and larger chest protectors.

It was hardly a surprise when cricketers began to wear shirts with their surnames on the back. The cricket uniform, created in the 1870s and little changed in a hundred years, underwent fundamental alteration. The growth, in both domestic and international cricket, of one-day limited overs matches, placed a greater and greater emphasis on the prevention of run-scoring by the use of brilliant fielding. Since the single object of this type of cricket is to score the most runs possible in a given number of overs, dismissing batsmen is relatively unimportant. Athleticism became a vital part of the game and with it came the need for new levels of fitness. Batsmen or bowlers, however gifted, of were little use if they were poor fielders. The medical profession moved in to fine-tune the players, and the practice of picking different players to represent national sides, depending on the type of cricket being played, became more widespread.

TV, ADVERTISING AND THE SPREAD
OF CRICKET

When, in August 1992, Bob Parish attributed the healthy state of Australian cricket to the enterprise of Kerry Packer, he could just as easily have given credit for the healthy state of world cricket to television.

The proliferation of television channels in the 1990s created vast numbers of viewing hours which the TV moguls had to fill with entertainment as cheaply as possible. There is a limit to the number of times old films and television programmes can be reshown. Many of the popular sports, such as the different types of football, can provide only a limited number of viewing hours, unless repeated.

Between September 1994 and September 1995, international cricket involving the nine Test-playing countries staged 276 days of top-level cricket at six hours a day. There were 124 matches, very few of which clashed with each other, making 1,656 hours in all, not to mention the usual preview and post mortem hours which normally accompany televised sport.

In harness with the television companies come the firms wishing to advertise their products. The advertising boards which encircle the Test Match grounds are not there for decoration, the television viewer will be catching glimpses of them all day. The ultimate board is the sight-screen itself. In most international venues, the screen now alternates between white, when facing the batsman, and an advert every other over. At Lord's there was a great debate about the tradition of allowing several rings of spectators to sit on the grass behind the boundary line. Then the marketing men explained that a ring of advertising boards produced more financial reward than spectators. After a year or two, the boards took preference. Television is introducing cricket to a public who would never dream of actually going to watch a match in person and this is occurring worldwide. After all, county scores have been read for years in newspapers by people who never go to county matches, rather in the same way that many English people claim to be Church of England without ever going to church.

This increased worldwide interest in cricket is plainly demonstrated by the number of countries joining the International Cricket Conference (see pages 244–5). In 1975 the

13

THE

1990s

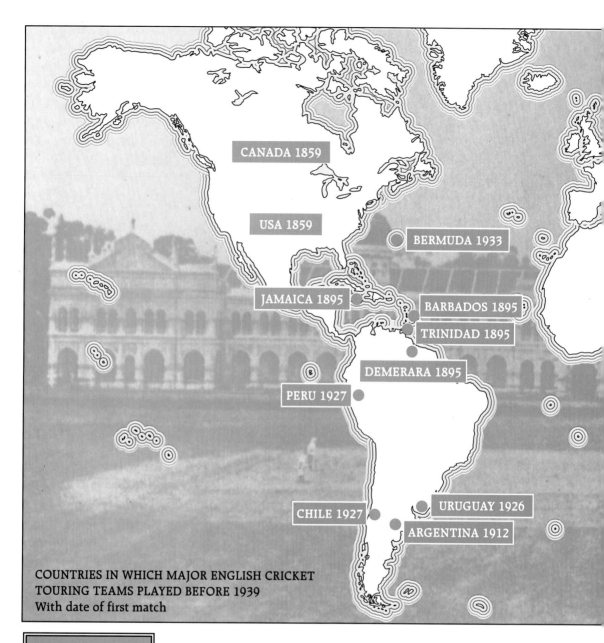

CANADA 1859

USA 1859

BERMUDA 1933

JAMAICA 1895

BARBADOS 1895

TRINIDAD 1895

DEMERARA 1895

PERU 1927

CHILE 1927

URUGUAY 1926

ARGENTINA 1912

COUNTRIES IN WHICH MAJOR ENGLISH CRICKET
TOURING TEAMS PLAYED BEFORE 1939
With date of first match

Countries which have been visited by major England touring teams, giving the year of the first visit.

Conference had 20 members; this grew to 27 by 1985, and by 1996 to 46. Just as important, Denmark and the Netherlands were joined by 11 other countries that had no direct connections with the old British Empire. In 1989 the European Cricket Federation was established, and had 12 members by 1995.

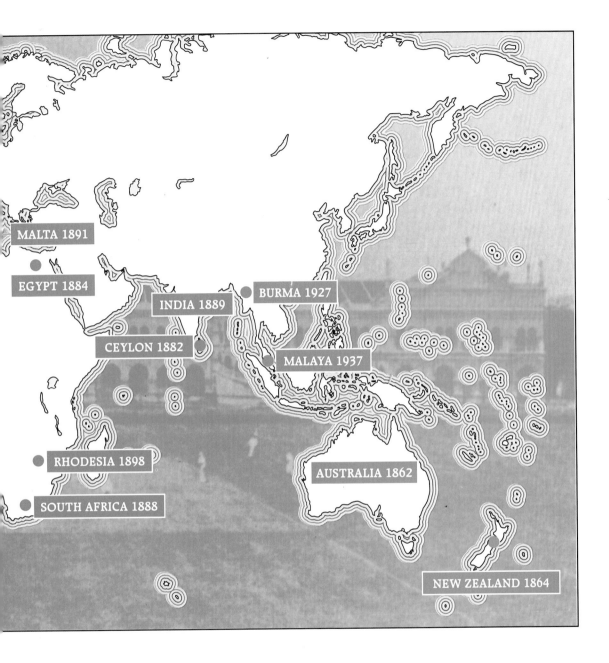

MALTA 1891

EGYPT 1884

INDIA 1889

BURMA 1927

CEYLON 1882

MALAYA 1937

RHODESIA 1898

AUSTRALIA 1862

SOUTH AFRICA 1888

NEW ZEALAND 1864

As cricket develops in Europe, the local clubs are trying to ensure that a reasonable percentage of their members are native-born, thus avoiding the creation of clubs simply for expatriates. For example, cricket may have been played in Portugal from the 19th century, but it has rarely involved the Portuguese, and until recently was confined to a very narrow section of the English community in that country.

Members
of the International
Cricket Conference.

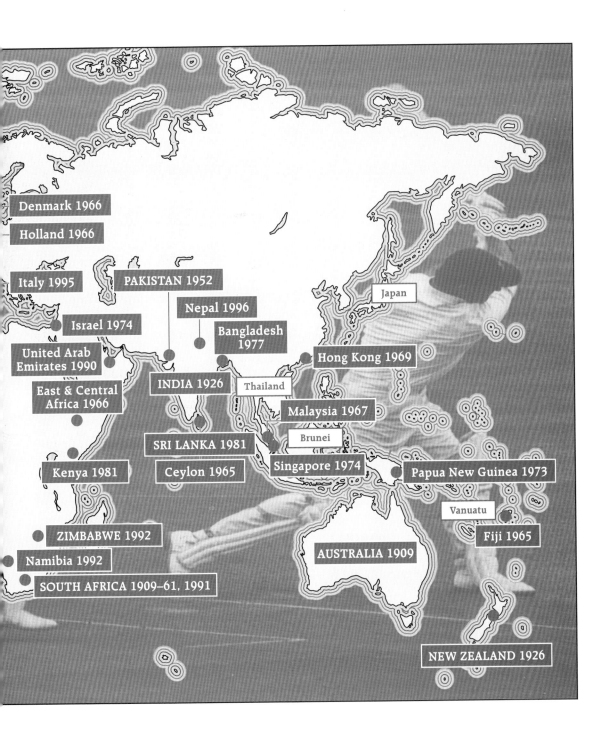

Denmark 1966

Holland 1966

Italy 1995

PAKISTAN 1952

Nepal 1996

Israel 1974

Bangladesh 1977

United Arab Emirates 1990

Hong Kong 1969

INDIA 1926

Thailand

East & Central Africa 1966

Malaysia 1967

SRI LANKA 1981

Brunei

Kenya 1981

Ceylon 1965

Singapore 1974

Papua New Guinea 1973

Japan

Vanuatu

ZIMBABWE 1992

Fiji 1965

Namibia 1992

AUSTRALIA 1909

SOUTH AFRICA 1909–61, 1991

NEW ZEALAND 1926

Meanwhile, the speed and comparative cheapness of air travel has helped cricketers to visit the southern hemisphere during the English winter and residents of the latter to come to England. The result is that touring sides now have a caucus of supporters wherever they travel. Similarly, many more club sides venture overseas. This can only be to cricket's advantage.

One hopes that cricket can spread again in North America. In Canada there is some cricket in schools and a scattering of well-established clubs. The recent upsurge in cricket, however, comes largely from emigrants from the South Asian subcontinent and the West Indies. The West Indians are also responsible for much cricket activity in the United States.

The 1995–6 season saw the Sixth World Cup, staged in India, Pakistan and Sri Lanka. Holland, Kenya and the United Arab Emirates joined the nine Test-playing countries (Zimbabwe was elevated to Test status in 1992). In the final, played in Lahore, the unfavoured Sri Lankans totally outplayed Australia, having previously overwhelmed India in the semi-finals, when Australia scraped through against the West Indies. Appropriately, Arjuna Ranatunga, the Sri Lankan captain, topped the batting averages for the tournament, followed by his colleague Aravinda De Silva. The enthusiasm for cricket in Sri Lanka has for some years been overwhelming; now it will know no bounds. Some commentators sent critical reports back home from the Cup, but they simply fail to comprehend that the subcontinent is not a part of the Home Counties, or indeed the Adelaide Oval. The staging of the World Cup there and its result can only advance cricket.

REVITALISING ENGLISH CRICKET

Meanwhile back in England yet more sub-committees and working parties have been formed to investigate the state of English cricket. The Murray Working Party, named after M.P. Murray, a former occasional member of the Middlesex county side, was set up by the TCCB in August 1991 to investigate the state of the domestic first-class game in England. Its three basic recommendations were that the counties should play only four-day Championship matches, instead of a mixture of three-day and four-day; that the zonal matches should be abolished for the Benson & Hedges Cup and that Sunday League matches should be 50 overs per side, not 40. It was agreed to try these recommendations for three years. One need hardly add that after one year, two of the three ideas had been abandoned. The four-day Championship matches remain, but in 1997 the days on which they are played have altered.

This initiative, however, was only part of the grand plan to revitalise English cricket. The other part was more radical: suggesting the total revision of the structure of English cricket, as set up in 1968 (i.e., the Cricket Council, TCCB and NCA). The plan was that the new structure for English cricket would be in place on 1 January 1996. When it became obvious that, because of differences of opinion, this would not happen, the TCCB set up another working party to assess the position and hopefully speed the process. The question of money from the National Lottery arose and minds were concentrated by the announcement that no money would be given to the professional game until cricket put its house in order. By late 1996, it looked as though the new England and Wales Cricket Board (ECB) was finally going to come into existence early in the new year.

NEW STARS

The whirligig of 1990s internationals threw up a new West Indian batsman, Brian Lara. For the West Indies against England at St John's, Antigua, Lara created a new Test batting record by scoring 375; the old record was 365 not out by Gary Sobers in 1957–8. Sobers came onto the field of play to shake Lara's hand when the new record was hoisted. Not content with this feat, a few months later Lara became the first batsman to score over 500 in a first-class match. Playing for Warwickshire against Durham at Edgbaston, he reached 501 not out. *Wisden* noted: 'The unparalleled glut of batting records that fell to Brian Lara between April and June 1994 amazed the cricket world and gained global attention beyond the game's narrow confines. It also prompted an outpouring of national pride in his native Trinidad and Tobago, where he was showered with honours and gifts.'

The previous first-class record had been 499 by the Pakistan batsman Hanif Mohammad in 1958–9. At the time of writing, Lara should have ten or more years of Test cricket ahead of him.

Many of the bowling headlines in the 1990s were, as is common, taken up by the fast men, in particular Curtly Ambrose and Courtney Walsh of the West Indies and the Pakistan pair, Waqar Younis and Wasim Akram. There was, however, one slower bowler who had consistent success – Shane Warne, the Australian leg-break bowler. His success revived interest in a largely forgotten breed.

Some idea of the proliferation of One-Day Internationals during the present decade can be gained by noting that the list of players who have appeared in over 200 such matches grows longer almost daily. Allan Border, the Australian captain, has logged 273, and within two or three years there will be more cricketers who have played 200+ One-Days than have played 100+ Test Matches.

Wasim Akram. On both the 1987 and 1992 Pakistan tours to England, Wasim was the side's most successful fast bowler. He has been equally successful when playing for Lancashire.

WOMEN'S CRICKET

Women's cricket both in England and overseas has raised its profile during the past 25 years. The first Women's Cricket World Cup was staged in England in 1973 with an odd mixture of sides competing: England, Australia, an International XI, New Zealand, Trinidad & Tobago, Jamaica and Young England. England beat Australia in the final and the whole competition was made possible by the generosity of the philanthropist Jack Hayward.

When it came to the fifth World Cup in 1993, the competing nations were New Zealand, England, Australia, the West Indies, Ireland, Denmark and Holland. England beat New Zealand in the final, staged at Lord's in front of some 4,500 spectators. The event achieved good television, as well as newspaper, coverage (see plate section).

Money in women's cricket has, however, remained a serious problem. Only a donation of £90,000 from the Foundation for Sports and the Arts prevented the 1993 competition being cancelled before it started. Women's cricket is still a minority sport in England, but if matches are televised on a regular basis, it will surely continue to grow.

BROADCASTERS

The increasing use of radio and television brings to the fore the commentators who in some cases have become better known than the players themselves. The broadcasting of Test cricket began in Australia in 1924–5, when England toured. In England itself the Revd F.H. Gillingham, a former Essex cricketer, made the first wireless broadcast of a first-class match, when Essex played the New Zealanders in 1927. Howard Marshall (1900–1973) was the first broadcaster to build a following among listeners for his cricket commentaries. He started broadcasting in the 1930s and continued up to the war. The best loved voice of cricket, John Arlott, began commentating in 1946. He retired in 1980. Almost as popular, but a complete contrast in style, was Brian Johnston, whose broadcasting continued until his death in 1994. Johnston's early broadcasts were on television, but he later switched to radio. E.W. Swanton's first Test series as a broadcaster was in South Africa in 1938–9. He was to continue until the 1970s on a regular basis, combining this task with his reporting for *The Daily Telegraph*. John Arlott reported mainly for *The Guardian*.

The best-known Australian voice was that of Alan McGilvray. He covered Australian Tests, but not normally the rest. The Australian, however, who has broadcast Tests from England every year from the mid-1960s is Richie Benaud, the former Test captain. In the mid-1980s the TV commentary team seemed to be an exclusive Test captains' club, with Tony Lewis, Ted Dexter, Bob Willis, Raymond Illingworth, Geoffrey Boycott and Tom Graveney, all of England, joining Benaud. Jim Laker, the former England spinner, also made a new career as a broadcaster, but died in 1986 aged 64. Tony Greig, another England captain, was frequently heard on Australia's airwaves.

THE WRITTEN WORD

This continuous broadcasting on radio and TV did not seem to affect the written word, or at least the quantity of words written on cricket. Neville Cardus's output reduced after the Second World War. John Arlott, whose first cricket book was published in 1947,

John Arlott. As a broadcaster he brought a new dimension to cricket commentating, just as Neville Cardus had done to cricket writing.

succeeded to the Cardus mantle. His portraits of cricketers were as evocative as those of Cardus but had the added dimension of Arlott's greater knowledge of cricket's history. Not so prolific as John Arlott, the literary figure who nevertheless stands beside him is Alan Ross. Ross was cricket correspondent of *The Observer* for nearly 20 years, retiring in 1972, and his main cricket books feature England on tour to various countries. Australia's most noted post-war cricket writer was Jack Fingleton (1908–1981), whose book *Cricket Crisis* is the outstanding description of the 1932–3 Ashes series. His *Brightly Fades The Don*, on Bradman's final tour to England in 1948, is of equal merit. Fingleton was trained as a journalist, but also made the grade as a cricketer, opening the batting for Australia in the 1930s.

The records and statistics of the game have come in for much scrutiny during the past 30 years and the production of books on the subject, which was once confined largely to a few fanatics, notably F.S. Ashley-Cooper (1877–1932), has developed into a small industry on its own. Most interested parties are members of the Association of Cricket Statisticians and Historians. Another post-war phenomenon is the growth of 'cricket societies'. These cater for followers who enjoy the social side of the game and meet during the close season to be addressed by guest speakers.

The story of cricket has been set out in this work and reveals that the game has altered in its minutiae constantly over the past 300 years – since William Goldwin published the first description of a match in 1706. Some of the changes, which are taken for granted in the 1990s, took years to become accepted, for example the move from under-arm bowling, or the acceptance in the south of England of league cricket. Tempers are frayed when coloured clothing is discussed, the traditionalists forgetting that the wearing of whites has been required for only a hundred years or so.

Opinions are divided as to whether the nostalgia element in cricket hinders or helps the overall development of the game. Does it, like the House of Lords, put a brake on the more idiotic sections of the radicals and let the sensible ideas come through, or does it merely attempt to prevent change at any cost?

The essence of cricket has not altered, only some of the manners. Whether the bowler is trying to outwit the batsman in a five-day Test, four-day County Championship match, two-day Minor County game or one of a myriad combinations of one-day limited overs contests does not change the concept of cricket.

No more was it changed in the second half of the 19th century when 'odds' matches were a regular feature on the fixture list. It is far better to play an odds match which balances up two sides than to play a game in which one side is utterly superior to the other. Another feature of 19th-century cricket that is no more was the single wicket match.

Both odds matches and single wicket matches may in the course of time return, and other previously unknown varieties of cricket may yet emerge. Change cannot harm the game to anything like the extent that placing a moratorium on it would. That would reduce cricket to a fossil.

If this book contains any message, it is that cricket will continue to fascinate those who understand it, and through television and the ease of travel more and more people in the world can have the opportunity to become fascinated. No longer will its enjoyment be confined to the heirs of the British Empire.

BIBLIOGRAPHY

In the course of researching this book, the author has had constant access to the cricket library at Trent Bridge, which contains over 6,000 books, as well as to his own personal library. It is impractical to list every book that has been used; the list below contains those volumes which have been most frequently consulted. In addition, the Association of Cricket Statisticians and Historians has published nearly 300 works of reference since 1973. These have likewise been a source of much information.

The 1789 Tour, J. Goulstone, I.R.P., 1972.
Australia 55, A. Ross, Joseph, 1955.
Australian Cricket, A.G. Moyes, Angus & Robertson, 1959.
Ball by Ball, C.D. Martin-Jenkins, Grafton, 1990.
Barbados Cricket Annual, ed. J.W. Gibbons, 1894–5 to 1913–14.
Barclays World of Cricket, ed. E.W. Swanton, Collins, 1980.
Beyond a Boundary, C.L.R. James, Hutchinson, 1963.
A Century of Philadelphia Cricket, J.A. Lester, University of Pennsylvania, 1951.
Chats on the Cricket Field, W.A. Bettesworth, Merritt & Hatcher, 1910.
Conflicts in Cricket, Jack Bailey, Kingswood, 1989.
Cricket, W.G. Grace, Arrowsmith, 1891.
Cricket, ed. H.G. Hutchinson, Country Life, 1903.
Cricket 1742–1751, F.S. Ashley-Cooper, Merritt & Hatcher, 1900.
Cricket, A Weekly Record of the Game, 1882 to 1913.
The Cricket Almanack of New Zealand, 1948 to the present day.
Cricket and I, L. Constantine, Allen, 1934.
Cricket Crisis, J.H.W. Fingleton, Cassell, 1946.
The Cricketer, a magazine published weekly, fortnightly, monthly, 1921 to the present day.
The Cricket Field, James Pycroft, Longman, Green, 1851.
Cricket Highways and Byways, F.S. Ashley-Cooper, Allen & Unwin, 1927.
Cricket: A History of its Growth & Development, Rowland Bowen, Eyre & Spottiswoode, 1970.
Cricket in the Fiji Islands, P.A. Snow, Whitcombe & Tombs, 1949.
Cricket in Ireland, W.P. Hone, The Kerryman, 1955.
Cricket in the Leagues, J. Kay, Eyre & Spottiswoode, 1930.
Cricket in Many Climes, P.F. Warner, Heinemann, 1900.
Cricket in Pakistan, S.M.H. Maqsood, Universal, 1948.

Cricket of Today & Yesterday, P.C. Standing, Caxton, 1904.

Cricket Prints, R.C. Robertson-Glasgow, Laurie, 1943.

The Cricket Quarterly, ed. Rowland Bowen, 1963 to 1970.

Cricket Scores, H.T. Waghorn, Blackwood, 1899.

Cricket Scores & Biographies, vols I–XIV, A.Haygarth, various years. (A 15th volume
    was published posthumously in 1925.)

Cricket: Sketches of Players, W. Denison, Simpkin, Marshall, 1846.

Cricket Tours at Home and Abroad, P. Wynne-Thomas, Hamlyn, 1989.

Cricket Who's Who, ed. H.V. Dorey, Cricket & Sports Publications, 1909 and 1910.

The Dawn of Cricket, H.T. Waghorn, MCC, 1906.

The Diary of Thomas Turner, ed. F.M. Turner, Lane, 1925.

Early Club & Village Cricket, J. Goulstone, The Author, 1972.

The Elevens of England, G.D. West, Darf, 1988.

The Elevens of Three Great Schools, W.R. Lyon, Spottiswoode, 1930.

Felix on the Bat, N. Wanostrocht, Baily Brothers, 1845.

A Few Short Runs, Lord Harris, Murray, 1921.

Fresh Light on 18th Century Cricket, G.B. Buckley, Cotterell, 1935.

Fresh Light on Pre-Victorian Cricket, G.B. Buckley, Cotterell, 1937.

Four Score and Ten 1879–1969, S.S. Perera, The Author, 1969.

Gentlemen v Players, P.F. Warner, Harrap, 1950.

The Hambledon Cricket Chronicle, F.S. Ashley-Cooper, Jenkins, 1924.

Hambledon's Cricket Glory, R.D. Knight, various years.

A History of Cambridge University Cricket Club. 1820–1901, W.J. Ford, Blackwood, 1902.

A History of Cricket, H.S. Altham, Allen & Unwin, 1926.

The History of Cricket, E. Parker, Seeley Service, 1950.

A History of Indian Cricket, M. Bose, Deutsch, 1990.

The History of Kent County Cricket, ed. Lord Harris, Eyre & Spottiswoode, 1907.

A History of Leicestershire Cricket, E.E. Snow, Backus, 1949.

A History of Oxford University Cricket Club, G. Bolton, Holywell, 1962.

A History of the Royal Engineers Cricket 1862–1924, R.S. Rait Kerr, I.R.E., 1925.

The History of South African Cricket, vols 1 and 2, M.W. Luckin, E.W. Hortor & Co.,
    1915, 1928.

A History of Tasmanian Cricket, Roger Page, Shea, 1958.

A History of West Indian Cricket, M. Manley, Deutsch, 1988.

Imperial Cricket, P.F. Warner, London & Counties, 1912.

Indian Cricket, annually 1946–7 to the present day.

The Iron Industry of the Weald, Cleere & Crossley, Merton, 1995.

Fred Lillywhite's Cricketers' Guide, 1849–66.

James Lillywhite's Cricketers' Annual, ed. C.W. Alcock, 1872–1900.

John Lillywhite's Cricketers' Companion, 1865–85.

The Jubilee Book of Cricket, K.S. Ranjitsinhji, Blackwood, 1897.

Kings of Cricket, Richard Daft, Arrowsmith, 1893.

The Language of Cricket, W.J. Lewis, Oxford University Press, 1934.

The Laws of Cricket: Their History and Growth, R.S. Rait Kerr, Longman, 1950.

Lord's, D.M. Rait Kerr and I.A.R. Peebles, Harrap, 1971.

Lord's and The MCC, Lord Harris and F.S. Ashley-Cooper, London & Co., 1914.

March of Indian Cricket, D.B. Deodhar, Roy, 1948.

More Cricket Prints, R.C. Robertson-Glasgow, Laurie, 1943.

New South Wales Yearbook, 1927–8 to the present day.

New Zealand Cricket 1841–1933, vols 1 and 2, T.W. Reese, Simpson, Williams, 1927, 1933.

North and South. Argentina, K.E. Bridger, Palleresgraficos, 1976.

Old English Cricket, six volumes, P.F. Thomas, Richards, various years.

Pageant of Cricket, D. Frith, Macmillan, 1987.

Parsi Cricket, M.E. Pavri, Marzbon, 1901.

Pre-Victorian Sussex Cricket, H.F. and A.P. Squire, The Authors, 1951.

Quilt Winders and Pod Shavers, H. Barty-King, MacDonald & Jane, 1979.

Recollections and Reminiscences, Lord Hawke, Williams, 1924.

Seasons in the Sun, R. Coleman, Hargreen, 1993.

Sir Julien Cahn's XI, E.E. Snow, The Author, 1964.

Sixty Years of Canadian Cricket, J.E. Hall and R.O. McCulloch, Bryant, 1985.

So This is Australia, W. Pollock, Barker, 1937.

South African Cricket Annual, 1951–2 to the present day.

The Sports and Pastimes of the People of England, J. Strutt, Methuen, 1903.

Sports Quarterly, J. Goulstone, 1977–82.

The Story of Warwickshire Cricket, L.B. Duckworth, S. Paul, 1974.

Surrey Cricket, ed. Lord Alverstone and C.W. Alcock, Longman, 1902.

Sussex Cricket, John Marshall, Heinemann, 1959.

Talks with Old English Cricketers, A.W. Pullin, Blackwood, 1900.

Twelve Years of the Ranji Trophy, S.K. Gurunathan, The Hindu, 1946.

Victorian Cricket Association Annual Report, 1895–6 to the present day.

West Indian Cricket, C. Nicole, Phoenix House, 1957.

Who's Who of Cricketers, P.J. Bailey, P.R. Thorn, P. Wynne-Thomas, Hamlyn, 1993.

Wickets and Goals, J.A.H. Catton, Chapman & Hall, 1926.

Wisden Cricket Monthly, ed. D. Frith, 1979 to the present day.

Wisden's Cricketers' Almanack, 1864 to the present day.

The World of Cricket, ed. A.C. MacLaren, weekly, 1914.

The Young Cricketers' Tutor, John Nyren, Effingham, Wilson, 1833.

Wimbledon House (Roedean School)
vs. Southdown on the South Downs
in Sussex in 1894.

THE HISTORY OF CRICKET

THE HISTORY OF CRICKET

Lancashire League   125, 151, 165, 176
Landsdown Club   57
Langton, A.B.C.   174
Lara, Brian   85, 134, 247, plate section
Larwood, Harold   155, 157, 158, pic. 159, 161, 162, 170, 177
Launceston, Tasmania   71, 72
Laver, Frank   129
Lawn mower   100
Lawrell, James   46
Lawrence, Charles   87
Lawrence, John   106
Lawrence, Sir Walter   167
Laws of cricket   7, 15, 18, 24, 25, 30, 31, 34, 35, 36, 44, 51, 52, 54, 56, 78, 100, 121, 160, 161, 225
Lawton, Joe   139
Lbw   18, 24, 100, 121, 156
League cricket (in England)   125, 165, 166, 249
Leeds   50, 63
Leer, George   22
Leicester   22, 23, 47, 50, 64
Leicester, Earl of   61
Leicestershire   30, 120, 121, 161, 165, 166, 213, 222
Lennox, Hon. Charles: see Richmond, 4th Duke of
Lester, J.A.   143
Letby, R.   53
Levant Company   40
Lever, J.K.   230
Leveson-Gower, H.D.G.   123, 137
Lewes   22, 28
Lewin, H.R.   68
Lewis, A.R.   248
Lewis, W.H.   57
Leyland, M.   162
Lichfield, Earl of   123
Lidster   53
Lillee, D.K.   230, 236, pic. 237
Lillywhite, Frederick   64, 66, 67, 78, 81
Lillywhite, James jnr   79, 89, 90, 91, 92, 93
Lillywhite, John   67, 68
Lillywhite, Shaw and Shrewsbury teams   92, 93, pic. 96, 97

Lillywhite, William   54, 76
Limbdi, K.S.   184
Lindwall, R.R.   203, 205, 206, 207, 236
Linley, T.   63
Linton   21
Lisbon   118
Literature   167, 249
Littleton, Dr Adam   28
Liverpool   64
Llewellyn, C.B.   150
Lloyd, C.H.   236
Lloyd's Evening Post   11
Lock, G.A.R.   206, 207
Lockwood, W.H.   123
Lockyer, Tom   67, 76
Lodge School   141
Logan, Hon. J.D.   130
Lohmann, G.A.   130, 131
Lombard World Challenge   plate section
London   9, 13, 24, 28, 29, 33, 42
London CCC   126
London Club   12, 14, 19, 28
London Counties   197, 202
London Gamesters   28
London Magazine   15
Long Robin: see Colchin, Robert
Lord's Cricket Ground   31, 34, 39, 45, 46, 47, 52, 54, 55, 56, 57, 64, 77, 78, 85, 92, 100, 122, 123, 150, 151, 158, 190, 197, 201, 202, 205, 223, 224, 236, 241, plate section
Lord, Thomas   14, 31-3, 50, 55
Loughborough   50
Love, James   15
Lowry, T.C.   178
Lucas, R.S.   141
Luckin, M.W.   131
Lyon, M.D.   191
Lyttelton, R.H.   99

Maadi Sporting Club   191
Mabbinck, Henry   27
Macartney, C.G.   140, 145, 168, 177, 188
Macdonald, R.   160, 161
MacDonald, Ramsay   160
Mackay, K.D.   207
MacLaren, A.C.   102, 122, 123, 126, pic. 134, 178
Macnaghten, Chester   111

Maddocks, L.V.   207
Madras   137, 179, 187
Madras Courier   42
Mahomedan CC   111
Maidenhead   21
Maidstone   27, 28, 75
Mailey, A.A.   168, 190
Malay CC, Colombo   111
Malaya   212, 213
Malaysia   225
Malden, Essex   26
Malden Wanderers CC,   223
Malietoa, King   117
Malling   28
Malta   192
Manchester   63
Manchester Guardian   167, 248
Manchester University   166
Mancroft, Lord   88
Mandela, Nelson   227
Manitoba   190
Manley, Michael   206
Mann, F.G.   236
Mann, Sir Horatio   21, 24
Mann, Noah   22
March, Cambridgeshire   39
Marchant, Thomas   6, 28
Marder, John   213, 214
Maritzburg   69
Marlborough   14
Marlborough Blues   105
Mars CC, Bombay   70
Marseilles   191
Marsh, R.W.   230
Marshall, Howard   248
Marshall, M.D.   236
Marsham, Charles   78
Martineau, H.M.   167, 191
Martingell, W.   62
Marylebone   31, 32, 35
Marylebone Cricket Club (MCC)   31, 34, 43, 45, 46, 47, 49, 52, 54, 55, 59, 78, 80, 82, 84, 86, 91, 100, 117, 119, 121, 122, 135, 140, 146, 147, 151, 158, 159, 160, 161, 162, 168, 172, 176, 179, 181, 197, 204, 213, 214, 217, 218, 236
Massie, H.H.   126
Matthews, Hon. R.C.   190
May, P.B.H.   206, 207
May, P.R.   140
McAlister, P.A.   pic. 129

Warwickshire 29, 41, 121, 208, 221, 247
Washbrook, C. 204, 207
Wasim Akram pic. 247
Waterloo 40, 41
Watson, F.B. 161
Waugh, Evelyn 124
Waugh, S.R. 169
Waymark, Thomas 13, 15, 16, 17
Wazir Ali, S. 180
Weald, The 4-6, 8, 69, 252
Weekes, E.D. 169, 204
Weekly Journal, The 12
Wei-hai-wei 70
Welbeck 22, 29
Wellington, New Zealand 73, 84, 140, 179
Wells, James 25
Wells, John 25, 54
Wensley, A.F. 165
West Bridgford 50
West, E.L. 184
Western Province CC 108, 173
West Horsley 27
West Indian team to England, 1900 141, 142
West Indies 42, 114, 115, 121, 135, 141-2, 171, 175-7, 196, 204, 216, 225, 226, 231, 233, 236, 246, 247, 248
West Malling 50, 80
West Meon 55
Westminster School 8, 19, 24, 28, 37, 57
Westover, Virginia 41
White Conduit Club 32, 33, 34, 35
White Conduit Fields 31
White Conduit House, Islington 31
White Hart Cricket Ground, Bromley 50
White Heather Club 194
White, Thomas 24

Wicket 6, 7, 10, 18, 24, 37, 121, 156
Wicket gate 6
Wickets in the West 88
Willcocks Sports Ground, Egypt 191
Willes, Christina 51
Willes, John 51, 52
Willingdon, Lord 179, 184, 185
Willis, R.G.D. 230, 248
Willow the King 125
Wills, Thomas 111
Willsher, E. 78, 79, 100, 112
Wilson, E.R. 162, pic. 163
Wilson, Rt Revd Cecil 117
Wilson, Revd Thomas 27
Wiltshire 17, 30, 55
Wimbledon Common 35
Winchester College 8, 41, 57, 102
Winchilsea, 9th Earl of 31, 35, 36, 47, 53
Windsor 30
Wirksworth 30
Wisbech 39
Wisden's Cricketers' Almanack 64, 100, 120, 133, 157, 162, 167, 168, 212, 247
Wisden, John 64, 67, 77, 79, 100
Woburn 16, 29
Wodehouse, P.G. 125
Wolfenden, Sir John 217, 218
Women's cricket 29, 30, 194-6, 248, plate section
Women's Cricket Association 194, 218
Women's Cricket World Cup 248
Woodforde 37
Woodfull, W.M. 158, 160
Woods, Float 141
Woods, S.M.J. 101
Woolley, F.E. 150, 168, 169
Woolmer, R.A. 230

Woolwich 61
Worcestershire 83, 121, 151, 212
Worcestershire, Gentlemen of 192
Wordsworth, Charles 57
World Cup 172, 224, 225, 226, 246
World of Cricket 150
World Series Cricket Pty Ltd 229, 230
World War, First 149, 179, 188, 194, 205
World War, Second 153, 164, 170, 191, 193, 197, pic. 198, 199, 200, 202
Worrell, F.M.M. 204, 205, 206
Wragg, C. 63
Wrecclesham 25
Wright 65
Wright, D.V.P. 174, 204
Wright, H. 63
Wrigley Cricket Foundation 223
Wyatt, G. 116
Wyatt, R.E.S. 180
Wycombe Abbey School 194
Wynyard, E.G. 140

Yalden, William 40
Yardley, N.W.D. 199
Yearwood, Hon. Laurie 172
York 53, 64
York, Duke of 35
Yorkshire 22, 30, 46, 55, 80, 81, 83, 101, 102, 124, 128, 151, 152, 153, 158, 161, 219, 222
Young Cricketers' Tutor, The 2, 10

Zaheer Abbas 232, 239
Zanzibar 147
Zia-ul-Haq, General 232, 235
Zimbabwe 225, 246
Zoroastrian CC 69
Zuoz College 192

THE HISTORY OF CRICKET